THE UNOFFICIAL GUIDE

JIM SANGSTER

Dedicated to Mum and Dad

First published 2002 by Contender Books
Contender Books is a division of
The Contender Entertainment Group
48 Margaret Street
London W1W 8SE

This edition published 2002
1 3 5 7 9 10 8 6 4 2

ISBN 1 84357 034 3

Printed in the UK by Butler & Tanner Ltd, Frome and London
Cover and text designed by seagulls
Typeset by seagulls
Edited by Wendy Hollas

THE UNOFFICIAL GUIDE

ACKNOWLEDGEMENTS

I'd like to say a big 'ta' to the following for their help, encouragement and inspiration in the writing of this book:

Scott Andrews, David Bailey, Alexander Graham Bell, Jason Boulter, Tim Berners-Lee, Paul Cornell, Martin Day, Gary Gillatt, Rebecca Levene, Steve Lyons, Steven Moffat, Richie Moosbally, Jim Smith, Keith Topping. And a big 'high-five' for Abi, Anna, Ashley, Linda, Natalie and Sam at h2g2 for cheering me on.

To Mrs Jones and Miss Riley of St Andrew's Junior School, Mr Cullen and Mr Young of St Edwards College, Mr Trevor Stent and Mr Sandy Gavin of Halewood Comprehensive, and Dr Jackie Miller and Mrs Petula Sawkins of Liverpool Institute of Higher Education – thanks for your encouragement throughout my education. Sorry I didn't listen to all of you at the time, but it did sink in... some of it...

Also, thanks to everyone at Contender, but specifically Michèle Brown, Lydia Drukarz, Wendy Hollas, Sasha Morton and Alison Parker. Special thanks to Lee Binding (for the recommendation) and Rebecca Gee (for her regular calls of encouragement and all-round enthusiasm).

Finally, I wouldn't have been physically capable of finishing this book without the help of Paul Condon, Ian Edmond, Dan Hogarth, Scott Matthewman and Louis Niebur for their help and patience, but especially Mark Wright who's been far too busy for his own good recently but was still generous enough to share the fun.

To all of you, just a very sincere thank you.

DID YA EVER HAVE ONE OF THOSE DAYS...?

00:00 13:41 07:24 22:38 10:09 17:59 09:13 21:01 04:45 14:12 07:57 13:41 07:24 22:38 10:09 17:59 09:13

After a visit to L.A. this January, a friend came back raving about a new show – the 'must see' fixture on American network TV. 'It's called ***24***,' he enthused, 'and every episode is one hour of real-time events in the life of Kiefer Sutherland.' It sounded as if someone, somewhere down the line, had gone a little too far with reality TV, stalking a celebrity for the entertainment of the masses. But then he explained that it was a fictional drama using multi-camera editing and more twists than a bowl of curly fries. Just the sort of show that I've traditionally adored.

Typically, by the time the first episode of ***24*** reached British shores I was trapped in a dog costume raising money for the Canine Protection League (honest!) and so I missed the whole thing. Big mistake – the next day almost everyone was talking about it and I was scrambling round trying to see if anyone had had the good sense to tape it...

Enough of the 'Dear Diary' moments – on with the book! This, as you might have guessed, is the unofficial guide to ***24***. By 'unofficial' I mean that I'm not a part of Fox or Imagine Entertainment's PR department but simply a writer who happens to be a fan. The fan's job has always been to obsess about detail, to scrutinise and pick apart the object of their affection to see how it all works and then piece it back together again. A bit like Frankenstein, though hopefully with less monstrous results. So while I'm obviously a bit biased when talking about the show, I'm not blind to its few faults as well. Luckily, such concerns are few and far between.

The ongoing story of ***24*** is a convoluted one, so this book is, first of all, your companion through the intrigue and mayhem of one day in the lives of the characters. Like other guides of this type, each episode is split into sections – cast list, summary and a few notes keeping track of the trivia for the obsessive in all of us. The breakdown is as follows:

Episode

Title – With the title being the times the episode is set between, e.g. '12:00 A.M. – 1:00 A.M.'

Production Code – The number by which each episode was known by the production team.

First US Transmission Date

Writer/Director Credits

Cast – All the credited actors aside from the core five.

Jack Bauer's intro – From 7:00 A.M. onwards, each episode is preceded by a brief recap of events that changes as the show progresses.

EPISODE SUMMARY – Scene-by-scene breakdown of the events in each episode, with the odd quotes and regular time checks thrown in for good measure.

Notes

- **Who's Who?:** A basic run-down of where you might have seen 'whatshisname' before, or where you can catch them again.

- **Time Checks:** Sometimes characters remind each other (i.e. the audience) when things occurred or are going to occur. This note just keeps a check of references to time, either necessary or just gratuitous reminders of the real-time aspect of the show.
- **Music:** All of the incidental music comes courtesy of the talented composer Sean Callery, but when music from other sources is heard, you'll find a reference here.
- **Death Count:** CTU must have shares in a body-bag company. Keep track of the growing list of corpses as they mount up.
- **Trivia:** Any odd bits of info, such as car licence plates, hotel room numbers, phone numbers and anything else that comes to mind.

COMMENT – Unlike with other guides of this type, this book does not contain individual reviews of each episode. Frankly, there are only two justifiable opinions of a ***24*** episode: great, and bloody great. Instead, I've chosen 24 topics to discuss, one per episode. If nothing else, they make this book perfect to read on the toilet, a chapter per sitting.

QUESTIONS ARISING – Finally, just some of the questions that have gone through my mind at the end of each instalment. Some of them are answered later on in the story, some remain unresolved. Some are just instances of me being bloody-minded, for which I apologise in advance.

24 is a complex, fast-moving show with many events happening at once, so while I've made every attempt to mention everything I think is of interest, inevitably there'll be the odd line of dialogue or small exchange that I've skipped for reasons of space. All I can say is you're just going to have to trust me... and we ALL know what happens to people who ask that!

If nothing else, I hope this helps you keep up with everything that goes on in the series.

Jim Sangster

London, June, 2001

WHO'S WHO?

00:00 13:41 07:24 22:38 10:09 17:59 09:13 21:01 04:45 14:12 07:57 13:41 07:24 22:38 10:09 17:59 09:1

Part I – The Characters

Jack Bauer

Jack Bauer is known as a man who can get things done – even if it means bending or even breaking the rules. Determined and focused yet compassionate and loyal, he has often been involved in operations that have not been reported in his personnel file due to their politically sensitive nature. After returning from one such mission two years ago, he found himself struggling to readjust to everyday life, a situation that put a strain on his marriage. Though he and his wife Teri separated for some time (during which time he enjoyed a brief affair with a work colleague), they have recently got back together, much to the relief of their teenage daughter Kimberly.

Jack is currently assigned to the Counter Terrorism Unit in Los Angeles, California. Having received a tip-off from one of their overseas agents about the likelihood of an assassination attempt on a candidate in the presidential primaries, Jack is awaiting confirmation of the suspected target any day now...

Teri Bauer

A sought-after interior design consultant, Teri has, not surprisingly, felt obliged to put her family before her career on a number of occasions. For some years now, she's enjoyed the freedom that being freelance has allowed her, though she has confessed to some of her friends that once her daughter goes off to college she hopes to return to full-time work.

Kimberly Bauer

The only child of Jack and Teri Bauer, Kimberly (also called Kim) is in her second year at Santa Monica High School. Though she is bright, she is currently experiencing a few difficulties at school – her parents have received a couple of letters about her behaviour, though this is possibly down to her feelings about her parents' break-up and subsequent reconciliation. She recently broke up with her boyfriend, Vincent, and, egged on by her best friend Janet York, she has agreed to go on a blind date with the best friend of Janet's new boyfriend, Dan.

Senator David Palmer

David Palmer is the Senator for California and is currently campaigning to win the Democrat party nomination for the presidential elections later on this year. David has previously served as a member of the Senate Appropriations Committee where he had responsibilities over the Department of Defence. He is married to Sherry, who he met in kindergarten, and has two children, Keith and Nicole.

Sherry Palmer

Sherry Palmer is more than just David Palmer's wife, she is his most dogged supporter. She has taken a keen interest in David's policies, specifically those relating to education, and plays an active role in the

National Youth Service. Having known David since they were both children, Sherry likes to cultivate the idea that they were 'childhood sweethearts' as part of her all-round image as a family woman. But insiders have often accused her of being ruthless to the point of being dangerous when crossed.

Keith & Nicole Palmer

No sign of sibling rivalry here, brother and sister Keith and Nicole are very close. However, that might have something to do with an event in their past that threw them together as a defence against the outside world...

Nina Myers

Nina Myers is a division leader at the Los Angeles Counter Terrorism Unit, reporting directly to Jack Bauer. Though she has always been thought of as truthful and by the book, her behaviour recently has led to some people questioning whether her rumoured affair with Jack Bauer might have made her too emotionally involved to be trusted to make serious decisions.

Tony Almeida

An Intelligence agent at CTU, it is well known that Tony resents Jack Bauer's unorthodox approach to the rule book. Though office rumours have suggested that Tony has recently become romantically involved with Nina Myers after her break-up with Jack, both parties deny that they have ever been anything more than work colleagues.

Jamey Farrell

Jamey Farrell – née Vasquez – is CTU's programmer. Having been abandoned by her husband, she relies on her mother to care for her young son Kyle while she is at work. She previously worked for Microsoft until she was dismissed for creating unauthorised intelligence-gathering software.

Part II – The Actors

Kiefer Sutherland (Jack Bauer)

The son of actor Donald Sutherland and stage actress Shirley Douglas, Kiefer William Frederick Dempsey George Rufus Sutherland was born in London, UK, on December 18 1966, along with his twin sister Rachel. After his parents split up, Kiefer was raised by his mother in Toronto, Canada – his maternal grandfather, Tommy Douglas, incidentally, had been Canada's first elected socialist Prime Minister from 1944-1961. At the age of 15, Kiefer decided to drop out of high school to live with a friend (without telling his parents) and take up acting. A few lucky breaks found him a part on Steven Spielberg's anthology TV show *Amazing Stories*, while 1986 saw him appear in *At Close Range* (dir. James Foley), opposite Sean Penn, the TV movie *Trapped in Silence* (dir. Michael Tuchner) and, memorably, as teenage thug Ace Merrill in *Stand By Me* (dir. Rob Reiner), an adaptation of a Stephen King short story. While making *The Killing Time* (dir. Rick King) the following year, Kiefer met producer Camelia Kath. The fact that she was 14 years his senior and had an 11-year-old daughter from a previous marriage didn't stop Kiefer from finding her attractive. A year later, they were married.

It was, of course, *The Lost Boys* (dir. Joel Schumacher, 1987) that cast Kiefer as the seductive leader of a gang of vampire punks terrorising a seaside town. It also turned Kiefer into a bona fide star. In 1988, Kiefer would appear in anti-war drama *1969* (dir. Ernest Thompson) with

Robert Downey Jnr and Winona Ryder, and *Bright Lights, Big City* (dir. James Bridges) with Michael J. Fox, which led to arguably the actor's biggest box-office success – *Young Guns* (dir. Christopher Cain). Doing for Westerns what *The Lost Boys* had done for gothic horror, *Young Guns* also starred Lou Diamond Phillips, who would later appear in the latter stages of ***24***. In 1990, Kiefer also worked with Dennis Hopper on *Flashback* (dir. Franco Amurri).

Having enjoyed the luxuries of stardom, Kiefer Sutherland briefly suffered the downside of celebrity when, after the breakdown of his first marriage, he became engaged to rising star Julia Roberts. Having met on the set of *Flatliners* (dir. Joel Schumacher, 1990), the couple were due to be married on June 14 1991, but just four days before the ceremony, Julia called it off and ran away to Ireland with Kiefer's best friend (and co-star from *The Lost Boys*) Jason Patric. The tabloids had a field day while all concerned parties went to ground until things blew over. Speaking to the *Radio Times* in 2002, Sutherland seemed stoical about the whole affair: 'I felt bad for both of us, but we asked for it. If two successful people, very much in the public eye, decide to have a very public fight four days before a very public wedding, things will come at you... you could drive yourself insane, though, if you take notice of silly stuff in the tabloids.'

Still, Kiefer continued to work, with *Article 99* (dir. Howard Deutch), *Twin Peaks: Fire Walk With Me* (dir. David Lynch), *A Few Good Men* (dir. Barry Levinson), *The Vanishing* (dir. George Sluizer) and *The Three Musketeers* (dir. Stephen Herek) in the space of three years, while additionally unveiling his directorial debut, *Last Light*, in which he also starred.

Sutherland was reunited with director Joel Schumacher in the 1996 film *A Time to Kill*, playing a vicious Ku Klux Klan leader. The film also boasted an appearance from Kiefer's father, though sadly neither of them had any scenes together. Soon after, however, he would appear with his mother in a stage production of the Tennessee Williams play *The Glass Menagerie* back in Toronto. The same year also saw Kiefer married for the second time, to former model Kelly Winn, though sadly the marriage ended four years later.

Although by no means as prolific as he once was, Kiefer Sutherland is still a talent very much in demand. In addition to directing *Woman Wanted* (which he subsequently disowned after conflict with the producers), he's appeared in *After Alice*, *The Last Temptation*, *Three Seconds*, *To End All Wars* and *Among the Thugs*.

Leslie Hope (Teri Bauer)

Born in Halifax, Nova Scotia, on May 6 1965, one of Leslie Hope's first major roles was playing Linda Martin in the soap opera *Knots Landing*. Her first American feature film was John Cassavetes' *Love Streams* in a role specially written for her, while other credits include Oliver Stone's *Talk Radio* (1988), *Bram Stoker's Shadow Builder* (dir. Jamie Dixon, 1997), and *The Spreading Ground* (dir. Derek Vanlint, 2000), which also starred Dennis Hopper. Prior to ***24***, she completed *Dragonfly* with Kevin Costner and Kathy Bates. In theatre, Hope was the founding artistic director of The Wilton Project in Los Angeles. Her official website can be found at http://www.lesliehope.com/.

Elisha Cuthbert (Kimberly Bauer)

Elisha Cuthbert was born in Calgary, Canada on November 30 1982. By the age of seven she was a model, and by fifteen she was a presenter on *Popular Mechanics for Kids*. It was through that show that Elisha met the then First Lady, Hillary Clinton. She later starred in the Nickelodeon series *Are You Afraid of the Dark?* After completing the first series of ***24***, she appeared in the film *Old School* (dir. Todd Phillips, 2002) opposite Luke Wilson, Vince Vaughan and Juliette Lewis.

Dennis Haysbert (Senator David Palmer)

Dennis Haysbert, born June 2 1954 in San Mateo, California, has been a professional actor since he graduated from the American Academy of Dramatic Arts and won a minor role in an episode of the politically-minded newspaper drama *Lou Grant*. His movie credits include *Major League* (dir. David S. Ward, 1989) and its two sequels, *Navy Seals* (dir. Lewis Teague, 1990), *Heat* (Michael Mann, 1995) with Al Pacino and Robert De Niro, *Waiting To Exhale* (dir. Forest Whittaker, 1995), *Absolute Power* (1997) directed by and starring Clint Eastwood, and Spike Lee's *Love and Basketball* (2000). For those who are curious, Dennis is 6' 4" tall.

Penny Johnson Jerald (Sherry Palmer)

Penny Johnson Jerald was a regular on the medical drama *ER*, playing Nurse Practitioner Lynette Evans, and was semi-regular on *Star Trek: Deep Space Nine*, as Captain Cassidy Yates. Like Dennis Haysbert, she was in *Absolute Power* and, credited as Penny Johnson, appeared in the life story of Tina Turner, *What's Love Got To Do With It*.

Sarah Clarke (Nina Myers)

Born in St Louis, Missouri, Sarah Clarke made her name in the theatre and as an architectural photographer. In her first short film *Pas de Deux* she won an award for Outstanding Performance at the Brooklyn Film Festival. She appeared in an award-winning advert for the VW Jetta and has guest-starred in *Sex and the City* and the films *The Accident* (dir. John Fletcher, 2001) opposite *Angel*'s Amy Acker, and *Emmett's Mark* (dir. Keith Snyder), which is due to be released in 2002. Sarah made a surprise announcement during the transmission of the series – she got engaged to her fellow ***24*** actor, Xander Berkeley (CTU's George Mason).

Carlos Bernard (Tony Almeida)

Carlos Bernard – born Carlos Bernard Papierski – is a graduate of the American Conservatory Theater in San Francisco. He went on to appear in many ACT stage productions, including *Good* with William Hurt, *The Diary of Anne Frank* and *The Cherry Orchard*. On television, Bernard has worked on *Walker, Texas Ranger* and the daytime soap *The Young and the Restless*. He also has an official website: http://carlosbernard.com/.

Karina Arroyave (Jamey Farrell)

Karina Arroyave was born on July 16 1969, in Colombia, South America. She graduated from the famous LaGuardia High School of Music and the Performing Arts in New York, and performed on Broadway in the Lincoln Center Theater's *In the Summer House*. She played Bianca Marquez Walsh in the soap *As the World Turns* for five years and has appeared in the films *Falling Down* (1993) and *Flawless* (1999) for Joel Schumacher, *The Cowboy Way* (dir. Gregg Champion, 1994), *Dangerous Minds* (dir. John N. Smith, 1995) and *187* (dir. Kevin Reynolds), amongst others. Arroyave's other TV credits include *NYPD Blue*, *Touched by an Angel*, *Law and Order*, *The Practice*, *All My Children*, *Chicago Hope* and *The Equalizer*.

Part III – Principal Production Crew

Joel Surnow & Robert Cochran

(series creators, writers & exec. producers)

Joel's television career includes stints on the 1980s glam-soap *Falcon Crest*, *Miami Vice*, *The Equalizer* and, most recently, the espionage thriller *La Femme Nikita* with Robert Cochran. Having trained as a lawyer, Cochran began writing for shows such as *L.A. Law* and later became a writer and producer on *Falcon Crest*.

Stephen Hopkins (director)

Hopkins' film credits include *A Nightmare on Elm Street 5: The Dream Child*, *Predator 2*, *Blown Away* and *Lost in Space*.

Brian Grazer, Tony Krantz, Howard Gordon & Ron Howard (producers)

The man behind *Liar, Liar*, *The Grinch Who Stole Christmas*, the *Nutty Professor* remakes, *Apollo 13*, *Ransom* and *From The Earth To the Moon*, Brian Grazer joined forces with film director Ron Howard back in 1986 to form Imagine Films Entertainment, Inc. Howard's *A Beautiful Mind* brought Grazer an Academy Award as producer in 2002.

Tony Krantz is founding partner, CEO and chairman of Imagine; the sister company Imagine Television was founded in 1997. Executive producer Howard Gordon has written for the CBS series *Beauty and the Beast* and acted as consulting producer on *Buffy the Vampire Slayer* and its spin-off, *Angel*. He was also executive producer and senior writer on the long-running FBI sci-fi series, *The X-Files*. Executive producer Ron Howard is a popular movie director, whose hits include *Splash*, *Cocoon*, *Parenthood*, *Backdraft*, *Apollo 13* and *A Beautiful Mind*.

TICK FOLLOWS TOCK FOLLOWS TICK:

00 13:41 07:24 22:38 10:09 17:59 09:13 21:01 04:45 14:12 07:57 13:41 07:24 22:38 10:09 17:59 09:13 19

THE MAKING OF *24*

I. The Concept

It was Joel Surnow who first played with the idea of a TV show filmed in real time. He pitched it to Robert Cochran, who Surnow had worked with regularly over the years. 'We did 96 episodes of *Nikita* together, 44 of *The Commish*, 22 of *Falcon Crest*. We've done hundreds of hours of story breaking together, which is the hardest part of our job.' Though the concept was a novel one, Cochran worried if it was even possible. 'I told him it sounded very clever,' Cochran revealed to *Directorsworld.com*, 'but it might be impossible to think of stories that would work with that premise.' However, the writing duo started thinking about what kind of story might require a full 24 hours to tell, one that wouldn't allow for food, sleep or even (eep!) toilet breaks. The idea of an assassination attempt on a presidential candidate came forth, but they knew they'd need to make the story more personal to be able to maintain a genuine level of intensity. 'Joel and I both have teenage daughters,' Cochran explains, 'and we thought one night if either of our daughters disappeared, we probably wouldn't get much sleep. So we put both of those things onto our hero and after that, everything started to flow.' From there, it was a natural leap to suggest that the group threatening the candidate and the group who are behind the daughter's abduction are one and the same.

Fox responded favourably to the script and, despite the existence of a number of similarly themed concepts flying round, they decided to commission a pilot of ***24***. Although they aired concerns over potentially alienating the audience by expecting them to watch every episode, Fox decided to take a risk and commissioned an initial series of 13 episodes with an option to extend the run to the full 24 that Surnow and Cochran had envisaged.

II. The Star

For the all-important role of Jack Bauer, Surnow and Cochran chose former brat-packer Kiefer Sutherland. 'First of all, I didn't know if he could pull off Bauer,' said Surnow:

> *'We loved him as an actor. What he has is a lot of anger. He sort of reminds me of Gene Hackman in a way: he's kind of a tough, angry guy. You channel that and turn him into a hero, you got a really volatile, potent character... What I didn't know that he could pull off was being the father and stepping into full manhood, which he has.'*

Sutherland himself had already made the decision to attempt a move towards television when he took the lead role in an unsuccessful pilot for a TV version of the hit film *L.A. Confidential*. Speaking to the British newspaper *The Observer*, he described the concept as 'incredibly innovative':

> *'We're approaching this as a 24-hour movie... Each scene on* **24** *has to be seamless. There's no time break between scenes. In a regular movie or TV series you play someone who has an argument with your boss or your wife, and the next scene is an hour or two later when you've come down from the argument. We don't have that luxury. The continuity is non-stop.'*

III. The Director(s)

For the pilot, the team managed to get director James Foley (who had previously directed the film *Glengarry Glen Ross* and the promo video for Madonna's 'Papa Don't Preach'). But then, a week before work began on the pilot, Foley was forced to abandon the project after a family tragedy and Stephen Hopkins was brought in as a last-minute replacement. Fortuitously, it was Hopkins and David Thompson, the editor, who came up with the idea of using split-screen in the pilot because of the number of phone calls. Eventually they started letting it creep in to help them keep track of all the concurrent storylines. Such a small decision eventually shaped the look of the show. Hopkins confesses:

> *'I am obsessed with American '70s movies, and they used to do this very well back then. I think now that we're living in the age of computers, where we are used to looking at lots of different screens at the same time, people might be ready to have another go at it.'*

Of the first 13 episodes, Hopkins directed seven, including the pilot. Three other directors, Winrich Kolbe (*JAG*, *Angel*), Bryan Spicer (*The X-Files*) and Davis Guggenheim (*NYPD Blue*, *ER*) took on two episodes each with a schedule of just 15 days to film two hours of drama. Everyone took their lead from Hopkins' dynamic hand-held camerawork for the pilot. Says Hopkins:

> *'I thought if we're going to get real time, let's try and make it feel gritty and documentary-like, so you don't know what these characters are doing. I wanted to try to follow these people around as if you didn't know where this story was heading.'*

Although it was a hectic schedule, the crew managed to get all the episodes in the can in time for their allotted 'first night'. What they could have never dreamed was that shortly before the transmission of the pilot, an event on September 11 that year would make their fictional thriller terrifyingly real for thousands of Americans...

Principal Production Team

Created by Joel Surnow & Robert Cochran

Executive Producers: Brian Grazer, Tony Krantz, Howard Gordon, Robert Cochran, Joel Surnow

Co-Producers: Robin Chamberlain, Michael Loceff

Co-Executive Producers: Stephen Hopkins, Ron Howard

Producers: Andrea Newman, Cyrus Yavneh

Consulting Producer: Michael S. Chernuchin

Associate Producer: Paul Gadd

Original Music: Sean Callery

Cinematography: Rodney Charters, Peter Levy

Film Editing: David Latham, Scott Powell, David B. Thompson, Chris G. Willingham

Casting: Debi Manwiller

Production Design: Carlos Barbosa, Joseph A. Hodges

Set Decoration: Ellen Brill, Claudia Rebar

Costume Design: James Lapidus

Principal Cast

Kiefer Sutherland as Jack Bauer

Leslie Hope as Teri Bauer

Elisha Cuthbert as Kimberly Bauer

Dennis Haysbert as Senator David Palmer

Mia Kirshner as Mandy

Sarah Lively as Nina Myers

Production Code 1AFF79

First US Transmission: Tuesday, November 6, 9/8C

Written by Robert Cochran & Joel Surnow
Directed by Stephen Hopkins

'The following takes place between midnight and 1:00 A.M. on the day of the California presidential primary... Events occur in real time.'

Cast: Mia Kirshner (Mandy), Carlos Bernard (Tony Almeida), Penny Johnson Jerald (Sherry Palmer), Michael O'Neill (Richard Walsh), Xander Berkeley (George Mason), Rudolf Martin (Martin Belkin), Richard Burgi (Alan York), Daniel Bess (Rick), Matthew Carey (Dan), Jacqui Maxwell (Janet York), Tanya Wright (Patty Brooks), Karina Arroyave (Jamey Farrell), Devika Parikh (Maureen Kingsley), Gary Murphy (Vincent), Jeff Ricketts (Victor Rovner), Karen Kim (Flight Attendant), Petra Wright (Flight Attendant).

EPISODE SUMMARY

It's **4:00 P.M.** in Kuala Lumpur, Malaysia. American Agent Victor Rovner rushes through the streets to his apartment to contact his agency back in the USA via a satellite link-up. Outside, he can hear banging on his door, but his message reaches its destination just in time. In Los Angeles, California, it's just turned **midnight**. **Richard Walsh**, a high-ranking agent in the Counter Terrorist Unit (CTU), receives notification of Rovner's communication – Rovner has uncovered a plot to assassinate **Senator David Palmer**. Palmer himself has no idea of this. Later on today, just a few hours after dawn, the 'Super Tuesday' presidential primaries will begin and he will face the Californian public vote. In another part of town, with his wife, **Sherry**, and his advisors by his side, Palmer makes final adjustments to his first speech of the day.

One of Walsh's agents, **Jack Bauer**, is at home playing chess with his teenage daughter, **Kimberly**. Though he and his wife **Teri** were recently separated, Jack has just moved back into the family home to attempt a reconciliation. Kim seems pleased that her father has returned, largely because she has always held her mother responsible for the split, something that Jack is all too aware of. Sending Kim to bed, Jack discusses the situation with Teri. She feels Kim is trying to play them off against each other, so Jack suggests to her that they show a united front to Kim in the hope she accepts her mother's authority as readily as she accepts his. But when the couple knock on their daughter's room they discover that she has defied them both by sneaking out of the house through her bedroom window without permission. Teri is furious and insists that when Kim returns she be grounded for a month and prevented from starting the driving lessons she wanted so much. But before Jack can come to terms with this, the phone rings. It's **Nina Myers**, Jack's chief of staff at the CTU office. Richard Walsh has summoned an emergency meeting. As Jack leaves the house for the office, he calls Kim's ex-boyfriend **Vincent** to ask him if perhaps he's arranged a secret rendezvous with Kim. Vincent, however, claims to have no idea where Kim might be. His daughter's disobedience will have to wait for now.

Kimberly is in fact with her friend **Janet York**, who has managed to arrange a double date for them with two guys, **Dan** and **Rick**, who are sophomores at San Diego University. Janet is a little stressed by the fact that she'd arranged to meet Dan and his friend at midnight and they're already six minutes late, but Kim reassures her, pointing out that they're both hot-looking girls and if these boys are as mature as Janet seems to think they are, they'll be sure to wait for them.

Jack reaches CTU headquarters by **12:09 A.M.** and calls home just to reassure Teri that everything will be OK. Nina has already assembled Jack's team, including agent **Tony Almeida** and computer programmer **Jamey Farrell**. Having already heard of reports of a possible assassination conspiracy, Jack has determined that the most likely subject is Senator Palmer, but it's an assumption that makes Tony uneasy:

Tony: 'If it leaks out that we're screening Palmer, people might think it's because he's black.'

Jack: 'Well, it is because he's black. It makes him the most likely target.'

Tony: 'I'm just saying it might not be interpreted that way on the outside.'

Jack: 'I don't care how it's interpreted on the outside. I just gave you an order and I'd like you to follow it, please.'

Despite Tony's concerns, Jack tells him and the rest of his team to pull out any information on Palmer they think might be relevant. At the same time as this, Kimberly and Janet reach their destination, a large furniture store where Dan works. Janet runs off inside with Dan, leaving Kim to introduce herself to Rick. There's a strong attraction for both of them, though Kim is determined to play it cool. But secretly, she's looking forward to a night of serious partying.

Grabbing a spare minute, Jack calls a friend of his at the Los Angeles Police Department to keep a lookout for Kimberly, explaining the situation. Walsh finally arrives just after **12.12 A.M.** and calls the team into a meeting room. Walsh tells them that, as Jack had suspected, intelligence has confirmed that an attempt will be made on Senator Palmer's life some time within the next 24 hours. They have no other information other than the probability that the assassination will be the work of a lone shooter from out of the country, probably funded by a hate group with a grudge. Walsh orders them to start immediately by checking all of Palmer's associates against their databases of known terrorists. As the team returns to work, Walsh holds Jack back to confide in him that he has reason to believe there is a mole within CTU and he needs Jack to find out who it is. Jack is reluctant to undertake the case – only last year, he brought a case against three of their own agents and busted them for taking bribes, something he suspects will stop him from getting anywhere near to the truth. But Walsh is insistent – Palmer is the first African-American with a serious chance of getting to the White House, and should anything happen to him it could tear the country apart. Jack is the only one Walsh feels he can trust and he alone will have to flush out the traitor or traitors. Walsh notifies Jack that District Director **George Mason** is on his way to brief him further. Jack asks him incredulously if he's expected to trust Mason and Walsh tells him in earnest:

12:00-1:00 A.M.

'Until we get a better handle on things don't trust anybody – not even your own people.'

At **12.22 A.M.**, renowned photographer **Martin Belkin** is on board an airplane heading for Los Angeles. Using the telephone handset in the seat in front of him, he calls Senator Palmer's campaign manager **Patty Brooks** to confirm that he will be meeting Palmer later that morning for breakfast. A young, attractive woman in the next seat to Belkin overhears his conversation and begins to quiz him about Palmer. He explains he's never met the man but that he soon will – he's due to photograph Palmer later that day.

By **12.25 A.M.**, Jack has informed Nina of the impending arrival of George Mason but refuses to explain further. Nina feels that Jack's shutting her out and playfully warns him that one day he'll ask too much of her. Their banter is cut short by a call from Teri who has just found three marijuana joints in Kimberly's desk. Jack suggests Teri opens Kim's e-mail to see what she might be up to, but Teri reminds him that they let her have her own password to show that they trusted her. Jack apologises for not being able to be with her and promises to call her later. Meanwhile, on the roof of the furniture store, their wayward daughter is getting close to Rick. To gain his sympathy, Kim tells him her father died six months ago.

It's **12:28 A.M.** Mason has arrived at CTU and is shown up to Jack's office. He tells Jack that their source has told them that the assassin is believed to be European, probably German, and either in the country already or arriving that day. Jack asks who his source is, but Mason is unwilling to tell him, claiming he too has his orders. Aware of the advice Walsh gave him, Jack asks Mason to at least try to get the authorisation to tell him the name of the source while he steps out of the office.

Leaving Mason to make the necessary phone call, Jack signals to Nina to tap into Mason's call and patch it into Jack's cellphone, only to hear the voice of the speaking clock on the other end of the line – just as he had suspected, Mason is not to be trusted. Jack heads over to an armoury store and equips himself with a tranquilliser gun. Returning to his office he allows Mason just enough time to lie to him about being unable to share his source before shooting him with a tranquilliser dart in the leg. Mason is unconscious within seconds. Nina enters Jack's office and is appalled, but Jack explains his actions. He tells her Mason is holding back information and he needs bargaining time to get that information. He reminds her of a previous case involving a convicted heroin dealer called Phillipe Darcet. Jack has always suspected that Mason had somehow stolen $200,000 from Darcet's assets and transferred it into his own account. Now he intends to use this information to blackmail Mason into revealing his source. But first, he needs evidence.

At Jack's home, Teri receives a call from a man introducing himself as **Alan York**. He's just got home from work to find his daughter, Janet, missing. Teri tells her that Kim is also missing and Alan suggests the likelihood of their daughters being together. He gives Teri his number and asks her to call him if she should hear anything.

Knowing how Tony feels about him, Jack asks Nina if she'll get Tony to unlock Mason's bank account details. But Tony accuses Nina of doing what Jack tells her because he believes she and Jack are having an affair. Nina refuses to confirm or deny the allegation but manages to convince Tony to do what she asks. Meanwhile, with the help of his computer expert, Jamey, Jack is able to get Kim's e-mail password – 'LIFESUCKS' – and he phones Teri with the news.

It's now **12:43 A.M.** and on the plane, Martin and his fellow passenger continue to chat flirtatiously. At around about the same time,

Senator Palmer gets a phone call from **Maureen Kingsley**, a TV news reporter. Sherry can't hear what's being said, but it's clear that Maureen has made an allegation and asked David to comment on it. David is furious and ends the conversation. Sherry asks him what Maureen wanted, but David dismisses it as 'more media nonsense... not important'. Sherry is unconvinced but David refuses to discuss it further.

Jack's behaviour is worrying Nina. Breaking into private accounts and shooting the district director are not ways to get his life back on track. Nina begs him to confide in her just what's going on. All Jack can offer as an explanation is that he refuses to look the other way when he's surrounded by corruption. The agents he brought a case against last year were just normal people who had compromised their position.

Teri phones Alan York to tell her she's broken into Kim's e-mail and found an address where she thinks the girls might have gone. She's going to head there straight away and Alan asks if he can come along too, offering to pick her up on the way. Meanwhile, Kimberly has turned on her cellphone to find five messages from her mother. The boys invite her and Janet to a party, but Kim tells them that she should probably go home. Janet, however, isn't ready to end the party and decides to go with the boys. Rick promises to drop Kim off on the way and, reluctantly, she climbs into their van.

By **12:52 A.M.,** Martin and the flirty passenger have just finished having sex in the bathroom of the aircraft. She tells him her name is **Mandy** and asks him if they might be able to meet up once they reach Los Angeles, but he tells her he'll be busy and sneaks back to his seat. Back at CTU, Tony gives Jack access to the Darcet account – now it's time to wake Mason. Once again, Jack asks who the source is, but when Mason threatens him, Jack shows him that he has uncovered the unauthorised transfer of $200,000 from Darcet's account into Mason's and the district director is forced to reveal his source at last. As Jack allows him to leave, Mason warns him he'll live to regret his actions.

Leaving Martin snoozing, Mandy tiptoes over to the back of the plane and puts the flight attendant out with a quick injection. Recovering her hand luggage, she inspects a wallet that she stole from Martin and takes his identification card before changing into a jumpsuit. Next, she removes a bomb that's been hidden inside a fire extinguisher and primes it. With just four seconds to go, Mandy casually ejects herself from the cabin as the plane explodes. Pieces of burning debris soar past her as she freefalls.

Teri calls Jack at **12:57 A.M.** to let him know she and Alan York are driving to the address she found on Kim's e-mail. Before she can tell him the address, her signal cuts out. Jack asks Nina to cover for him as he attempts to leave the office, but just then Tony gets news that a 747 has blown up over the Mojave Desert. Initial reports suggest it was a bomb. Jack tells Tony to locate a passenger list and Nina to get Walsh on the phone. It dawns on Jack that he won't be able to leave the office any time soon.

Kim realises that Dan has driven past the turning to her house, and when she asks him to turn back, Rick tells her to relax: 'The night's just getting started.' Kim sits back in her seat, visibly worried.

High above the Mojave Desert, a lone figure releases a parachute to guide her safely to the ground...

NOTES

- **Who's Who?:** Richard Burgi (Alan York) served his time in daytime TV, playing Chad Rollo on *Another World* (1986-1988), Glen Harrington in *As the World Turns* (1988-89) and Phillip Collier on *Days of Our Lives* (1992-93). Michael O'Neill (Richard Walsh) might be familiar to viewers of *The West Wing*, where he plays Secret Service Agent Ron Butterfield, while in the same show, Devika Parikh plays Bonnie. Rudolf Martin [Martin Belkin] played Anton Lang in the US daytime soap *All My Children* from 1992-1995, and appeared in an episode of *Buffy the Vampire Slayer* as Dracula.

- **Time Checks:** Walsh – 'For the next 24 hours I want you all over this.' Jack tells Nina that Mason will be unconscious for about 30 minutes [translation: 'he'll be out until towards the end of the episode...'].
- **Music:** As Jack and Kim talk over chess in the living room, we hear 'It's All Good' by The Fearless Freep; when Kim sneaks out, she leaves The Dirtmitts' 'Fix And Destroy' playing in her room, while when Jack phones Vincent, he's deafened by Sugarcult's 'Bouncing Off The Walls'; Janet plays 'Compromise' by Mean Red Spiders on the way to the furniture store, and when they get there we hear 'Live At E's' by Sublime and 'Chair On A Wire' by Krome; inside the store, Dan is blasting out 'Everything And Nothing' by Rocket Science; Mason is tranquillised by Jack to the accompaniment of Gustavo Santaolalla's 'Iguaza'; Kim and Rick kiss to The Angel's 'Destiny Complete', while back at Dan's van we hear 'Feelin' Irie' by Jazz Pharmacy. Finally, as Dan's van drives off into the night, the episode ends with 'Christiansands' by Tricky. Incidentally, for the untransmitted pilot, filler music was used, including 'Californication' by the Red Hot Chilli Peppers, 'Ray Of Light' by Madonna and 'Butterfly' by Crazy Town.
- **Death Count:** The passengers of Flight #221, including Martin Belkin and the air stewardesses [all at 12:57 A.M.].
- **Trivia:** Jack's home phone number is 310 555 3067, the licence plate number of his car is 4RHI 384, and his office is 248. Kim has Coldplay and 2Pac posters on her bedroom walls. According to Kimberly, the Bauers live on 10th Street, which would appear to be

less than ten minutes away from CTU H.Q. David Palmer's hotel is on Sunset Boulevard, opposite the famous Argyle Hotel where Bette Davis once lived.

COMMENTS

Without in any way attempting to make a crass link between the events of September 11 2001, and the success of ***24***, it is nevertheless clear that the existence of terrorist organisations intent on targeting the American people was, more than ever, at the forefront of every mind in the country, even two months later. The world had witnessed the destruction of the Twin Towers of the World Trade Center live on CNN and every other TV news service across the globe. With the loss of life reaching into the thousands, the effect of this one event would be far-reaching.

The entertainment industry was quick to react. Instantaneously, films and TV shows scrambled to remove any material that might be considered inappropriate. Films about terrorism were slipped back in the schedules or shelved completely. Old favourites such as *The Towering Inferno*, *Die Hard* and even the *Airplane* movies were suddenly untransmittable. And while all this was taking place, Imagine Television were putting the final touches to an hour of drama that had, at its heart, a terrorist conspiracy that involved the destruction of a 747. ***24***'s planned plane bomb sequence was, of course, trimmed down slightly for its first broadcast out of respect; the original cut had included a shot of the plane visibly exploding, which was replaced with clever editing and sound to suggest the plane's demise without showing it. But even this was an incredibly strong image to be showing so soon after 11/9. And it's to ***24***'s credit that, from the outset, it set itself apart from other shows by not being afraid to tackle difficult subjects.

QUESTIONS ARISING

- How did Victor Rovner uncover the assassination plot in the first place? Was his information in any way correct? Who is he actually working for? What happened to Rovner after he made his transmission?
- Why did Jack and Teri split up? Does it have anything to do with the alleged relationship between Jack and Nina, and if so, why does Kim blame her mother?
- Why was Mason withholding the identity of his source?
- What is the allegation Maureen Kingsley made to David Palmer, and why won't he tell his wife about it?
- Why did Mandy go to all that trouble and expense to steal Martin's ID?
- ...and how exactly did Janet get from Santa Monica to the Valley in just under six minutes without getting caught by the traffic police for speeding?

07:24 22:38 10:09 17:59 09:13 21:01 04:45 14:12 07:57 13:41 07:24 22:38 10:09 17:59 09:13 19:47 05:20

Production Code 1AFF01

First US Transmission: Tuesday, November 13, 9/8C

Written by Michael Loceff & Joel Surnow
Directed by Stephen Hopkins

'The following takes place between 1:00 A.M. and 2:00 A.M. on the day of the California presidential primary... Events occur in real time.'

Cast: Penny Johnson Jerald (Sherry Palmer), Carlos Bernard (Tony Almeida), Richard Burgi (Alan York), Mia Kirshner (Mandy), Michael O'Neill (Richard Walsh), Michael Massee (Ira Gaines), Rudolf Martin (Jonathan – the fake Martin Belkin), Daniel Bess (Rick), Matthew Carey (Dan), Jacqui Maxwell (Janet York), Karina Arroyave (Jamey Farrell), Vicellous Shannon (Keith Palmer), Megalyn Echikunwoke (Nicole Palmer), Kim Murphy (Bridgit), Glenn Morshower (Agent Aaron Pierce), Scott Denny (Scott Baylor), Tanya Wright (Patty Brooks).

EPISODE SUMMARY

Walsh is not answering his phone. While Nina continues trying to reach him, Tony quizzes Jack about Mason's visit. He noticed that Mason was limping when he left Jack's office and asks Jack to explain what's going on. Nina jumps in and tells Tony within earshot of the rest of the department that Mason is holding a grudge against Jack for what happened last summer with the corrupt agents and chose his moment to make accusations against Jack and other members of his team.

In the Mojave Desert, the terrorist, Mandy, burns her parachute to remove any evidence, then places the identity card she stole from Martin Belkin inside a metal case that sends out a homing signal. She buries the case in the dirt shortly before a car comes to collect her. Once the car is out of sight, a motorcyclist uses a homing device to unearth the case.

Back at CTU, Tony accuses Nina of lying about what happened with Mason and Jack. Nina reminds him that Palmer's life is at stake and that he should just get on with his work. Jack phones Teri just as she and Alan reach the Palladio furniture store in Van Nuys, the address Teri found on Kim's e-mail. Janet's car is still outside the store and Teri tells Jack she'll call him back as she and Alan begin to explore inside. Upstairs in the bed section, Alan finds an empty condom wrapper.

Kim becomes worried about Janet, who appears to have been drugged by Dan. Becoming increasingly frustrated by the guys, she reveals that she lied about her father being dead and tells them that he's a government agent. The guys don't seem too impressed and tell her to 'chill'.

Just before **1:10 A.M.**, Richard Walsh makes his way to 2350 Dunlop Plaza to meet with **Scott Baylor**, a CTU analyst. Baylor has been secretly working for Walsh and tells him he has acquired a security keycard, the kind commonly used to gain access to CTU. This keycard, however, is special: hidden in the card's magnetic strip is a file that can be used to smuggle sensitive, even restricted, information in and out of the building with ease. Baylor believes the card contains top-secret information about Senator Palmer. Walsh is grateful for Baylor's help, but needs him to continue working for him. Baylor is reluctant – he doesn't know what the information is, but he knows it's something serious and has already taken the precaution of sending his family away just in case anything happens. Walsh persuades him to give him just one more day, but at that point, Baylor is shot dead by unseen gunmen and Walsh is wounded. Walsh calls Jack to tell him what has happened. Jack leaves the office to rescue him.

Kim tries to reason with Rick, who claims that they're just involved in a fraternity stunt until he lets slip that other people are involved. Still unconscious, Janet begins to choke, and as Rick opens a window to get her some air, Kim leaps at Dan and tries to wrestle the wheel from him. Dan pushes her away and regains control of the wheel as Rick restrains the now-panicking Kim.

By **1:20 A.M.**, news of the plane crash has reached the TV stations. David and Sherry Palmer watch the report while they wait for their son and daughter to return from a political rally. David apologises for shutting Sherry out earlier, saying he's just overreacting to everything at the moment. This seems to set Sherry's mind at rest and she decides to go to bed.

Mandy arrives safe and well at an old house not far from her landing site. There, she collects her payment from **Ira Gaines**, who invites her to join him in the summer on another operation. Mandy is not interested; she just wants to lie low for a while. Gaines asks her about the I.D. and she tells him it's on its way.

Having arrived at Dunlop Plaza, Jack calls Nina and asks her to get him the entry code for the garage's security gates. Unbeknownst to either of them, Tony is reading the automatic log of their call and grows even more suspicious of the pair's actions. Jack makes his way to the roof of the Plaza and finds Walsh wounded but safe. Back at Gaines's hideout, Mandy is astounded to meet **Jonathan**, a marksman who has been made to look like the photographer Martin Belkin through extensive plastic surgery. She realises that Jonathan has been hired to kill David Palmer.

Jack uses Walsh's tie as a makeshift tourniquet for Walsh's arm. Walsh apologises for dragging him into this, but as far as Jack's concerned, he owes Walsh his life. The men head towards the foyer, but on the way they find themselves under fire from the shooters. Between them, they manage to shoot two men down. Using a retractable knife, Jack removes a thumb from one of the bodies and wraps it in a handkerchief.

The motorcyclist – a woman called **Bridgit** – reaches Gaines's house by **1:37 A.M.**, but instead of handing over Belkin's I.D. to Gaines, she hands him a polaroid photo of it, telling him she wants another $1 million in addition to the million already promised. Even the threat of a gun to her head doesn't frighten her – she knows she's the only one who knows where the I.D. is. Gaines concedes, but Mandy is furious with Bridgit for even trying such a stunt.

As they clear up the mess left by their daughters, Teri tells Alan that her husband works for the government and calls Jack to see if he can use his contacts to help them. Jack has turned off his cellphone, meaning Teri is unable to reach him. Instead, she calls Nina to ask for her help in finding the owner of the furniture store.

At **1:44 A.M.**, Sherry hears her children, **Keith** and **Nicole**, get back from the campaign rally. Nicole decides to go straight to bed, but Keith is too excited. Evidently the rally went well. David steps into another room to take a call from one of his aides, **Carl Webb**. David tells Carl about

Maureen Kingsley's call earlier that morning. Not wishing to discuss it over the phone, David insists that Carl meets him immediately.

While she waits for Nina to get back to her, Teri tells Alan that she and Jack were recently separated, though they're now back together. He in turn tells her that when he and his ex split up, she went home to Australia and hasn't spoken to him or Janet in ten years. Nina calls Teri back with the owner's name – Mr Naraste – and phone number. Teri calls Naraste but gets his answer machine so she leaves him a message, hoping to find out more about the boys that Janet and Kim are with.

Aaron Pierce, a Secret Service agent, comes to Palmer's hotel suite only to find Palmer has slipped out unnoticed. Pierce tells Sherry and Keith that he has clear evidence that an attempt will be made on David Palmer's life some time that day.

1:53 A.M. Jack and Walsh head towards Jack's car. A sniper lurking in the shadows begins to hail them with bullets and Walsh is hit, apparently fatally. Walsh throws the keycard to Jack, telling him to get it to Jamey, who he is certain can be trusted. She should be able to see which CTU computer terminal the card is linked to and flush out the dirty agent. As Jack makes for his car, more shots ring out and he is forced to abandon his friend to die. He drives off to safety, tears blurring his vision. Eventually, he feels composed enough to call Jamey to inform her of the death of two agents and the existence of the keycard. Jamey tells him he can use the mobile scanner in his card to transmit the keycard's data to her so she can begin tracing the computer that encoded it.

At **1:56 A.M.** Dan pulls his van over to the side of the road. He orders Kimberly to phone her mother and tell her she's at a party. Kim refuses and Dan makes to hit her but Rick reminds him that 'Gaines said not to hurt her'. Instead, Dan breaks Janet's arm with a crowbar, which instantly convinces Kim to do exactly as she's told. Teri is, naturally, relieved to hear from Kim and that she and Janet are apparently alright. As she signs off, a tearful Kim tells her mother that she loves her. Dan thinks it's just a cute touch, but Teri rightly interprets Kim's words as a sign that something is wrong – she tells Alan that Kim never tells her she loves her.

It's one minute before **2:00 A.M.** and Jamey thinks she's traced the terminal that encoded the keycard. She calls Jack and breaks the news to him – it's Nina's. Meanwhile, within the grounds of Gaines's hideout, Jonathan indulges in a little target practice.

NOTES

- **Who's Who?:** Michael Masse (Ira Gaines) played a character called 'Funboy' in the film *The Crow*. Kim Murphy (Bridgit) appeared in a couple of episodes of the US series *Party of Five* and the sitcom *Cybill*. You can catch a young Vicellous Shannon (Keith Palmer) in the surprisingly entertaining *D2: The Mighty Ducks* (where he's credited as Vicellous *Reon* Shannon). Glenn Morshower (Agent Pierce) was a semi-regular in the series *JAG* and has also appeared in episodes of *The West Wing* and *CSI: Crime Scene Investigation*.
- **Time Checks:** Scott agrees to work for Walsh for just 24 hours – the gunmen shoot him to death less than 24 *seconds* later.
- **Music:** In Dan's van, at various points in the episode, we hear 'Did You Forget' by Perry Farrell, 'Losing An Edge' by Rocket Science and 'Darker' by The Doves. According to Keith, the band Green Day played 'A Time Of Your Life' at the rally.
- **Death Count:** Scott Baylor (killed by shooters at 1:11 A.M.), two unidentified shooters (shot by Jack and Walsh at 1:35 A.M.) and Richard Walsh (shot by a sniper at 1:45 A.M.).
- **Trivia:** The entry code for 2350 Dunlop Plaza is 91367*. Gaines's hideout is just 16 minutes away from where Mandy landed in the

Mojave Desert. The home phone number of Mr Naraste (the owner of the Palladio furniture store in Van Nuys) would appear to be 555-2927 (though Alan York clangs his dustpan and brush to mask the last two numbers).

COMMENTS

A blonde woman lies tied to a rail track screaming as she sees the 3.15 express come relentlessly chugging into view. Safe on the railway embankment cackling with laughter stands an oily middle-aged man with a waxed moustache. Suddenly, from nowhere, a handsome young hero leaps onto the man's back – there is a fight and the hero manages to punch the villain, knocking him out. He runs swiftly to untie the woman and frees her just as the train hurtles by...

Silent movies were full of this kind of rubbish; damsels in distress, strong, reliable men always around to save them and a nasty villain, motivated by greed, revenge or lust (often all three) vowing to return. Audiences loved it – it didn't matter if it was formulaic or if we knew the hero would escape week after week from sawmills, burning cars or exploding laboratories. We watched because we enjoyed being kept in suspense for a week to see *how* he escaped.

Though we'd probably like to think otherwise, we haven't really matured much as an audience 70 years on. We still want our spills and thrills; we're addicted to that fix of adrenalin. We still want our heroes and heroines to escape the clutches of death by a gnat's whisker only to find themselves in peril once more, just in time for the closing credits. We need it because, without once putting ourselves at risk, it's a reminder of that basic human necessity – survival. The bigger the threat to the fictional characters, the greater the relief when they escape unharmed. We might deny it, but we don't *want* Kim to escape her kidnappers just yet; we don't want Jack to find her with just one call on his cellphone, and we definitely don't want David Palmer to win the election without first being seen to suffer. If they're to achieve their goals, they have to *earn* them. Of course, just to keep things exciting, and because all viewers are, at heart, sadists, we also need there to be casualties along the way...

QUESTIONS ARISING

- If Nina was having an affair with Jack until recently, why did she feel the need to lie about coming into work early with Tony a month ago? Is she now seeing Tony too? Was she two-timing them?
- Who are the shooters, and why do they want to stop Walsh getting the keycard?
- What previous incident resulted in Jack feeling indebted for his life to Walsh?
- Is Nina a traitor?

7:24 22:38 10:09 17:59 09:13 21:01 04:45 14:12 07:57 13:41 07:24 22:38 10:09 17:59 09:13 19:47 05:20

Production Code 1AFF02

First US Transmission: Tuesday, November 20, 9/8C

Written by Michael Loceff & Joel Surnow
Directed by Stephen Hopkins

'The following takes place between 2:00 A.M. and 3:00 A.M. on the day of the California presidential primary... Events occur in real time.'

Cast: Penny Johnson Jerald (Sherry Palmer), Carlos Bernard (Tony Almeida), Richard Burgi (Alan York), Mia Kirshner (Mandy), Michael Massee (Ira Gaines), Daniel Bess (Rick), Matthew Carey (Dan), Jacqui Maxwell (Janet York), Rudolf Martin (Jonathan – the fake Martin Belkin), Karina Arroyave (Jamey Farrell), Vicellous Shannon (Keith Palmer), Zach Grenier (Carl Webb), Kim Murphy (Bridgit), Keram Malicki-Sanchez (Larry Rogow), Glenn Morshower (Agent Aaron Pierce), Stephen DuVall (Rocco), Marcus Brown (Teenager #1), Joe Nieves (Teenager #2), Carmen Mormino (Businessman).

EPISODE SUMMARY

Using the scanner in his car, Jack sends a print of the thumb to data services to see if they can find a match. Teri calls to tell him about Kim's call. She mentions the way Kim said 'I love you', but Jack thinks this is just Kim's way of trying to get out of being grounded. He asks Teri to put Alan York on the phone and pressures him into staying at the store to wait for the girls.

At the hideout, Gaines is furious with Bridgit for trying to change the agreement, especially because his bosses are rushing him to proceed to the next stage of the plan. Jonathan needs to leave soon, so the retrieval of the I.D. is now imperative. Gaines blames Mandy for Bridgit's amateurish stunt and tells her to explain to Bridgit why she can't have any more money.

As David has received a number of unfounded death threats since he announced his candidacy, Sherry can't understand why this latest one is being taken so seriously. Agent Pierce explains that his unit is only ever called when the situation is serious. Sherry asks him why he let David slip past him but immediately apologises; she's all too aware of how much her family needs their protection. Keith decides to go looking for his father but Agent Pierce prevents him from leaving by pointing out that they consider a threat on a candidate's life to include his family.

At **2:08 A.M.**, Dan drives up to an airfield. Gaines calls him to check up on 'the Bauer girl' and to let him know that he's running late and that Dan should wait for him. Janet is still in agony with her broken arm and Kim demands they take her friend to the hospital. Rick suggests they should give her something to dull the pain, but Dan refuses to use any of his drugs on her. Rick defies Dan and prepares a syringe. To Kim's disgust, Rick injects Janet directly into her arm to help her with the pain.

David Palmer pulls into an underground parking garage just before

2:15 A.M., where two thugs are smashing car windows for kicks. They recognise David and begin to harass him.

Thug: 'What you gonna do for me, Mr President?'
Palmer: 'See, that's your problem. You want everyone else to do the work. What are you going to do for yourself?'
Thug: 'See man, all y'all, y'all got the same rap.'
Palmer: 'Keep going like this, and you'll be dead in five years.'
Thug: 'What you know of my life?'
Palmer: 'More than you think...'

The boys are less than impressed by David's lecture and in an act of defiance they smash the rear windscreen of his car.

Jack returns to the Counter Terrorist Unit at **2:17 A.M.** Lurking in the shadows, he phones Nina and, pretending he's still a block away from H.Q., he asks her to fetch the passenger reports on the plane crash from Tony and wait for him in his office. With Nina out of the way, Jack sneaks over to Jamey and passes her the keycard he got from Walsh. He tells her to search Nina's workstation to confirm whether or not it really was encrypted there and in turn prove that Nina is a traitor. He then heads up to his office to keep Nina distracted. Nina is annoyed that he's not keeping her informed. He asks her if she thinks it's possible that there's a traitor in their team to gauge her reaction, but Nina seems surprised at the idea. Jamey signals to Jack to keep Nina talking so he turns his attention to Nina's love life by asking her if she's seeing Tony. Understandably, Nina is annoyed that he could pry like that and suggests he's only asking to see if she's over him yet. At that moment, Jamey calls Jack on an internal line to let him know she's got a positive confirmation that the encrypted key came from Nina's computer. Jack lets Nina go. While he changes his shirt, he gets a call-back from data services. They've been unable to get a match on the thumbprint from Dunlop Plaza.

Mandy spells out the situation to Bridgit. Her greed could get them both killed.

Bridgit: 'They hired you to blow up a plane. Another million dollars doesn't mean anything to these people.'

Mandy: 'You're wrong – money is the only thing these people care about.'

Bridgit however is very persuasive and plays on Mandy's feelings for her. The women kiss passionately and Mandy agrees to insist on the additional million from Gaines.

At the airfield, Kimberly rouses the drugged Janet and explains that they have been kidnapped. Janet doesn't believe her until she sees the mess her arm is in – only then does the pain begin to kick in again. Kimberly convinces Janet that they have to escape and, while Dan and Rick are distracted, the girls run off across the airfield but the guys spot them and give chase. Meanwhile, Jamey quizzes Jack about his former relationship with Nina. Jack admits that, while he and his wife were separated, he and Nina had an affair. Jamey persuades him that, as Nina is a possible security risk, she should have her network access shut down. Jack reluctantly agrees.

Kim and Janet escape down a dark back alley. Trying to find a place to hide, the girls interrupt a young male prostitute who is servicing a businessman. Embarrassed, the suit runs off without paying and the boy is livid. However, when Dan and Rick ask him about the girls, he claims not to have seen them.

It's now **2:39 A.M.** Palmer meets up with **Carl Webb** and tells him about Maureen Kingsley's evidence against his son, Keith. Carl is well aware that, several years ago, Nicole was raped. It had always been thought that the accused rapist had committed suicide, but now Maureen claims to have evidence that Keith murdered him. Carl agrees to help him suppress Kingsley's story to help David's campaign. Just then, the Secret Service agents arrive and David is forced to go with them while Carl leaves to begin his work.

With Dan and Rick's search blocking their only escape route, Kimberly and Janet follow the rentboy into a warehouse. The boy resents the fact that the girls clearly come from privileged backgrounds and refuses to help them. Meanwhile, Jack finally confronts Nina over her treachery. Nina swears her innocence but Jack is not convinced. And out at the hideout, Gaines concedes to transfer an additional million dollars into the bank account of Mandy and Bridgit. Satisfied that her stunt worked, Bridgit agrees to take Gaines to where she hid the I.D. – but insists that only he and Mandy accompany her.

Kim and Janet run into a pimp talking on a cellphone. They ask for his help but the man wants paying and the girls have no money on them. The pimp is unsympathetic towards the girls' situation and makes a move on Janet. From nowhere, the rent boy attacks the pimp and shouts at the girls to take his cellphone and run. As the pimp begins to beat the boy savagely, Dan and Rick arrive. The pimp turns on them, blocking their route to the girls.

At **2:52 A.M.**, a CTU memorandum is circulated reporting Walsh's death. Tony can't believe it and asks Jamey to help him find out what happened. As Jamey is still working on something for Jack, she grants him special access on his own terminal so he can investigate further without disturbing her.

Bridgit leads Gaines and Mandy out to the desert. But once she hands over the I.D., Bridgit is shot in the back by a sniper – Jonathan, who has been hiding on a nearby hillside all along. Gaines repeats his offer of a job for Mandy in the summer. Aware that she's not in a position to refuse, she accepts.

Jamey shows Jack and Nina the evidence that links the keycard to Nina's terminal. The records show that the card was burned on January 14 that year. Jack dismisses Jamey and hurriedly apologises to Nina – he and Nina had gone away together to Santa Barbara that weekend, so there's no way Nina could have been responsible. It looks like someone deliberately set Nina up, but she's more upset that Jack would even doubt her in the first place. Tony, meanwhile, informs head office that Jack is out of control and should be replaced.

Using the pimp's cellphone, Kim calls her mother to admit that she's not at a party but in danger. She tells Teri where they are but then hangs up when she sees Dan and Rick running towards them. While Teri phones 911, the girls try to run for safety but Janet, dashing out into the road, is hit by a speeding car which then drives off. Kim hugs Janet and tries to revive her but then Dan and Rick catch up with her and drag her away, leaving Janet lying lifelessly in the road.

Unseen, Janet's eyes flicker open – she is still alive...

NOTES

- **Who's Who?:** Zach Grenier (Carl) appeared in *Fight Club* (dir. David Fincher, 1999) as the narrator's boss. But we don't talk about that. Keram Malicki-Sanchez (Larry Rogow) had a small part in *American History X* as a skinhead neo-Nazi, and also appeared in 'Earshot', a controversial episode of *Buffy the Vampire Slayer*.
- **Time Checks:** Data services remind Jack that he called them about

an hour ago when in fact it's been less than 20 minutes. When it's announced that Richard Walsh is dead, Jamey says that Walsh was just there an hour before – it was more like two and a half hours (although, considering the events so far this morning, it's understandable she's confused).

- **Death Count:** Bridgit, shot by Jonathan at 2:55 A.M.
- **Trivia:** Jack has a number of tattoos, including a sword or dagger and a Celtic band on his upper right arm, and a band of barbed wire on his upper left arm (actually Kiefer Sutherland's own tattoos). His authorisation number for data services is 4393-CTU. The Palmer suite is in room no. 1439.

COMMENTS

Despite the seemingly contrary evidence of shows like *Oz*, *Queer as Folk*, *Sex and the City* and *The Sopranos*, America remains a doggedly conservative nation when it comes to their television. Ellen DeGeneres has all but been driven off prime-time TV since her public declaration of her sexuality. And while on the surface the land of opportunities optimistically embraces differences in colour, belief, ability and sexuality in the pretence of equality, in truth the religious right has a stranglehold on what people see and how they can see it. It's alright to have a lesbian couple as the only stable relationship in *Friends*, just so long as they're not seen very often and only then so long as they're never seen to do anything other than hold hands. In *Dynasty*, they turned one character gay only for both of his boyfriends to be murdered (one by his father, one as only two casualties in the Moldavian 'massacre') before he himself 'reverted' to straight less than a year later. Even in DeGeneres's ground-breaking *Ellen*, the gay men were always of the non-threatening, non-sexual variety.

When television does dip into the sexuality pool to any extent, as in this episode, the outcome is inevitably the same. Gay men are instinctively *wrong*, so they're depicted as seedy, degenerate and selfish. Gay women are, of course, sexy – every straight man's fantasy – but still, they must be punished for not being loyal to men. The 'confused' Mandy, who only two hours earlier enticed a man into an airplane bathroom for a frenzied shag just to get at his wallet, is clearly capable of being 'straight', so she must be shown the error of her ways for dabbling with the corruptive Bridgit. Bridgit, being the temptress who leads Mandy astray, must die, so that Mandy can be sent on her way, once more under the control of Ira Gaines – who is, naturally, the avenging angel sent to right the world of its wrongs.

Of course, this view ignores the fact that the majority of ***24*** episodes feature the death of one or more characters, and corruption in the story extends way beyond the merely sexual. But it's easy to see why organisations such as G.L.A.A.D. (Gay and Lesbian Alliance Against Deformation) become upset by the constant misrepresentation of homosexuality when the only gay characters in this show are an alleyway prostitute and two terrorists. Whether or not that's the fault of the show's creators or the network they're trying to sell to is another matter.

QUESTIONS ARISING

- Who used Nina's terminal to create the encrypted keycard?
- Why does Gaines want Kim and who does he report to?
- Is Keith Palmer guilty of murder and if so, how did Maureen Kingsley find out about it?
- What is this 'job' Gaines has for Mandy?

3:00 A.M.

7:24 22:38 10:09 17:59 09:13 21:01 04:45 14:12 07:57 13:41 07:24 22:38 10:09 17:59 09:13 19:47 05:20

4:00 A.M.

Production Code 1AFF03

First US Transmission: Tuesday, November 27, 9/8C

Written by Robert Cochran
Directed by Winrich Kolbe

'The following takes place between 3:00 A.M. and 4:00 A.M. on the day of the California presidential primary... Events occur in real time.'

Cast: Penny Johnson Jerald (Sherry Palmer), Carlos Bernard (Tony Almeida), Richard Burgi (Alan York), Michael Massee (Ira Gaines), Daniel Bess (Rick), Matthew Carey (Dan), Vicellous Shannon (Keith Palmer), Jacqui Maxwell (Janet York), Karina Arroyave (Jamey Farrell), Yolonda Ross (Jessie Hampton), John Hawkes (Greg Penticoff), Xander Berkeley (George Mason), Zach Grenier (Carl), James MacDonald (Cop), Glenn Morshower (Agent Aaron Pierce), John Cothran Jr (Officer #3), Wiley Pickett (Simms), Kathy Byron (Woman), Mike Siegal (Agent), Johnny Vasquez (Janitor).

EPISODE SUMMARY

Dan and Rick take Kimberly back to the van unaware that Janet is alive and struggling to remain conscious. Passers-by assume she's a junkie or a drunk and leave her where she is. At CTU, Jack is still apologising to Nina for not instinctively trusting her and tells her that Walsh was killed because he had evidence that people in their own agency are involved in the planned hit on Palmer. He reassures her that she and Jamey are the only people he can trust, so the three of them will have to work together in exclusion of the others.

David Palmer returns to his hotel to find Sherry waiting for him. She tells him what Pierce had said about the believed assassination attempt but David is dismissive of the whole thing.

Inspecting the passenger records of the crashed 747, Tony discovers that there was an empty seat in first class, which, considering there was a waiting list for the flight, strikes him as odd. Jamey also has some success – uncovering a part of the encrypted file on the keycard to reveal an address – 18166 San Fernando Road. Sadly, that's all she's been able to decrypt and it could take her hours to completely unlock the keycard. Just then, the external phonelines and network access all go down. District Director George Mason storms the building with back-up and declares a lockdown – no-one is to enter or leave the building until he gives the signal. Thinking quickly, Jack sneaks out of a back entrance and heads over to the address Jamey found. As Mason briefs the team on the reasons for the lockdown, Nina accuses Tony of calling in Mason and challenging Jack's authority because of his own feelings for her. Tony insists he did it because he believes Jack is out of control.

At Palmer's campaign headquarters, Agent Pierce manages to convince Palmer that they are taking the threat against his life seriously. Pierce is concerned by the planned breakfast scheduled for first thing that morning, but Palmer insists it will go ahead. As the top labour leaders in the country will be attending, he can't afford to cancel it. Keith can't sleep so he decides to sit up and watch TV for a while. He's worried about the threat on his father's life, unaware that David is also worried about what might happen to his son if Maureen Kingsley's allegations prove to be true.

Kimberly tries to work on Rick to persuade Dan to turn back for Janet. If there's even a chance that she could be alive, Kim doesn't want to abandon her. Dan does indeed decide to go back to check – but to kill her just in case she can identify him and Rick. Dan orders Rick to tape up Kim's mouth to stop her screaming. Alan and Teri drive towards North Hollywood to where Kim said she and Janet were, but en route they get stopped by a traffic cop for speeding. Though they try to explain that their daughters are in danger, the cop refuses to listen and instructs them to stay in the car while he checks their documents. Teri tells him that she placed a 911 call just a few moments ago and begs him to check with his operator. The cop duly goes to radio in for confirmation, but Alan is impatient to leave and gets out of his car to remonstrate with the officer. Seeing Alan disobey a direct instruction, the cop feels duty-bound to arrest and cuff him. As Teri grows more and more worried, she fails to notice Dan's van drive past her.

At **3:23 A.M.**, Nina is summoned to speak to Mason, who has commandeered Jack's office for the duration of the lockdown. She claims she doesn't know where Jack is, though Mason rightly suspects she's simply playing dumb. He tries to get under her skin by alluding to her past relationship with Jack, claiming Jack frequently brags about it and suggesting that he couldn't have thought that much of her if he's prepared to leave her to take the rap for his actions.

In the meantime, Jack has found the address Jamey gave him. As he explores, he sees a man lurking in the shadows. He shouts to the man not to move but instead he darts off, firing a shot at Jack as he runs. The gunshot alerts a policewoman who is patrolling the estate. She calls for back-up before leaving her vehicle. Though she misses the fugitive, she intercepts Jack and tells him to freeze. Carefully, Jack puts his gun down and throws her his CTU I.D., explaining that he's after a suspect and entreating her to help catch him. As Jack and the policewoman hunt down the suspect, Jack's phone rings, drawing the gunman's attention to them. Jack tells the officer to switch off her radio as she's already phoned for back-up (which Jack wishes she hadn't done as the police need to play by the rules, something Jack realises he won't be able to do). As they explore further, a janitor strolls into the line of fire of the suspect. Jack shouts for him to hit the floor just as the suspect fires before running off. Realising that the janitor speaks Spanish, the officer tells him in his own language to stay put.

Dan drives back to where he left Janet to find her lying quite still in the middle of the road. He drives up to one side of her while holding a gun out of the window with the intent of shooting her as he passes by. But when an ambulance approaches from the opposite direction, Dan speeds past, leaving Janet behind.

At about **3:40 A.M.**, Nina warns Jamey that Mason will try to turn her against Jack, and reminds her that as their orders came from Walsh, his take priority over Mason's. In his suite, Palmer finally confides in Sherry that the news reporter Maureen Kingsley claims to have new evidence that ties their son Keith to the murder of Lyle Gibson, the 19-year-old boy who raped Nicole a few years ago. Until now, they had always believed that Lyle had committed suicide, but Carl thinks that during counselling Keith confessed his involvement in Lyle's death to his therapist, George Ferragamo. Sherry refuses to believe it and tells her husband he needs to get their lawyers onto this straight away. Palmer knows Maureen

Kingsley of old; she has an excellent reputation as a responsible journalist. Could Keith really be guilty of murder as she suggests? Meanwhile, the traffic cop detaining Alan York finally receives confirmation of Teri's 911 call and grudgingly releases Alan, who can't resist muttering 'idiot' under his breath. He and Teri return to his car and speed off while Teri tries to phone Jack.

Jack and the police officer split up, but just then a police helicopter overhead mistakes Jack for the gunman and fixes him in a spotlight. Jack leaps for cover as a series of shots ring out. The officer, meanwhile, is distracted by the janitor, who ignored her earlier instruction to stay out of the way. The man's innocent disobedience provides the suspect with the perfect opportunity to grab her and try to use her as a hostage. He calls out to Jack and draws him out into the open. Jack warns the officer in Spanish to drop to the floor when he gives the signal, then tells the gunman that he is going to put his gun down. Swiftly, Jack jumps at the man – a shot is fired but Jack manages to wrestle the man away and restrain him. Calling out to the officer, Jack is saddened to see that she has been hit by the stray bullet and killed.

At **3.53 A.M.**, as they near the place where Kim was, Alan and Teri pass an ambulance driving at speed in the opposite direction. They learn from a bag lady that a young girl was knocked over by a car and has been taken to St Mark's, the nearest hospital. Dan and Rick, meanwhile, have met up with Gaines at last. When he asks about Janet, they claim that she became 'a problem' so they had to kill her and dispose of the body. Gaines takes Kim to his car and tells her that if she does what he tells her, she'll be freed in a day or two, otherwise... she won't. At CTU, Mason tries to convince Jamey that she's being used by Jack and Nina but he is interrupted when he learns that Jack has been spotted on a police frequency. He ends the lockdown and withdraws his agents to find Jack.

At **3.58 A.M.**, Jack learns from her fellow officers that the dead policewoman's name was Jessie Hampton. Jack persuades the arresting officers to give him a minute with the suspect, but his man refuses to talk unless Jack can get him freed. Jack refuses, and it's then that the suspect reveals that he knows who Jack is. As the police officers take him away, he shouts over his shoulder: 'If you ever want to see your daughter again, get me out of this!'

NOTES

- **Who's Who?:** John Hawkes appeared as Dave in the slasher movie *I Still Know What You Did Last Summer* (Danny Cannon, 1998) and as Bugsy in *The Perfect Storm* (Wolfgang Petersen, 2000).
- **Time Checks:** The traffic cop gets confirmation that Teri's 911 call was received 'approximately' half an hour ago (it was nearly 50 minutes earlier).
- **Death Count:** Officer Jessie Hampton, shot at around 3:52 A.M., though she's not called in as a DOA until 3.57 A.M.
- **Trivia:** Alan York's car licence plate number is 4IEH 746. Officer Hampton's ignorance of the existence of CTU ('What the hell's *that*?') suggests that the department is not common knowledge outside of the Secret Service. Nina has been with the agency for seven years.

COMMENTS

It's all too easy to dismiss ***24*** as a one-gimmick concept, promoting itself so heavily on the fact that it's a drama running in real time. Then again, people levelled the same criticisms at Alfred Hitchcock's intellectual murder thriller *Rope* (1948) – and they were right.

Hitchcock would often tire of the actual process of film-making – by the time he'd worked it all out in his head, his interest would wane. To keep himself focussed, he would often come up with a trick, a gimmick, such as setting the entire story in a lifeboat, filming in 3D or killing off the female lead before the end of the second reel. So, for *Rope*, the idea was to set it not only in real time but in one long, continuous shot, like a stage play. Each scene would be played out in eight-minute blocks, with action timed to the second so that the actors, stagehands and cameramen all hit their marks exactly. To mask the join between scenes, actors would be directed to cross the line of the camera so that the edit could be made in the half-second of blackness provided. Though *Rope* was well received, the flat, single-camera direction meant that it boasted none of Hitchcock's customary flair.

Such an accusation cannot be directed at ***24***, with its frantic, often relentless direction. But it has to be said that the real-time element is every bit as much a gimmick here as it was over 40 years ago. That's not to say it's a bad thing, but it's the concept by which the show succeeds or fails. If the viewers begin to lose faith in the idea that the events onscreen are advancing exactly one hour at a time, the show sinks. But if they maintain a decent level of continuity from episode to episode, even if it's just the occasional time check between characters, the show works. In later episodes, they even use this to their advantage by announcing the imminent arrival of a character an episode before we get to see them, building anticipation and suspense, which were, of course, Alfred Hitchcock's greatest strengths.

QUESTIONS ARISING

- What part does Hampton's killer play in the conspiracy? How does he know Jack?
- Is Janet York still alive?

0:00 13:41 07:24 22:38 10:09 17:59 09:13 21:01 04:45 14:12 07:57 13:41 07:24 22:38 10:09 17:59 09:13

5:00 A.M.

Production Code 1AFF04

First US Transmission: Tuesday, December 11, 9/8C

Written by Chip Johannessen
Directed by Winrich Kolbe

'The following takes place between 4:00 A.M. and 5:00 A.M. on the day of the California presidential primary... Events occur in real time.'

Cast: Penny Johnson Jerald (Sherry Palmer), Carlos Bernard (Tony Almeida), Richard Burgi (Alan York), Michael Massee (Ira Gaines), Daniel Bess (Rick), Matthew Carey (Dan), Vicellous Shannon (Keith Palmer), Jacqui Maxwell (Janet York), Karina Arroyave (Jamey Farrell), John Hawkes (Greg Penticoff), Xander Berkeley (George Mason), David Barrera (Officer Phillips), Tanya Wright (Patty Brooks), Glenn Morshower (Agent Aaron Pierce), Megalyn Echikunwoke (Nicole Palmer), Davika Parikh (Maureen Kingsley), Tony Perez (Douglas Newman), Sharon Madden (Receptionist), James Healy, Jr (Dr Kinnard), Ray Hale (Intern), Nynno Ahli (Abbot).

EPISODE SUMMARY

Teri and Alan reach St Mark's hospital and frantically try to find which of their daughters it was who was in the ambulance – it's Janet, which brings relief for Teri but more worries for Alan as his daughter is put on the operating table to save her life. While they hover by the operating theatre, Jack follows the squad car with his suspect to the police station. Teri phones him to tell him about Janet; Jack tells her he'll keep looking for Kimberly and promises to get back to her as soon as he knows anything.

Rick and Dan bundle Kimberly into Gaines's car. Gaines tells them they'll be able to collect their payment from him at the compound. Once Gaines is out of earshot, Rick suggests to Dan that they should just get away, but Dan reminds him that Gaines is paying them $20,000.

It's **4:07 A.M.** – After ordering his exhausted assistant Patty to go to bed, David Palmer tries to warn his daughter Nicole about the allegations that Maureen Kingsley is threatening to air on television. Before he can say anything, Nicole tells him she's worked out that he can't lose the election, so she's invited Suzy and Rachel Brenner, two of her best friends, to fly in for his victory party – such is her faith in her father. David doesn't have the heart to spoil her good mood just yet; he knows that, should this all come to light, Nicole will have to relive the hardest time of her life.

Jack calls Nina and asks her to contact the CTU police liaison to help him get his suspect from the police. As her access to the network is still blocked, she's forced to ask Tony for the liaison's number. Tony still can't understand why Nina won't trust him yet is so loyal to Jack. Jack, meanwhile, convinces the desk sergeant at the police station to let him talk to his suspect – who has been identified as Greg Penticoff. As Jack heads towards the interview room where Penticoff is being kept, Mason storms in and takes over. Mason asks Jack to explain his actions so far this morning, warning him that if his answers are unsatisfactory, he'll be forced to consider Jack the prime suspect in Walsh's murder. Jack tells him that Walsh's evidence led him to Penticoff, and that Walsh was killed while getting his information to Jack. Should Mason obstruct Jack in his enquiries – and should anything happen to Palmer later in the day – Jack threatens to make sure his superior officer is held responsible. Mason backs down, but insists on interviewing Penticoff himself.

Tied up on the rear passenger seat of Gaines's car, Kim tries to attract the attention of a passing truck driver, but Gaines calmly points his gun at her and tells her to be quiet. Tiring of her crying, he decides to lock her in the trunk.

At just before **4.20 A.M.**, Palmer phones Maureen Kingsley who, it turns out, is staying in the same hotel as Palmer. He asks if he can talk face to face with her about her accusation and they arrange to meet in an unused conference room in the hotel.

Jack phones Teri to let her know that the police have arrested a man who might know where Kim is and instructs her to speak to Janet as soon as she possibly can. His call is interrupted by Mason, who informs him that the prisoner refuses to speak to anyone but Jack. Penticoff has been placed in an observation room with a two-way mirror at one end. While Mason and the police officers watch, Jack whispers something to Penticoff that enrages him and he tells Jack to 'go to hell'. Jack attacks Penticoff, pulling his hair back and covering his mouth, prompting the police officers to interrupt the interview and drag Jack out of there. Penticoff begins demanding his right to a telephone call. Mason can't understand what Jack is up to, asking him 'What's the plan?', but Jack walks off to get some air.

Penticoff is led to a phone booth where he surreptitiously removes a sliver of paper with a number on it. He dials a number, and on the other end of the line Jack answers his cellphone. The fight was just a ruse to enable Jack and Penticoff to speak to each other without other people listening in. Penticoff tells Jack that he has arranged to speak to the people who have his daughter via a public telephone near to where he was arrested. If he's not there to answer then Kim's life might be at risk. He repeats his warning that Jack needs to get him out of there. Jack instantly calls Nina and instructs her to put a trace on the call box nearest to the San Fernando address Jamey gave him.

4:29 A.M. Jack speaks to Officer Phillips, who had been the partner of the deceased policewoman Jessie Hampton, and asks if he might be able to get access to Penticoff for just a few minutes. Phillips uses his electronic keycard to unlock Penticoff's cell and lets Jack in, but almost instantly Jack and the suspect are fighting again. Phillips becomes involved and Jack needles him by asking him where he was when Jessie needed him. Jack is escorted out of the cells by other officers and Penticoff is left alone with Phillips's security card, which Jack stole and passed to him during the struggle. Once he's sure it's safe, he lets himself out.

At **4:36 A.M.**, Palmer meets with Maureen Kingsley. He's a little annoyed at all the security checks she's made to go through as they've been friends for many years. Palmer comes straight to the point – why does she believe Keith murdered Lyle Gibson? He believes the accusation is just a rumour started by his enemies. At first, Maureen stalls, claiming she can't reveal her sources, but David talks her round:

> *'C'mon, Maureen. We're not in court here. I'm just an old friend with a career and family you just might destroy. You owe me that much.'*

Maureen tells him that she has both the testimony of Keith's therapist, **George Ferragamo**, and a sample of handwriting from an African-American boy who went to a nearby hospital the night of Gibson's death with marks that matched those found on Gibson during his autopsy, suggesting they had fought each other that night. Though the boy called himself 'Edward Johnson', in subsequent tests by experts, the signature matched the handwriting of Keith. Palmer is disgusted and warns Maureen to 'be prepared to accept the consequences' of her actions should she air her accusations.

A few minutes later, David wakes Keith and quizzes him about the night that Nicole was raped. Keith refuses to discuss it, but suggests that he felt that David had left them all to fend for themselves as he was out of town at the time. David is furious and makes to strike Keith but then pulls back, realising he has already gone too far, and leaves him alone.

Teri confesses to Alan how Kim had been doing badly in school and that she's been so wound up by Kim's insolence towards her recently she'd thought to herself that she couldn't wait for Kim to get her own place and move out. Alan reassures her that all parents have moments like that. Seeing how upset she is, Alan promises that he'll stay with her until Kim is found.

At around **4:43 A.M.**, Officer Phillips finally discovers that his security card, his prisoner and Jack Bauer are all missing. Mason taps into surveillance equipment in the station to see video footage of Jack leaving with Penticoff some minutes earlier. On San Fernando Road, Jack and Penticoff locate the payphone where the call is expected. However, it is a cellphone hidden in the booth that rings, meaning Nina cannot get a trace on the call. Penticoff is told to locate some car keys stuck to the back of the payphone and then use them to dispose of a body inside the trunk of a car nearby. Jack's first thought is clearly that the body might be his daughter, but to his relief the body turns out to be that of a man. Mason arrives with back-up. As Mason's agents swarm on the area, Jack finally confides in Mason that there are people inside CTU who might be involved in the plot against Palmer, hence his unorthodox behaviour of the last few hours. Jack believes the man in the trunk is linked to the investigation and asks Mason for his help. Mason agrees to take Penticoff back for questioning while Jack takes the body back to CTU for identification. As Jack leaves, Mason warns him that, as far as he is concerned, this conversation never took place.

As Jack drives the car with the body back to the office, he speaks to Teri on his cellphone and tells her that he's on his way over to the hospital to be with her.

Rick and Dan reach the compound shortly before Gaines. As soon as Gaines arrives he begins questioning Dan about Janet York, telling him he knows that she is not dead as Dan led him to believe. Dan tries to suggest that Janet might not have been completely dead when they left her, but Gaines is not convinced:

> *'You're either dead or you're not dead; there's no such thing as "sorta dead"'..'*

To prove his point, Gaines shoots Dan, killing him instantly.

At just before **5:00 A.M.**, Janet York's heart monitor flatlines as Alan and Teri look on helplessly...

NOTES

- **Who's Who?:** David Barrera (Officer Phillips) played Dr Carreras, a recurring character in the cop show *NYPD Blue*.

- **Time Checks:** Maureen Kingsley arranges her meeting with David Palmer: 'I just need about ten minutes to get dressed – see you in ten'... so, just after the next ad break? Penticoff tells Jack he has just 20 minutes to get him back to where he was first arrested to receive the call from his associates, while, just before 5:00 A.M., Jack tells Teri that he'll be with her in 20 minutes.
- **Music:** 'New Noise' by Refused.
- **Death Count:** Dan (4:59 A.M.).

COMMENTS

To many viewers, there would appear to be little difference between the Secret Service and the F.B.I., largely because cinema and TV tends to depict them in similar ways – plain clothes, badge, gun held at shoulder height chasing after bad guys. Of course, their responsibilities are quite different. The Secret Service came first, formed in 1865 merely to combat counterfeit money, though that remit was later widened to cover any acts of 'frauds against the government'. At the time this would have included the activities of the Ku Klux Klan, bootleggers, smugglers, bank robbers and counterfeiters.

In 1894, the Secret Service was called upon to offer part-time protection of President Cleveland, though the President's safety would not become a permanent part of their responsibilities until 1902, a year after the assassination of President William McKinley. And it would be another five years before Congress would allocate the Secret Service a budget for this duty.

On November 3 1907, Joseph Walker became the first Secret Service agent to be killed in the line of duty while investigating western land frauds. The following year, President Roosevelt assigned eight Secret Service agents to the Justice Department in a move that formed the genesis of the modern Federal Bureau of Investigation.

In 1917, Congress authorised the use of the Secret Service to protect not only the President but his family. Any person or persons issuing threats to the President would also find themselves violating federal law. On November 1 1950, Puerto Rican nationalists launched an attack on President Truman. Though the President was unharmed, Officer Leslie Coffelt of the White House police was shot dead. This prompted legislation to authorise Secret Service protection of the President, his immediate family, the President-elect, and the Vice President. In the 1960s, this was expanded to include Vice Presidents-elect, as well as former Presidents, their spouses during their lifetime, and their children until the age of 16. After the assassination of Robert Kennedy in 1968, this would also include major presidential and vice-presidential candidates and nominees – such as David Palmer in ***24***. Though Sherry, Nicole and Keith would not be automatically covered by the Secret Service's protection, as Agent Pierce suggests, any threat to them could be perceived as a threat to Palmer himself.

In 1984, Congress enacted legislation making the fraudulent use of credit and debit cards a federal violation. The law also authorised the Secret Service to investigate violations relating to credit and debit card fraud, federal-interest computer fraud, and fraudulent identification documents. This presumably explains why Jamey and Tony are able to access private telephone, e-mail and financial accounts so readily.

The gradual increase in the Secret Service's involvement in the safety of presidents past and present was, however, halted in 1994 by an act of Congress that reduced the previous lifetime protection of former presidents to just ten years from their last day in office. This act came into effect in January 1997, just as Bill Clinton began his second term as President.

'Here endeth the lesson...'

QUESTIONS ARISING

- What happened between Rick and Dan in Phoenix for Dan to feel that Rick 'owes' him?
- Who is the man in the trunk?
- Can George Mason be trusted?
- How does Gaines know that Janet York is at the hospital?

5:00 A.M.

7:24 22:38 10:09 17:59 09:13 21:01 04:45 14:12 07:57 13:41 07:24 22:38 10:09 17:59 09:13 19:47 05:20

6:00 A.M.

Production Code 1AFF05

First US Transmission: Tuesday, December 18, 9/8C

Written by Howard Gordon
Directed by Bryan Spicer

'The following takes place between 5:00 A.M. and 6:00 A.M. on the day of the California presidential primary... Events occur in real time.'

Cast: Penny Johnson Jerald (Sherry Palmer), Carlos Bernard (Tony Almeida), Richard Burgi (Alan York), Michael Massee (Ira Gaines), Daniel Bess (Rick), Matthew Carey (Dan), Jacqui Maxwell (Janet York), Karina Arroyave (Jamey Farrell), Jude Ciccolella (Mike Novick), Zach Grenier (Carl), Eric Balfour (Milo Pressman), Kim Miyori (Dr Collier), Todd Jeffries (Claude Davenport), Chuck Walczak (Bob), Norma Maldonado (Nurse), Suzan Brittan (Anchorwoman), Ariel Feld (Anesthesiologist), Linda Klein (Surgical Nurse).

EPISODE SUMMARY

While Janet fights for her life in hospital, Jack warns Teri that the critically ill girl might be under threat from some people he is investigating. He reaches CTU and Nina collects the body in the car, noting that whoever killed him has mutilated his face, teeth and hands to make it harder to identify him. Jack asks her to cover for him as he requisitions a helicopter for personal use. Then he phones St Mark's hospital to warn them that someone might try to harm their patient, Janet York. As he flies off, Tony notes with increasing frustration that Jack is again flouting protocol.

At the compound, Gaines gives Rick a shovel and makes him bury Dan's body. Gaines walks back into the compound, leaving Kim and Rick alone. Kim tries to convince Rick to escape with her but, for the moment, he is not in the mood to listen to her and tells her to shut up.

At **5:06 A.M.**, Carl comes to Palmer's hotel suite. David tells him that he knows that Keith was somehow involved in the death of Lyle Gibson, the boy who raped Nicole, and that someone altered his hospital records to cover it up – someone like Carl. Carl tells him that Keith came to him the night that Nicole was raped to tell him that he'd been to see Gibson. Gibson had apparently pulled a knife on him, so what happened was, in fact, self-defence. Sherry was at the hospital with Nicole and David was flying back to be with his family, so Carl stepped in and made it look like Keith had never been there. David doesn't understand why, if Keith was innocent of any crime, Carl didn't just go to the police. Carl spells it out for him – Gibson was white: Keith wouldn't have stood a chance, and that would have been the end of David's career as a consequence. David is furious and tells Carl never to come near him or his family again. As Carl leaves, however, he has one last thing to say:

'Before you're finished crucifying me, save some nails for your wife.'

Carl explains that it was Sherry who sent Keith to him in the first place. Carl walks out, defiant.

It's **5.15 A.M.** Kim grabs a spare shovel and begins helping Rick dig the grave. Rick is upset about what's happened. Their instructions were just to hang out with Kim and, he says, he can't understand why all this has happened. Kim tells him he needs to stop feeling sorry for himself and start thinking up a way for them to get out of the compound.

Arriving at the hospital, Jack is greeted by the head of security. He thanks him for mobilising his guards at such short notice, but apologises that he can't explain what's going on. Teri is overjoyed to see Jack and after an emotional reunion she introduces him to Alan. Almost instantly, Jack begins to question Alan as if he's a suspect. Teri is embarrassed by his rudeness and tries to speak with him alone, but Jack is distracted by a commotion going on down the corridor, He walks over to a man and begins quizzing him about the contents of a briefcase he is carrying. The man refuses to answer him and Jack pushes him against a trolley and restrains him while he checks out the case – but it turns out the man is here visiting his sick brother and, concerned that the doctors aren't looking after him, he's just trying to smuggle painkillers in. Jack lets the man go. Teri can see now that Jack is upset and the couple hug while Jack repeatedly apologises to his wife.

David tells Sherry that he knows about Keith's involvement in Gibson's death. At first, Sherry tries to make out it is just a story that Carl's trying to pass off, but David refuses to let her pass the buck – he knows Sherry is a strong, independent woman. Sherry admits she did what she felt was right, to protect him and her family. But David angrily accuses her of only looking out for her own interests, her own desire to move into the White House. She in turn asks him if he's prepared to send their son to jail.

By **5:27 A.M.**, Kim and Rick are beginning to open up to each other again. Rick feels that Dan's irresponsibility always got him into trouble; Kim feels the same way about Janet. Kim can't help thinking about her mother:

> *'I've spent every day trying to get away from my mother. Now I can't stop wishing she were here. She must be freaking...'*

She again suggests to Rick that they should try to get away, but then Gaines comes to take Kim up to the house. As he leaves, he warns Rick that when he returns he wants Dan's body buried.

Nina informs Jack that their pathologist believes the dead body died just a few hours ago – some time between 11 and midnight. Jack tells her he needs her to hurry up with the I.D. on the body and that she should bring Jamey on board to speed things up. Hanging up, Jack takes Teri to one side to explain everything. He tells her he believes that Janet was hurt by someone trying to kidnap Kim – they must know he's been assigned to protect David Palmer:

> *'I know this is all happening because of me. I've tried to keep a wall between my work and my family. The wall's coming up and I don't know what to do...'*

Jack tries to reassure her that Kim is probably safe, but Teri suddenly realises that the situation is much worse than she's feared and breaks down sobbing.

Nina pulls Jamey off the keycard as Jack instructed, telling her that she's bringing in **Milo**, an outside contractor. Jamey is not happy about this as she feels she's close to cracking the card, but Nina is pragmatic and knows that Milo will be quicker. As she briefs Jamey, Tony watches them suspiciously.

Alan is told by the doctors that Janet is making good recovery and is being moved from recovery to the Intensive Care Unit (ICU). Jack apologises to him for being rude earlier, but Alan says he understands what Jack is going through. They are interrupted by a call from Nina who tells Jack that she thinks they are close to getting an I.D. on the dead body – he had a surgical pin in his ankle that was one of a kind. Jamey is checking with the manufacturers. Jack tells her to call him the minute she gets confirmation.

David speaks with his chief of staff, **Mike Novick**. Mike explains that if Maureen breaks the story, David's party will try to cut their losses and drop him. David interprets this as Mike telling him he should withdraw from the election, but Mike is not so defeatist. He feels that, handled carefully, the situation can be turned to David's advantage. Right or not, he says, David's making history. David can't get past the fact that his family has been involved in covering up Keith's involvement. Mike admits it's a 'hard sell' but the election is still six months away. He recommends that David must somehow break the story before Maureen has the chance. David's ignorance of the facts prior to now will stand in his favour, so Mike advises him to announce the story at his breakfast meeting later that morning. He'll be able to survive this – so long as his entire family is standing with him when he makes the announcement.

A doctor explains to Alan that Janet has extensive bone damage and suffered a cardiac arrest in theatre, but is confident that she will make a full recovery. Jack asks the doctor if Janet might be up to answering a few questions as soon as possible, explaining that she might know where their missing daughter is. The doctor defers to Alan, who gives his consent, but only after he's spoken to Janet first. The doctor takes Alan to ICU, leaving Jack and Teri alone. Just then, Jack's phone rings again. At first he thinks it'll be Nina calling back with the I.D., but it's Gaines. He warns Jack to do what he tells him if he wishes to see his daughter again. He tells Jack not to worry Teri, but to walk outside slowly. He guides Jack out towards a nearby exit.

The doctor leaves Alan alone to speak to his daughter. Walking in, he sees that Janet is dazed but conscious. As he approaches her, Janet tries to focus on his face but does not recognise him. 'Who are you?' she asks weakly. 'Where's my father?' Moving slowly, the man calling himself 'Alan York' closes his fingers around Janet's air pipe, then holds his hand over her breathing mask, suffocating her. Switching off the sound on her heart monitor, he coldly watches her die. Checking that nobody is around, 'Alan' leaves the room, closing the door behind him.

At **5:51 A.M.** Gaines directs Jack by phone to a car waiting in the car park. To prove that Kim is still alive, Gaines lets her speak very briefly to her father before silencing her. Next, he leads Jack towards a small metal container in the glove compartment of the car. Inside it is a small transmitter, which he instructs Jack to place inside his ear. Now Gaines has a direct audio link to Jack, so he orders him to throw his phone out of the window before telling him to make his way back to CTU.

'Alan' returns to Teri, claiming Janet told him that they'd been with a couple of boys who got a bit rough with them at a party held at a house in Bel Air. He tells her the doctor said that Janet is in no danger, and that as she's asleep, he could drive Teri out to the house to pick up Kim. Teri tries to call Jack to let him know what's happening, but Jack's phone keeps diverting to his voicemail. Distressed, she decides to leave with 'Alan'.

It's **5:57 A.M.** and while Jamey works with Nina in the pathology lab on the dead body, Milo, the outside contractor, has arrived at CTU and already worked out a better way to unlock the keycard than the way Jamey had tried. Jamey barely masks her contempt for Milo, but then Nina gives her some good news: the hunch that she had about the pin in the dead body has come up trumps – the AMA (American Medical Association) have positively identified the dead man.

It's sunrise, just before **6:00 A.M.** As 'Alan' drives them both out to Bel Air, Teri notices a scratch on his arm that she hadn't seen before. He tells her that he did it at the furniture store, though in fact he got it when he killed Janet York. Just then, Teri's phone rings – it's Nina trying to get in touch with Jack. Teri explains that Jack left her a while ago to take a phone call, which she'd assumed was from Nina, but Nina says she hasn't spoken to him in half an hour. Knowing how Jack is at the moment, Nina changes the subject and asks her to pass a message onto him when she next speaks to him. She explains about the murder victim that Jack asked them to identify and tells Teri that his name is Alan York, an accountant from the Valley. Teri is instantly alarmed and asks Nina to repeat the name, but there's no mistake. She switches off her phone and tries to act calm. Whoever the man sitting next to her is, he is not Alan York...

NOTES

- **Who's Who?:** Jude Ciccolella (Mike Novick) played a guard in *The Shawshank Redemption* (dir. Frank Darabond, 1994) and in 2003 is slated to appear in the long-awaited movie version of the superhero *Daredevil* (dir. Mark Steven Johnson). Eric Balfour (Milo) might be familiar to fans of *Buffy the Vampire Slayer*; he played Xander's best friend Jesse in the first two episodes of the series. He also played the boyfriend of Mel Gibson's on-screen daughter in the romantic comedy *What Women Want* (dir. Nancy Meyers, 2000) and is a regular in the HBO series *Six Feet Under*. Kim Miyori (Dr Collier) appeared in *St Elsewhere* from 1982-4 and played John Lennon's wife Yoko Ono in the TV movie *John and Yoko: A Love Story* (Sandor Stern, 1985).

- **Time Checks:** Nina reminds Jamey that she's been trying to crack the keycard for two hours (episodes). The doctor tells 'Alan' that the next six hours could be critical (not that it has any bearing on Janet's life after this episode anyway) while, during their phone call, Gaines rushes Jack, ominously telling him: 'I don't have all day...' Nina tells Teri that she and Jack haven't spoken for almost half an hour.
- **Death Count:** The real Alan York (though it happened before midnight, we only learn this now) and his daughter, Janet (5:46 A.M.).
- **Trivia:** Mike Novick's hotel room is 1218.

COMMENTS

The twist. The shocker. The thing that frazzles your head and makes you shout 'What the...?' at the screen. It's the hook in the script that – pulled off correctly – will make the piece become legendary.

(By the way, in about 100 words' time, I'll start revealing the twists of *Citizen Kane*, *Rebecca*, *Psycho*, *The Usual Suspects* and *Boxing Helena,* so if you haven't seen any of these films, don't say I didn't warn you!)

It's one of the most commonly known surprise endings outside of the *Star Wars* trilogy. After the newspaper giant Charles Foster Kane utters the word 'Rosebud' on his deathbed, a journalist tries to piece together the man's life in an attempt to find out who 'Rosebud' was and why he should recall this person right before he meets his maker. The ironic twist of *Citizen Kane* is that we, the audience, discover what the journalist never will – that Rosebud was Kane's sled when he was a boy.

Twists frequently rely on irony or hidden information to make their mark. In the Daphne du Maurier novel *Rebecca*, for instance, we're led to believe that Maxim de Winter is still morbidly in love with his deceased first wife, Rebecca, and it's only when his second wife tries to emulate her that he reveals that he had hated Rebecca all along. It's a shocking turn of events, as everything up to that point has convinced us to believe otherwise. It's also a turning point in the novel, because the second wife suddenly feels empowered at the exact moment she needs her strength most – for soon after, it's revealed that the first Mrs de Winter's body has been found floating in the sea, and Maxim is now a prime suspect for her murder.

Another type of twist comes in the form of the shock unmasking of a person's true identity, whether it be that sweet, nervous Norman Bates (Anthony Perkins) is, in fact, a cold-blooded transvestite killer, or that sweet, nervous, Verbal Kint (Kevin Spacey) is, in fact, a cold-blooded criminal mastermind and bloody good liar too! Secret identities always make good twists, but only if they've been played believably all the way through. With 'Alan York' here, we suddenly realise that his supposed irritation at being delayed by the traffic cop a few hours ago was itself a delaying tactic to make sure Teri didn't reach Janet in time; his reluctance to let Jack interview his 'daughter' was a way of maintaining his cover for a bit longer; and his promise to Teri to stay with her no matter what suddenly takes on a chilling air.

With any luck, you'll have been able to watch ***24*** without anyone spoiling any of the main twists. When a programme such as this relies on the ability to shock its audience and make them wonder just who they can trust, it would be cruel to ruin that for anyone else, which is why, up to this point, I've played fair and not revealed the real name or identity of Teri's travelling companion 'Alan'. All I will say about what is to come over the next 18 hours/episodes is that – unlike the woeful *Boxing Helena* – all of this will not turn out to have been a rather tacky dream…

QUESTIONS ARISING

- How did Gaines gain access to the hospital security? And how long has he had Jack's cellphone number?
- Why was the real Alan York killed? What does he have to do with this?
- How long will it take for Janet York's body to be found?
- Who the *&@# is 'Alan York'?

6:00 A.M. – 7:00 A.M.

:24 22:38 10:09 17:59 09:13 21:01 04:45 14:12 07:57 13:41 07:24 22:38 10:09 17:59 09:13 19:47 05:20

Production Code 1AFF06

First US Transmission: Tuesday, January 8, 9/8C

Written by Andrea Newman
Directed by Bryan Spicer

'The following takes place between 6:00 A.M. and 7:00 A.M. on the day of the California presidential primary... Events occur in real time.'

Cast: Penny Johnson Jerald (Sherry Palmer), Carlos Bernard (Tony Almeida), Richard Burgi (Kevin/'Alan York'), Michael Massee (Ira Gaines), Daniel Bess (Rick), Vicellous Shannon (Keith Palmer), Karina Arroyave (Jamey Farrell), Rudolf Martin (Jonathan – the fake Martin Belkin), Silas Weir Mitchell (Eli), Eric Balfour (Milo Pressman), Glenn Morshower (Agent Aaron Pierce), Megalyn Echikunwoke (Nicole Palmer), Suzan Brittan (Anchorwoman), Jesse Corti (McLemore), Steve O'Connor (Phil).

EPISODE SUMMARY

At **6:00 A.M.**, Gaines's assassin, Jonathan, who has been altered to look like the photographer Martin Belkin (including dyed brown hair and brown contact lenses), prepares for his mission and leaves Gaines's compound for the Palmer breakfast. Simultaneously, Gaines gives his instructions to Jack via the earpiece. Behind the sun visor in the car Jack is driving, there is a keycard, similar to the one Jack left with Jamey to decrypt. Unbeknownst to Jack, Milo, the contractor Nina hired, is having greater success than Jamey had in cracking the encryption.

Palmer is still upset about what he has been told about his son, Keith. Believing Mike Novick's solution to be the best, he asks Keith to stand by him when he makes his announcement to the press about the incident in just an hour or so. But Keith still blames his father for everything that happened and refuses to help him drag old problems up again.

Kimberly, meanwhile, tries again to work on Rick, pointing out her suspicion that Gaines won't let him just walk away with his money as he promised. She begs him to help her escape.

Jack reaches CTU at **6:08 A.M.** Nina rushes over to him to ask him how Kimberly is. Jack fobs her off by telling her that Kim is safe, that she'd just been to a party where things got out of hand. But when Nina tells him that the body he found has been identified as an 'Alan York', Jack begins to worry for Teri also. Making his excuses with Nina, Jack goes to his office and immediately starts to threaten Gaines. A gunshot and a threat from Gaines instantly silences Jack and places Gaines very much back in command. He tells Jack to switch the keycard from the car with the keycard that Walsh gave him – the one Milo is close to breaking. Having heard Nina's conversation with Jack through the transmitter, Gaines then phones his associate Kevin – the man who until now has been known as 'Alan York' – to warn him that his cover has been blown.

Fortunately for Teri, Kevin's cellphone is out of range and the message goes straight to his voicemail. At that precise moment, Teri begins to act as if she's going to be sick and convinces 'Alan' to pull over and let her out. As she scrambles up an embankment towards some bushes, Kevin notices his cellphone message indicator blinking. He checks the message and, although the message breaks up a little, he can deduce from it that Teri almost certainly now knows he's not the real Alan. Kevin removes his car keys and heads after Teri, but she's nowhere to be seen. From behind a tree, she leaps out at him and hits him across the head with a rock. She tries to grab the car keys but Kevin throws them right into some bushes where she'll never find them. Teri manages to retrieve the rock and smacks Kevin out cold. Within a few minutes, the resourceful Teri has tied Kevin to a tree with jump leads and other cables from his car. Certain her attacker won't be going anywhere, she tries to use her cellphone, but of course, she can't get a signal.

Egged on by what Kim said to him, Rick tries to get Gaines to pay him so he can 'get out of everyone's way'. Gaines tells him he needs him for some more work, implying that Rick won't be leaving the compound any time soon.

At CTU, Jack tries to scrawl a note to Nina to warn her he has been bugged, but Gaines warns him to shred the message, revealing for the first time that he can see everything Jack does via a camera mounted right outside his office. Meanwhile, Palmer finally tells Nicole about the possibility that Maureen Kingsley will reveal Keith's involvement in the death of Lyle Gibson. Nicole is visibly upset – she'd just reached a point where she could almost pretend she'd never been raped in the first place, only for her past history to be dragged up again.

Jack goes to introduce himself to Milo and manages to deftly swap the keycards while Milo's not looking. But within a few minutes, Milo begins to notice a difference in the decoding programmes. While he desperately attempts to recover what he'd achieved before Jack distracted him, Kevin taunts Teri as she tries to get the attention of a passing motorist:

> *'You flag down that car, you bury your daughter. I'm your only hope of getting her back. If I don't deliver you in half an hour, Kimberly's dead.'*

Teri continues to try for a signal on her cellphone while Kevin threatens her.

At **6:31 A.M.**, on Gaines's orders, Jack arranges security clearance for himself so he can get into Palmer's breakfast meeting. At the same time, Rick tells Kim that she was right, that Gaines won't let him leave. As they plan to escape, one of Gaines's henchmen, **Eli**, disturbs them. Thinking quickly, Kim pulls Rick on top of her and begins to struggle, making it appear to Eli as if Rick was trying to rape her. Rick convinces Eli to wait outside while he 'finishes up', then tells Kim he'll distract Eli so she can make her escape and meet him elsewhere in the compound.

By **6:36 A.M.**, having realised that the keycard is 'lying' to him, Milo works out that it is, in fact, an entirely different keycard that he's working on. He tells Nina about his discovery and explains that the only person who could possibly have made the switch is Jack. Nina goes up to Jack's office to confront him and threatens to report him if he doesn't hand the card over. Gaines tells Jack to get her out of the office, so reluctantly Jack acts as if he's flipped out and pulls a gun on Nina. Removing a jacket from a closet, he drapes it over her shoulders to hide the gun in her back and leads her out of the office. On their way towards the exit, however, Tony intercepts them and asks them where they're going. Jack tells him they're off to an official jurisdiction meeting and he and Nina leave. Tony does not appear impressed that he is again being excluded.

Teri finally gets a signal on her phone at **6:42 A.M.** and tries Jack's phone only for it to be answered by somebody at St Mark's hospital, who tells her he found the phone in the hospital garage. Even more concerned than she already was, she calls Nina, but Jamey answers. Teri tells Jamey what's happened and where she is and Jamey tells her she'll send someone right away to pick her up. Across town, Sherry Palmer suggests to David that they blackmail Maureen Kingsley into dropping the story about Keith. David knows that Maureen is clean and can't be got at that way, but Sherry tells him she's prepared to do anything to save both her family and his candidacy. And at the compound, Rick keeps Eli talking while Kim makes her escape. She reaches a small shed and waits there for Rick as arranged.

Teri is relieved when a car full of agents arrives to pick her up, but instead they untie Kevin/Alan and grab her. Too late, Teri realises these men are colleagues of Kevin, not Jack. Screaming, she is taken to the car...

Tony asks Jamey about this 'jurisdiction meeting' that Jack and Nina have gone off to, but Jamey knows nothing of it. Worried about Nina, he tells Jamey to get the security footage from Jack's office.

At **6:49 A.M.**, Nina is driving Jack according to instructions he's being fed through the earpiece by Gaines. Jack notices they are being followed by another car. Nina accuses him of making up all that's happened to Kim and says she thinks there might not even be a mole at CTU. Just then, Gaines orders Jack to kill Nina. His reaction to the instruction alarms Nina, who realises for the first time that Jack is communicating with someone else. They reach a huge industrial estate. Jack bundles her out of the car at gunpoint and tells her to turn round to face a large mined-out crater. Nina refuses to turn her back on him, saying if he's going to shoot her, she wants to see his face. Jack grabs her by the jacket he gave her and shoots her at point-blank range in the chest. She falls down the embankment of the crater. Gaines sees all this via surveillance cameras in the second car. Satisfied that Nina's dead, Gaines orders Jack to get back in the car and drive off.

Kim and Rick have found a loose section of perimeter fencing and are about to scramble underneath when they see a car arrive at the main gates. When Kim sees her mom, she insists on going back for her and, reluctantly, Rick goes with her.

Tony reviews the security tape to see Jack pulling a gun on Nina before handing her a bulletproof flak jacket. While Tony can't comprehend what's just gone on, the dazed Nina at the bottom of the embankment is beginning to work it out. Pulling compacted bullets from the outer layers of the jacket, she begins the long walk back trying to piece it all together...

NOTES

- **Who's Who?:** Silas Weir Mitchell (Eli) has made the usual rounds on *ER*, *NYPD Blue* and *The X-Files*. Jesse Corti (McLemore) voiced LeFou, Gaston's henchman in Disney's adaptation of *Beauty and the Beast* (dir. Gary Trousdale & Kirk Wise, 1991).
- **Time Checks:** Gaines tells Jonathan he'll be seeing the President in an hour, and gives Jack a three-minute ultimatum over the switch of the keycard.
- **Trivia:** Jack's clearance code for the breakfast is Q22 Q17 and the registration number of the car Gaines gives to Jack is 4IMV486.

COMMENTS

24 would be screwed if it weren't for technology. Not just the super-futuristic stuff such as fingerprint thingies and networks of decoders.

Even the simple things like cellphones. The show's reliance on technology to tell its story is a perfect example of the American people's long-standing need to be able to communicate with each other across long distances. And yet significantly, the technological invention that started it all off is nowhere to be seen. Pay attention, class...

In 1831, Professor Joseph Henry of Princeton University invented the telegraph, a method of using electrical impulses and a network of wires to send messages over long distances. So far, so good. Sadly, Henry didn't bother to patent his system, leaving Samuel Morse, a scientist and ambitious politician, to jump in and effectively steal the idea. Brazenly, Morse even consulted Henry on a number of occasions as to how he might perfect the telegraph system. The first test message was sent on May 11 1844 and, almost instantly, Morse forgot all about Professor Henry's involvement. Within four years, America had a network of over 5,000 miles of telegraph wires and Morse was a very wealthy man. Henry, conversely, wasn't.

In a rather nice example of poetic justice, Morse's system would ultimately be superseded by another attempt to improve upon it, this time in the form of Alexander Graham Bell's invention, the telephone. Although Western Union initially dismissed Bell's telephonic system as an 'electrical toy', it would soon make Bell's corporation, American Telephone and Telegraph (or AT&T as it's now known), the largest in the USA. Today, America is the most phone-dependent nation on earth with over 90 per cent of Americans having at least one phone, which goes some way to explaining why, of all nations, America is also becoming the most internet-reliant too.

The race for the internet truly began in 1957 after USSR launched Sputnik, the first artificial earth satellite. Not to be outdone, the US government set up the Advanced Research Projects Agency (ARPA) to try to put America ahead of the technological competition in fields related to the military. In the midst of the Cold War, it was felt that a computerised network would benefit the government in the event of a war. Just over a decade later, the ARPANET was unveiled, running across four servers, located at UCSB, UCLA, Stanford Research Institute and the University of Utah (one other major innovation at this time, courtesy of Doug Engelbart, was the mouse, a device invented to make hypertext browsing and editing easier). By 1972, this small network of four servers had expanded to more than 30. The same year, electronic messaging – or e-mail – was slowly introduced, and by 1973 e-mail accounted for more that 75 per cent of the system's usage (presumably to help people waste company time with jokes and office gossip, much like today). But by the 1980s, the internet (a term not coined until 1982) had grown away from its governmental purpose to become a general public access system. By 1990, with the introduction of Tim Berners-Lee's 'World Wide Web' concept, the original ARPANET was killed off, putting an end to government ownership and control of the internet's usage and content. Hurrah!

So, although it might have been possible to tell the story of ***24*** decades earlier, it's unlikely it could have been told as concisely, with many plot points depending on the internet, telephones or even just the amount of times a character is *unable* to access such modern marvels. But for an idea of how our awareness of technology can actually *ruin* our enjoyment of a show, read the **COMMENT** section in two episodes' time.

QUESTIONS ARISING

- How did Gaines's men get that surveillance shot of Nina's body down the slope?

7:00 A.M.

7:24 22:38 10:09 17:59 09:13 21:01 04:45 14:12 07:57 13:41 07:24 22:38 10:09 17:59 09:13 19:47 05:20

Production Code 1AFF07

First US Transmission: Tuesday, January 15, 9/8C

Written by Joel Surnow & Michael Loceff
Directed by Stephen Hopkins

'The following takes place between 7:00 A.M. and 8:00 A.M. on the day of the California presidential primary... Events occur in real time.'

Cast: Penny Johnson Jerald (Sherry Palmer), Carlos Bernard (Tony Almeida), Michael Massee (Ira Gaines), Daniel Bess (Rick), Vicellous Shannon (Keith Palmer), Karina Arroyave (Jamey Farrell), Rudolf Martin (Jonathan – the fake Martin Belkin), Silas Weir Mitchell (Eli), Eric Balfour (Milo Pressman), Jackie Debatin (Jessica Abrahms), Glenn Morshower (Agent Aaron Pierce), Jesse D. Goins (Alan Hayes), Rick Garcia (News Anchorman), Mark Clayman (Man at bus stop), Ron Roggé (Jared, Gaines's thug at the power plant), Al Leong (Neill – not credited).

EPISODE SUMMARY

At **7:00 A.M.** the polls for the 'Super Tuesday' primary elections finally open. David Palmer tells his wife and son that he has decided to come clean to the press at his breakfast conference about Keith's involvement in Gibson's death. Sherry and Keith are furious, and accuse him once more of putting his precious career before his family.

David: 'We have to put this thing behind us, Keith.'
Keith: 'Oh, by me being in prison and you in the Oval office?'

Meanwhile, posing as the photographer, Jonathan, the assassin, arrives at the San Clarita power plant where the breakfast is to be held. Despite the stringent security measures in place, Jonathan's new face and identity gain him swift entry.

Gaines directs Jack to drive to a bus stop where a man who seems to know him gives him a briefcase. Jack starts to show signs of resistance to being bossed around so Gaines reveals that he now also has Jack's wife as his hostage. Hearing her voice briefly is enough to convince Jack to drive to the power plant as instructed.

At CTU, Jamey receives a message on her PDA (personal digital assistant) and goes to the bathroom. There she begins to communicate with Gaines, telling him that Milo has worked out he's got a fake keycard and that Jack must have the real one. She then tells him that she will sort things out for him, but then Gaines gives her new instructions. He tells her that Nina is dead, and that Jamey must cover for her.

Dragged into the shack in the compound, Teri is finally reunited with her daughter, Kimberly.

7:17 A.M. Nina breaks into an office on the edge of the industrial estate and uses a phone to call Jamey. When Jamey doesn't answer,

Nina tries Tony instead and asks him to pass her onto Jamey, but then he overhears Jamey telling Milo that Nina is out of the office at an all-day meeting. Tony asks Jamey how she knows this and Jamey tells him she's just spoken to Nina. Realising she's lying, Tony instead returns to Nina and tells her what Jamey has said. Nina tells him that Jamey is lying and therefore cannot be trusted. She confides in Tony that Jack suspects there's a traitor in their team and apologises for not trusting him earlier. Tony tells her he'll come and fetch her, but she tells him instead to send a car and wait for her at the back entrance to CTU.

Jack reaches the power plant at about **7:25 A.M.** and meets Agent Pierce, who's searching everyone as they enter the complex. He asks Jack to open up his briefcase and, with no idea what the case might contain, Jack is forced to comply. Inside is a laptop. Jack thinks quickly and tells Pierce that it contains all the information they've collated since they first became aware that Palmer was in danger. Pierce asks him to turn the laptop on and, satisfied that Jack is telling the truth, he grants him entry. As he mills through the crowd, Jack bumps into **Jessica**, Palmer's press secretary, who Jack knew in high school. But reunions are not on the agenda today and Gaines orders him away while he waits for his contact. Palmer has already arrived and as he makes his way through the crowd he sees Jack. The two men lock eyes but Jack restrains himself from warning the Senator of what might be about to happen. Palmer is introduced to the photographer 'Martin Balkin'...

Teri lets Kim catch some much-needed sleep. Rick enters the shack and Teri hits him. Rick tries to explain his actions but then Eli walks in and, thinking Rick is now trying to rape Teri, tells him not to get too close to the women, hinting that neither of them will be alive for much longer.

As Jack awaits his contact he meets Jessica again. As they make small talk, he tries to scrawl a message to her on the reverse of a business card; using the security cameras, Gaines realises he cannot see Jack and orders one of his men to find him. Sure enough, one of the thugs strides in between Jack and Jessica, giving Jack a hard, warning glare. Gaines now directs Jack to make his way towards a closet towards the rear of the complex.

Nina arrives safe and well at CTU – much to Tony's relief. Knowing she must not be seen by Jamey or the rest, Tony has already looped the security cameras between the back door and the 'ITS' room. Nina tells him all about Teri and Kim's abduction and the reasons for Jack's odd behaviour. Recognising that this must be connected to the threat against Palmer, Tony and Nina agree to warn the Secret Service.

At **7:36 A.M.**, Jack finally meets his contact – Jonathan. He opens up the briefcase and reveals under the laptop the parts for a gun. He tells Jack to assemble the gun for him while he himself places small latex pads on his fingertips to mask his own prints. With the gun assembled, Jonathan makes to leave. Jack pulls his own gun on the man, but Jonathan casually reminds him of the threat against Jack's family and walks out, leaving Jack seething.

Tony tells Milo that Jack definitely took the original keycard – making sure Jamey is within earshot. Next, he calls Agent Pierce at the power plant to warn him that Jack Bauer's position has been compromised and that Pierce should take whatever action he feels necessary. Nina, meanwhile, uses internal security cameras to track Jamey. She sets one of the cameras to a 20-second loop and speaks to Tony via an earpiece, giving him his cue to move in. Once Jamey has snooped off to the bathroom, and the loop is in effect, Tony makes his way into the cubicle next to Jamey's and, seeing her communicating to Gaines via her PDA, he pulls a gun on her and leads her out of the bathroom all within the 20-second loop.

Following Tony's tip-off, Pierce speaks to Palmer, warning him about the threat on his life. He again urges him to cancel the breakfast, but Palmer, now single-mindedly determined to make his announcement, once more refuses. Pierce is forced to warn his fellow agents about Jack but take no further action. At CTU, Tony takes Jamey into the office where Nina is waiting for her. Jamey's visibly surprised to see Nina alive, but tries to pretend she doesn't know what's going on. Nina and Tony begin to pressure her, telling her they'll make sure she faces charges of treason and the murders of Agents Walsh and Baylor. Reluctantly, Jamey confesses that she was made to tap into the CTU surveillance and, later, to pass information to a third party. Tony tells her he'll make sure whatever information she gives them will be taken into consideration to cut her a deal, but Jamey refuses to say any more without legal representation.

Teri makes sure that Kim knows she loves her, an act that ends up worrying the already-scared Kim even more. Teri comforts her daughter, trying to reassure her that no matter how bad things get, nothing will sway her love for her.

Jonathan lines up his rifle while Jack waits nervously. Gaines instructs him to join Jonathan. Once the gunman has shot Palmer, he intends to hand Jack the gun, and with his prints all over the murder weapon, he'll be the prime suspect for the assassination. Jack is aghast. Knowing he can't intervene directly, he instead heads over to one of the Secret Service agents and makes for his gun. The agent overpowers Jack and calls for assistance while Pierce swiftly bustles Palmer and his wife to safety. Aware that his family's lives are at stake, Jack announces loud enough for Gaines to hear that he has done nothing. In the struggle with the agent, Gaines's earpiece becomes dislodged from Jack's ear and skids across the floor out of reach.

Furious that the assassination has not gone to plan, Gaines orders Eli to kill the women. Just then, a message comes through from Jamey. Gaines phones her to learn that Jack did not intentionally disrupt the hit – since Jack has been wanted by CTU for breaking protocol ever since Gaines first got to him, someone must have given the Secret Service the tip-off. Gaines ends the call and instantly receives another, this time from his superiors.

Eli and **Neill**, another of Gaines's men, drag Teri and Kim through the woods towards an open grave. With both women screaming for mercy, Eli places a gun to the back of Kim's head. Gaines calls and, just in time, calls Eli off; he still needs them alive after all.

At the power plant, Jack is placed under arrest...

NOTES

- **Who's Who?:** Maybe Jackie Debatin (Jessica Abrahms) has one of those faces; she played a prostitute in an episode of *Dr Quinn, Medicine Woman* and a stripper in the *Friends* episode 'The One With The Stripper'. She also played a character called Simone in two episodes of *Caroline in the City*. Jesse D. Goins (Alan Hayes) seems to have appeared in most American shows from *Diff'rent Strokes*, *The Dukes of Hazzard* and *Buck Rogers in the 25th Century* to *Hill Street Blues* and *Ally McBeal*. Rick Garcia is a real-life anchorman, currently hosting Fox TV's sports news show, *Fox Overtime*. Mark Clayman (Man at bus stop) was in a number of episodes of the high-school sitcom *Saved By the Bell*, while Ron Roggé (Jared) can be seen playing Captain Mitchell in the *Power Rangers* spin-off series, *Lightspeed Rescue*.
- **Time Checks:** Jack tells Agent Pierce that the dummy laptop contains all the information they've collected on Palmer in the last

eight hours. Gaines reminds Jack that the assassination will be over in just five minutes... that's what he thinks, anyway.

- **Trivia:** The San Clarita power station is at 417 Ridgeway Road. Gaines's telephone dialler on his PC lists Jamey's number as 485 698 175 64. Incidentally, Gaines's contact list includes members of the production crew: Michael Loceff (writer and co-producer on the show), Virgil Williams (writer), Nicole Burke (second assistant director), Tony Pacheco (production accountant), as well as the names Todd Wasserman, Doug Miller, Jason Savage and Randy Engle. Jessica Abrahms reveals that Jack used to be a motorcycle racer before his daughter was born, and according to Agent Pierce, Jack is 160 lbs and 5' 11".

COMMENTS

So far in ***24*** we've seen an aeroplane packed to capacity blown to smithereens – that's a good 500 people – plus a family man, a lesbian courier, a teenager, a police woman and a great deal of government agents shot dead. Yet until this episode, the public seemed to accept these murders, however tragic, as acceptable events in the narrative of an action-packed thriller. But in this episode, Kim and Teri are threatened with a bullet in the back of the head in front of an open grave. Though the threat is withdrawn fairly quickly and the women survive, all of a sudden the show comes under fire from people declaring its makers 'sick'. Why? Because the camera *lingered*.

The question has often been asked: Does television have a responsibility to protect its audience from unsavoury or corruptive influences? On the whole, I think many people would concede that although much of the responsibility rests with the individual or, in the cases of minors, with their parents, yes, to some extent the TV companies do have a duty to ensure that what they are broadcasting is fit for its intended audience. But what if its actual audience is comprised of people who have become desensitised to volumes of violence and death in fiction thanks to the action movies of Schwarzenegger, Stallone, Van Damme et al? How do you get across the fact that this drama, this situation the characters have found themselves in, is not just another predictable goodies vs. baddies show? Well, you make it painful to watch. You *show* the suffering of the characters. And then, maybe, you let them live another day. Or maybe you don't.

I'm going to dive back to Hitchcock for a second. In 1964, the master of suspense made a 'sexual thriller' called *Marnie* about a frigid kleptomaniac with a traumatic past trapped inside her head. Hitchcock had insisted on the inclusion in the script of a scene where the woman (played by Tippi Hedren) was raped by her husband (Sean Connery). Hitch was reputed to have said to his scriptwriter, Evan Hunter: 'When [Connery] sticks it in her, I want the camera right in her face.' Hunter refused to script the scene and walked. Watching this episode of ***24***, some fans have suggested that writers Joel Surnow and Michael Loceff should have offered to do the same.

The implied emotional and physical torture of the two women here seems to have hit a bum note with some, who feel it was just too much. Certainly, the scene in question is distressing, helped in part by Stephen Hopkins' decision to film it with hand-held cameras that are usually reserved for real-life documentaries – or people trying to emulate them. Leslie Hope and Elisha Cuthbert should also be praised for emotional performances that help to convince anyone watching that this is happening for real. But really, it's the camera that is under scrutiny here, because, so his critics claim, Hopkins insulted his audience by showing them something they *didn't* want to see in a way that seemed exploitative and cheap.

It didn't do much harm to the ratings, though... Funny that.

24

QUESTIONS ARISING

- Why hasn't the murder of Janet York made the news headlines yet?
- And why no mention of the plane crash just six hours ago?

00 13:41 07:24 22:38 10:09 17:59 09:13 21:01 04:45 14:12 07:57 13:41 07:24 22:38 10:09 17:59 09:13

9:00 A.M.

Production Code 1AFF08

First US Transmission: Tuesday, January 22, 9/8C

Written by Virgil Williams
Directed by Stephen Hopkins

'The following takes place between 8:00 A.M. and 9:00 A.M. on the day of the Californian presidential primary... Events occur in real time.'

Cast: Penny Johnson Jerald (Sherry Palmer), Carlos Bernard (Tony Almeida), Michael Massee (Ira Gaines), Vicellous Shannon (Keith Palmer), Karina Arroyave (Jamey Farrell), Jude Ciccolella (Mike Novick), Silas Weir Mitchell (Eli), Eric Balfour (Milo Pressman), Michael Bryan French (Frank Simes), Kathleen Wilhoite (Lauren Proctor), Jesse D. Goins (Alan Hayes), Glenn Morshower (Agent Aaron Pierce), Devika Parikh (Maureen Kingsley), Talitha Peters (Anna), Al Leong (Neill – not credited).

EPISODE SUMMARY

Agent Pierce escorts David Palmer and his wife to safety. Meanwhile, now free from Gaines's control, Jack tries to explain his actions to **Special Agent Simes** of the Secret Service, telling him that he intentionally caused the disruption to the breakfast in order to save Palmer. He tells them that he is on a restricted information assignment and has been tracking the real assassin since midnight. Agent Simes does not appear to believe him, largely because of the call he received from Tony Almeida warning him about Jack.

At CTU, Tony and Nina are still questioning Jamey, who has finally decided to tell them that it is Ira Gaines who she's been feeding information to. She tells them that she needed the money but that she didn't think anyone would die. She admits to setting up the surveillance cameras and offers to call Gaines on a landline so that they can get a trace on him. After the failure of the assassination attempt, all Gaines is worried about is the location of Jonathan. Jamey is able to pacify him slightly by telling him she'll try to find out what has happened to Jack. Meanwhile, Nina tells Milo to forget about the keycard and puts him on all of Jamey's projects.

David and Sherry leave the power plant in the back of a limousine. David gets a call telling him that a man has been arrested for the disturbance at the breakfast. Sherry is shaken by what has happened and tells him that she really doesn't want him taking chances.

At around **8:07 A.M.**, Jack is still trying to convince the Secret Service Agents to let him go, telling them that he can identify the would-be assassin. When Simes tells Jack that he is to be handed over to the FBI for questioning, Jack confides in him about the abduction of his wife and daughter. However, Simes claims he doesn't have the authority to intervene and remains unconvinced by Jack's claims that he was trying to avert an attempt on Palmer's life. Instead, Simes orders that he be taken to the district office for further questioning. He is led, handcuffed, through the power station. Seizing his chance, Jack grabs a valve and lets a blast of steam into his captors' faces. He steals an agent's gun, sprints out of the plant, climbs over a perimeter fence and rolls down an embankment towards a road. There he carjacks a terrified waitress and orders her to drive him away. With Jack directing her at gunpoint, the waitress eventually drives into a building site. They park up and Jack tells her he has to make one phone call before he can let her go. Together, they break into the site office.

08:19 A.M. Under interrogation, Jamey tells Tony that she was paid $3,000 by Gaines for information. Tony scoffs at such a small price for Jamey's treachery, but the young woman points out that as a single mother, abandoned by her husband, her paltry wages are barely enough for her to make ends meet. Nina enters the office and Jamey again insists that she will not give them any more information unless they can guarantee her immunity, signed by their superior, **Chappelle**. Just then, Jack calls. Apologising for shooting her, he explains to Nina that Gaines had ordered her dead after she had got close to piecing everything together. She accepts his apology, aware of the strain he must have been under, but then regretfully informs him of Jamey's betrayal. This comes as a serious blow – Jack is aware that Jamey knows everything. Nina lets him speak to Jamey. He tells her that he will make sure she gets out of this mess as long as she helps him find his family, but Jamey is resolute – no immunity, no help. Mindful that time is not on their side, Jack tells Nina to bring Jamey's son Kyle in: maybe that will convince Jamey to talk. He also asks Nina to have a new car, gun and phone sent out to him at the building site. Through all this, the waitress, **Lauren**, has been listening intently. Once Jack has finished his call, she asks him who he is and he explains as much as he can to her, but she tells him she doesn't want to be involved:

> *'You're not the only one who has problems, Jack. Y'know I've just come off of a hellatious night-shift, I'm due in court in 45 minutes on a DUI charge of which I'm* guilty, *so... good luck with your own crisis, OK?'*

She makes to leave, but Jack pulls his gun on her and tells her to sit down.

The Palmers return from the breakfast at around **8:30 A.M.** a little shaken but otherwise fine. They're concerned that Keith is not home. Sherry tries to persuade her husband to put a stop to Maureen Kingsley's story. David turns this on his wife, telling her how furious he is with her for keeping Keith's involvement in Gibson's death a secret for seven years.

At **8:31 A.M.**, Jack speaks to Tony on the phone. Now fully aware of the situation, Tony apologises for undermining him earlier, while Jack tells him he regrets not confiding in him; by telling the Secret Service about his presence at the breakfast, Tony might well have saved Palmer's life. Hanging up, Jack gets Lauren to help him use a pair of bolt-cutters to remove his handcuffs.

Speaking with his chief of staff, Mike Novick, David Palmer learns that the incident at the breakfast was down to a CTU agent called Jack Bauer who insists he was trying to save Palmer, not kill him. The name 'Bauer' rings a bell with David, though for the moment he can't place it.

At the compound, Eli decides to follow Rick's example and tries to take Kim into another part of the shack to have sex with her. Kim struggles with him, but Teri, realising that Eli is a very strong man, offers herself in Kim's place, telling him she won't fight back. Saving her daughter from Eli's advances, she takes her place and consents to go into the other room with him, to Kim's utter horror.

Just 20 minutes before she is due to go on air, Maureen Kingsley returns a call from Sherry Palmer. Against her husband's wishes, Sherry asks Maureen to hold off for a few weeks on the story about her son. Maureen tells her what she told her husband, that she will not suppress the story – until Sherry tells her about the government agent's assassination attempt on David's life that morning, and that he might not be acting alone. Suddenly, Maureen appears much more willing to listen. She tells her she won't suppress the story, but she agrees to hold off on it for a couple of days.

Teri returns to the cell where her distraught daughter is waiting. Kim sobs in her mother's arms, aware of the sacrifice Teri has made to save her from Eli, but Teri appears almost unnaturally calm. Making sure none of Gaines's men are around, she reveals that she has been able to steal Eli's cellphone. She begins to call Nina for help, but no sooner has she connected than she is forced to hang up because Neill, the guard, comes into the cell looking for something.

Keith Palmer returns to the suite and appears unimpressed by his father's assurances that his lawyers will help him clear his name. Just then, Mike Novick comes in to tell David that for some unknown reason Maureen Kingsley has agreed to hold back on her story about Keith. David immediately detects Sherry's hand in this, but his wife pretends she knows nothing about it.

Jack and Lauren chat and he learns that her husband left her after she decided to look after her sick sister. Referring to her court appearance later that day, Jack asks her if she has a problem, and she laughs bitterly:

'A drinking problem? I wish it were that simple. At least then I'd have a support group... No, what I'm afraid I have is bad luck...'

As she talks, Lauren notices that Jack is growing sleepy. She waits until he looks settled then makes to leave, but his eyes snap back open and he points his gun at her again. Not wanting to fall asleep, he stands up and waits by the window for his car to arrive.

Tony and Nina turn up the pressure on Jamey, telling her that if she doesn't co-operate, her son will see her go to prison arrested for being a traitor. They point out that if Gaines can't get to her, he would not hesitate to hurt her son if it stopped her from testifying against him. A sobbing Jamey tells them she's confused and needs time to think. They decide to leave her alone – handcuffed to a chair – to mull over what they've said.

Jack notices that the car from CTU has arrived – and so have the Secret Service. Jack tells Lauren to pick up the car and drive it round to the side of the building site so he can leave without being seen. Still only half-convinced his story is true, Lauren agrees to help him. He watches as Lauren walks out of the building site towards the car, but then, changing her mind, she turns and goes straight to the agents to tell them where Jack is. Jack is forced to make a quick getaway via a back window. Evading the Secret Service agents, he runs to the CTU car and drives off at speed.

By **8:57 A.M.**, Milo has made some headway in identifying Gaines, but is perturbed by the news that Jamey's son is being brought in. Nina denies anything is wrong, but tells Tony in private that Milo will probably work out what has happened and suggests they bring him in permanently. Nina and Tony return to Jamey to find her lying on the floor, her wrist gushing with blood from a severe cut made with a shard from a broken cup. Nina and Tony run over to her and try to bring her round. Milo calls through to tell Nina that Jamey's son has arrived but Nina tells him not to bring him into the room. As Tony tries to resuscitate Jamey, her PDA begins to ring – Gaines is trying to contact her...

NOTES

- **Who's Who?:** Michael Bryan French (Frank Simes) played Doctor Smith in the slasher-horror film *I Still Know What You Did Last Summer* (dir. Danny Cannon, 1998) and also appeared in an early episode of *The X-Files*. Kathleen Wilhoite (Lauren Proctor) played Patricia in Steve Bochco's ill-fated police musical series *Cop Rock*, Rosalie in *LA Law* and Chloe Lewis in *ER*. More recently, she appeared in the film *Pay It Forward* (dir. Mimi Leder, 2000). She is also a composer, having written music for many shows, including *Buffy the Vampire Slayer*.
- **Time Checks:** Jack tells Agent Simes that he's been tracking the assassin since midnight. Sherry points out that Maureen Kingsley is due to broadcast her show at 9:00 A.M., pointing out that this is just 40 minutes away. Lauren the waitress moans that she's done a nightshift and is due in court in four hours, but Jack points out he hasn't slept in 24 hours and has killed two people since midnight. Dispatching the new car to Jack, Tony tells him it should be with him in just ten minutes.
- **Trivia:** Palmer experienced a similar security alert in Annapolis, though that was proven to be a false alarm. Jamey has a son called Kyle.

COMMENTS

As mentioned earlier, ***24***'s strength is its ability to shock with twists and turns that seem to come from left-field and only on reflection appear to make sense. So pity viewer Dean Browell, a keen-eyed web designer and Mackintosh computer enthusiast from Virginia, USA, who, while watching **24** with his wife, noticed that all the good guys use Macs, while the villains seem to prefer IBM PCs (what, for instance, did Gaines hide Jonathan's gun underneath? Yup, an IBM laptop). In an interview with Wired.com, the online computer magazine, Browell noted how Jack Bauer is seen to use an Apple Cube while most of his colleagues use PowerBooks, iBooks or PowerMacs. Even Tony – who early on is signposted as the obvious traitor – is a loyal Mac user, which convinced Browell that the character was a deliberate red herring. Yet Jamey, the one person Bauer's boss Walsh had claimed they could trust, uses a Dell PC. 'I thought my theory had been blown,' said Browell. 'My wife was quite entertained when my theory was shot down.'

So of course, by the time this episode was broadcast, Dean Browell could rightly claim to be the smuggest of **24**'s many viewers. 'It is really odd,' Browell admitted. 'It almost seems like a visual clue that was there from the beginning. It would be a really big coincidence if they didn't put that in there intentionally.' Yes indeed. But as if an intelligent production team would think of such a thing...

In an e-mail to Wired.com, **24** writer and co-producer Michael Loceff played along with the theory, sarcastically pointing out that in the show 'the bad guys use Nokia and the good guys, Ericsson. The good guys play chess and the bad guys play Go. The good guys eat popcorn and reconstituted soy protein and the bad guys eat red meat...' and so on. Loceff may mock, but it's not uncommon for characters in TV shows and movies to favour Mac to PC, adding an interesting dimension to the wider PC vs Mac debate. The young student characters in *Buffy the Vampire Slayer*, for instance, somehow have the money to work on Mac iBooks instead of the more likely PCs – though when one of their number turned 'evil' recently, it was noted that she still relied on a Mac, suggesting that redemption wasn't out of the question.

Dean Browell's theory could well have ruined his enjoyment of the show's twists and turns, but he has continued to watch, scrutinising every shot for any clues to help him second-guess future plot revelations. Indeed, while everyone else breathed easy after Jamey was unmasked as the dirty agent, Browell's attention was distracted by another character who just happens to have started using a Dell laptop...

QUESTIONS ARISING

- How long has Jamey been a traitor, and who recruited her?
- How does Palmer know Jack's name?
- What happened to Jonathan after the failed assassination attempt?

9:00 A.M.

:24 22:38 10:09 17:59 09:13 21:01 04:45 14:12 07:57 13:41 07:24 22:38 10:09 17:59 09:13 19:47 05:20

Production Code 1AFF09

First US Transmission: Tuesday, February 5, 9/8C

Written by Lawrence Hertzog
Directed by Davis Guggenheim

'The following takes place between 9:00 A.M. and 10:00 A.M. on the day of the Californian presidential primary... Events occur in real time.'

Cast: Penny Johnson Jerald (Sherry Palmer), Carlos Bernard (Tony Almeida), Michael Massee (Ira Gaines), Tamara Tunie (Alberta Green), Zeljko Ivanek (Andre Drazen), Daniel Bess (Rick), Karina Arroyave (Jamey Farrell), Jude Ciccolella (Mike Novick), Zach Grenier (Carl), Silas Weir Mitchell (Eli), Eric Balfour (Milo Pressman), Currie Graham (Ted Cofell), Ivar Brogger (Frank Ames), Tracy E. Wilson (Cofell's Assistant), Desmond Bull (Kid), Martin Morales (Attendant), Manny Perry (Cop), Maurice Dunster (Security Guard), Burke Stuart (Mark, Cofell's Chauffeur).

EPISODE SUMMARY

Jamey is taken out of CTU by paramedics while Nina informs the team that Jamey tried to commit suicide. Everyone is understandably shocked, but Nina urges them to all return to work – the threat against Palmer isn't over yet. Jack calls her to ask for her help in evading the roadblocks that the Secret Service have set up to catch him. Nina tells him that Teri has just called her but she got disconnected almost immediately. Pragmatically, Jack realises that he can't help Teri while he's still trapped by the roadblock. Nina urges him to give himself up, but Jack is banking on Gaines keeping Teri and Kim alive for as long as he still believes Jack can be of use. If he's in custody, Gaines won't hesitate to kill both of them. He asks if Jamey has been able to give them any more information and it's then that Nina regretfully tells him about Jamey's suicide attempt. The news comes as a terrible blow to Jack, but he nevertheless gives instructions for Nina to send someone to the hospital to question Jamey just in case she makes it. On another line, Teri calls Nina again; Nina tells her to leave her phone on so they can trace her call and quickly connects her to Jack. But before she can speak to him, she hears Eli and Rick entering the outer door to the shack. Teri hides the phone on a beam. Eli enters the cell and begins frantically searching for his phone. Rick quickly spots the phone up on the beam but says nothing. The two men leave the cell and continue their search elsewhere.

David makes his way to his next public fixture, a visit to an elementary school. Sherry goes with him but insists on criticising him for wanting to make his grand confession about Keith to the press.

Milo works hard to track Teri's location, but even with their sophisticated tracking equipment it's not good enough to make a positive trace. Searching Jamey's e-mail, Tony finds an encrypted message which he gets Milo to decrypt. Just then, Tony gets a call from the hospital – Jamey has died.

Back at the shack, Teri gets the phone back from the beam and tries to give Jack some clues as to where she is. Jack is driving while speaking to her on the cellphone and soon attracts the attention of a pair of traffic cops. The cops signal for Jack to pull over, but as they approach his car, Jack speeds off, leaving the officers to run back to their car and give chase. Jack parks up in a busy car park and moves from car to car, talking to Teri as he goes. Hiding under a car, Jack promises Teri he'll find her and is able to grab just a few reassuring words with Kim before Eli returns. Teri hides the phone back on the beam, but the phone's battery is running low and its warning beep alerts Eli to where she's hidden it. He hits Teri and then puts the still-connected phone to his ear to hear Jack threatening him. The phone's battery chooses that moment to die. Eli is raging and makes towards Gaines's office to tell him what has happened, but Rick points out that Gaines will not be happy with him if he learns that the women were able to phone Jack just because he stupidly lost his phone. Eli decides to take Rick's advice and say nothing. Back at CTU, Nina tells Jack that they were unable to trace the signal in time.

Jack manages to hotwire one of the cars in the parking lot and drives off unseen by the increasing numbers of policemen looking for him. He calls Nina back to learn about Jamey's death. Nina puts him through to Tony who tells him that Milo has deciphered the name '**Ted Cofell**' from the message on Jamey's e-mail. Armed with Cofell's address, Jack decides to go to him and see what he can find out.

Gaines is concerned that he has been unable to get a response from Jamey for some time. But then he gets a call from his employer, Andre Drazen, who tells Gaines that he and his brother are disappointed that

Palmer has not been killed as planned. Gaines tries to convince Drazen that he can still pull off the assassination and implicate Bauer, but Drazen is unimpressed:

> *'If Plan A doesn't work, you should have a Plan B – not Plan A recycled...'*

Gaines promises that the job will be done by the end of the day, but Drazen warns him that they can order their contact, Cofell, to remove all the funds from the bank account Gaines has been using so far to fund the operation... and that if things continue to go badly, the money won't be the only thing he'll lose.

Sherry calls Palmer's former colleague, Carl, and asks him to stop Maureen Kingsley from running her story, only to be told that Carl has already 'taken care of everything'.

By **9:38 A.M.**, the CTU team have worked out that Ted Cofell is Gaines's money-man – Jamey's e-mail revealed a bank transfer to Gaines of $1 million. Jack calls Cofell's office and speaks to his secretary, posing as an old friend. The secretary tells him that Cofell is in a meeting and then due to leave the office at 10:00 that morning. Meanwhile, Tony and Nina learn that their superiors have decided to replace Jack with **Alberta Green**, an agent who Nina once worked with. Tony can tell that Nina is not impressed by the news.

As Teri and Kim try to comfort each other, Kim chooses the moment to ask what prompted her father to move out. Teri tells her that Jack went away on a mission a couple of years ago, only to come back a shell of what he was, 'distant and preoccupied, and at other times he was just angry'. He left her to sort his head out though they eventually decided to get back together.

Though he can't prove a link to Gaines, Tony discovers that Cofell is booked on a private plane destined for Denver, Colorado. Alberta Green arrives to brief the team. She announces that Jack has been dismissed, pending an investigation. As a fugitive from the Secret Service, Jack is now considered to be connected to the assassination attempt on Palmer. The team's first priority therefore is to find Jack.

At the school, Palmer's talk with the children is interrupted by a call from one of his main sponsors, **Frank Ames**. Having heard of Maureen Kingsley's case against Keith, Ames is threatening to withdraw his support for Palmer. He tells Palmer that he has also learned that Carl plans to remove Maureen's chief witness, Dr Ferragamo – permanently! Ames hangs up leaving David stunned. He orders Mike to contact Carl...

Alberta Green takes over Jack's office and summons Nina for a chat. Perfectly aware that Nina and Jack once had an affair, Alberta accuses her of knowing where Jack is, though Nina denies everything. Jack, meanwhile, has made his way into Cofell's office. He speaks to Cofell's secretary, who tells him that Cofell has just left via the elevator. Jack sprints down the stairs and sets off a fire alarm to delay the elevator momentarily. Working to a strict schedule, Cofell leaves the elevator at the garage level and heads straight towards his limo. Rushing to get to his destination, he fails to notice that his regular driver has been replaced by Jack.

At the shack, Teri begins to experience stomach pains. Kim asks her if Eli hurt her, but Teri plays it down, pretending she is OK. But as she cradles her daughter in her arms, Teri is clearly trying to hold back the agony...

NOTES

- **Who's Who?:** Tamara Tunie (Alberta Green) played Lillian Fancy in a number of episodes of *NYPD Blue* and Jessica Griffin in *As The World*

Turns on and off for 13 years, she has also appeared in the films *Wall Street* (dir. Oliver Stone, 1987), *Rising Sun* (Philip Kaufman, 1993), *City Hall* (dir. Harold Becker, 1996), The Peacemaker (dir. Mimi Leder, 1997) and *The Devil's Advocate* (dir. Taylor Hackford, 1997). Zeljko Ivanek (Andre Drazen) has appeared in the daytime soaps *The Sun Also Rises*, *All My Children*, the TV series *The Edge of Night*, *Homicide: Life on the Street* (as Ed Danvers), *Oz* (as Governor Devlin) and Imagine's *From the Earth To the Moon*, and movies including *School Ties* (dir. Robert Mandel, 1992), *Donnie Brasco* (dir. Mike Newell, 1997), and, for director Ridley Scott, *Hannibal* and *Black Hawk Down* (both 2001). Currie Graham (Ted Cofell) played Nate in the comedy *Suddenly Susan*.

- **Time Checks:** Nina tells Jack their trace on Teri's call will take 20 minutes. Tony gets advance word that Alberta Green is expected at 9.45. Jack learns that Cofell is due to leave his office by 10.00 A.M., while Drazen tells Gaines that he will join him at 10.30 A.M. When Jack sets the fire alarm off, Cofell reassures his fellow passengers in the stationary lift that the alarm works to a 30-second reset before the lift continues moving automatically – the spoilsport.
- **Death Count:** Jamey Farrell (9:12 A.M.).
- **Trivia:** Ted Cofell is a CEO at an investment bank at 21500 Riverside Drive, Burbank.

COMMENTS

In 1999, Kweisi Mfume, President of the National Association for the Advancement of Colored People (or NAACP), accused the major American networks of a 'virtual whitewash' for failing to provide leading roles for African-American artists in their autumn schedule. At the time, black actors were estimated to account for ten per cent of the characters on TV. This might appear only slightly unfair when taking into account that African-Americans comprise just 13 per cent of the entire population of the USA. However, they also happen to make up for more than 20 per cent of the entire viewing population, and it's this statistic that should cause the most concern to TV executives.

Over the years, there have been a few TV shows on the major networks with predominantly black casts: *Sanford & Son* (a reworking of the British comedy series *Steptoe & Son*), *The Cosby Show*, starring America's most popular black TV actor, Bill Cosby, and Fox's own *In Living Color*. The connection with all these is not just that they were all comedy shows; they all depicted a world *separate* to that of the whites. *In Living Color*'s sole white performer, the now mega-famous Jim Carrey, was hired more as a statement against similar tokenism in predominantly 'white' shows than a genuine attempt at integration. In the music business, though, things have improved. When MTV first started up, there was resistance to allowing 'black music' onto the station; the first video by a black artist to be played was Michael Jackson's 'Billie Jean', almost 18 months after the station commenced broadcasting. Now, 22 years later, MTV is recognised as being the nearest America has to an integrated TV channel.

But while TV executives seem open to the idea of blacks as entertainers – a stereotype that's barely removed from the Black and White Minstrels of the 1920s – less common is the 'black' drama. Alex Haley's celebrated mini-series *Roots* (first shown in 1977) is the notable exception. But certainly by the dawn of the 21st century, Kweisi Mfume's complaint seemed to be justified, with the 'Big Four' (ABC, CBS, NBC and Fox) preferring to target the largest audience – mainly white – rather than cater for all. Coupled with this was the rather curious problem of the 'politically correct' lobby refusing to allow blacks to play villains (traditionally the best roles in any drama) for fear of being insulting to minorities. So the black population was becoming marginalised from all directions.

24 represents a considerable step forward. While a black president, even a *non-white* president, is, perhaps, still very idealistic in real life, the positioning of David Palmer and his family in the show is important. In the first episode, Jack Bauer and his superior both admit that the prospect of an African-American presidential candidate is something that is almost guaranteed to cause them problems, that Palmer's skin colour is reason enough for someone to see him as a viable target. The show takes a stance by stating that, yes, this is wrong, but that we have to accept racism as a reality rather than sweeping it under the carpet and pretending it doesn't exist. When Palmer himself later learns that the assassination bid is not racially motivated, it takes him by surprise because he's so used to being seen as a black man.

The kind of roles that populate ***24*** could easily be played by an all-white cast: Alberta Green would be ambitious whatever her background; Officer Jessie Hampton's death would still be a tragedy. In fact, even the villains of the piece, the Drazens, are shown to be evil men who happen to be Serbian rather than *because* they're Serbian. And despite Sherry's misguided obsessing about her husband's place in history as, potentially, the first black president, the show is at pains to show him as a credible presidential candidate, a good father and an honourable man, while at no point claiming that his race is insignificant with regards to who he is.

QUESTIONS ARISING

- What went on between Nina and Alberta to cause such suspicion between them?
- What's wrong with Teri's stomach?

24 22:38 10:09 17:59 09:13 21:01 04:45 14:12 07:57 13:41 07:24 22:38 10:09 17:59 09:13 19:47 05:20

Production Code 1AFF10

First US Transmission: Tuesday, February 12, 9/8C

Written by Robert Cochran
Directed by Davis Guggenheim

'The following takes place between 10:00 A.M. and 11:00 A.M. on the day of the Californian presidential primary... Events occur in real time.'

Cast: Penny Johnson Jerald (Sherry Palmer), Richard Burgi (Kevin Carroll), Michael Massee (Ira Gaines), Tamara Tunie (Alberta Green), Zeljko Ivanek (Andre Drazen), Daniel Bess (Rick), Jude Ciccolella (Mike Novick), Zach Grenier (Carl), Silas Weir Mitchell (Eli), Currie Graham (Ted Cofell), Carlos Bernard (Tony Almeida), Jenny Gago (Principal).

EPISODE SUMMARY

The CTU staff are finally informed by Alberta Green that Jack Bauer, along with the photographer Martin Balkin, is now a suspect in the assassination attempt on Palmer. Jack is, of course, in the driving seat of Ted Cofell's limousine. It doesn't take long for Ted to realise that Jack is not his usual driver and as he begins to dial a number on his cellphone, Jack locks the doors, pulls over and draws a gun on him. He asks Cofell who he's working for, but the businessman claims he doesn't know what Jack is talking about. Jack calls Nina and asks her to find out all she can about Cofell while he finds somewhere to lie low for a while.

Eli sends Rick to the shack to interrogate Teri and Kim, but Rick tells the women that he has no intention of asking them anything – that way he can't lie when he tells Eli that they told him nothing. When Rick leaves the shack, his lack of success angers Eli, who takes his frustrations out on him with a severe beating.

In the middle of obtaining information about Ted Cofell, Nina is forced to switch to another task when Alberta comes to speak to her about the passenger list of the crashed 747. Apparently, the empty seat that Tony had identified was actually booked for Martin Balkin, the photographer, which would suggest that the Balkin at Palmer's breakfast meeting was in fact a lookalike. This would appear to corroborate Jack's claim that Balkin was the assassin. At that moment, Nina gets a call from Jack – she pretends it's an FBI agent for Alberta's benefit, only for Alberta to ask to speak to him. Fortunately, Tony realises what's happening and calls Alberta over to his desk, which gives Nina enough time to tell Jack all she knows about Cofell; Cofell is, it seems, on medication for a weak heart. She guesses that, as a typical passive-aggressive control-freak, the threat of pain would be more persuasive to him than actual violence.

Climbing into the passenger area of the limo at around **10:17 A.M.**, Jack begins to interrogate Ted and learns only that he was en route to a meeting with a machine salesman by the name of Kevin Carroll. Trying to make him talk more, Jack tells Ted about a trick he knows which involves stuffing a water-soaked handkerchief down someone's throat and then, when the stomach begins to digest it, the handkerchief is pulled out taking the stomach lining with it. Ted is clearly terrified, but still claims he cannot tell Jack anything.

A dissatisfied Andre Drazen arrives at Gaines's compound. Unhappy with the way Gaines has messed up the assassination attempt, Drazen offers Gaines just a half-hour to find and kill Jack before he puts into action an alternative plan. Working nearby, Rick overhears Drazen tell Gaines that ultimately it will be his responsibility to kill Jack's family.

Still at the school visit, Palmer gets a call from Carl. His former advisor at first refuses to meet with him to discuss the Ferragamo problem, but by suggesting he can incriminate him, Palmer manages to convince Carl to meet him face to face. At the compound, Teri once again begins to experience stomach pains but tells Kim that it's nothing.

At just on **10:23 A.M.**, Nina calls Jack to tell him that out of the six likely 'Kevin Carrolls', just one works for a machine tool company, which might suggest that Cofell was telling the truth or that the partial evidence on Jamey's e-mail is not as reliable as Jack is banking on. Jack is still desperate to stick with Cofell, so far his closest link to his family's abductors. He decides to take Cofell to meet with this 'Kevin Carroll'. Unseen by Jack, Cofell removes a knife from a compartment in the back seat.

David Palmer manages to grab a minute alone with his wife at the school meeting. She claims that she spoke to Carl recently and he hinted that he has been able to 'take care' of their problem over Keith but that, as she wasn't sure what Carl meant by that, she didn't think to mention it to David. This worries David greatly. Learning only recently that Sherry has kept the knowledge of Keith's involvement in Gibson's death from him, David feels disinclined to believe Sherry's claims of innocence now. Mike Novick calls him aside to let him know that he's run a check on the agent at the breakfast – Jack Bauer – and discovered that his personal file contains a number of 'gaps' that seem to be restricted information. Much to Mike's surprise, David asks him if there might have been a gap two years ago. Without explaining how he might have known this, David tells Mike that they have more important things to worry about.

Jack drives to the multi-storey car park where Cofell's meeting with Kevin Carroll is due to take place. Stepping into the back of the limo, Jack is taken by surprise by Cofell, who attacks him with his knife. But Jack's training is superior to Cofell's and he manages to overpower him easily. He is surprised enough that a businessman would have a Microtech Halo knife, but even more surprised when Cofell curses him in a foreign language Jack recognises as Serbian, suggesting Cofell is from Belgrade or has family there. Jack immediately challenges Cofell, and the man gloats that Jack deserves what he's getting. Just then, Cofell suffers a massive heart attack. Jack tries to force him to take his heart medicine but Cofell refuses; he dies leaving Jack even more distraught about his family's safety.

Speaking to Nina a few minutes later, Jack reasserts his belief that this whole mess is down to a personal connection to himself. He asks her to cross-check any connections between Cofell and 'Operation Nightfall', a mission Jack was on a couple of years ago in Belgrade and Kosovo. Aware that Kevin Carroll could arrive at any moment, Jack props Cofell's dead body up in the back seat so that, from the back, he will look alive.

Ever the pragmatist, Tony suggests to Nina that they should involve Alberta in Jack's case, especially as she suspects so much already. But after the revelation of Jamey's treachery, Nina tells him they should play safe and not risk exposing themselves or Jack to any additional moles in CTU. Reluctantly, Tony agrees.

Though Kim is exhausted, Teri stops her from falling asleep, mindful that Jack could turn up at any moment and they'll need to move quickly. Rick comes to the cell. He's managed to salvage Dan's gun from the back of his van and smuggle it into the shack to Teri and Kim. Teri takes this as a sign that Gaines plans to have them executed. Meanwhile, with the clock ticking towards **10:45 A.M.**, Jack sees a car arrive at the car park and pull up behind the limo. A man steps out and gets into the back of Cofell's vehicle; Jack's only partly surprised to discover that this man is the person he formerly knew as 'Alan York'. Jack locks the doors and Carroll sees for the first time who's behind the wheel; he pulls a gun and fires at point-blank range, unaware that Jack is protected by bulletproof glass. Jack decides to take Carroll for a drive, speeding round the garage frantically and sending Carroll sprawling around the back of the limo. He breaks suddenly, sending Carroll head first into the glass, knocking him out. Jack quickly binds Carroll's wrists with tape. When Carroll finally comes round a few minutes later (at **10:52 A.M.**), Jack immediately starts asking him about the whereabouts of Teri and Kim. Carroll tells him that there's no reason for Gaines to keep his hostages alive now Jack is free from his control. But if Jack agrees to let him go, Kevin will lead him to Gaines. Jack transfers Kevin to his own car and drives towards the compound. With the time limit up, however, Drazen has ordered Gaines to dispose of Jack Bauer's family, and Eli has already been dispatched to do the job.

Carl arrives at the elementary school and is led to a private area away from the reporters. Palmer rebukes him for threatening someone just to help his presidential candidacy, but Carl claims he was only acting in the interests of the people who they both work for, people who are eager to see Palmer in office and will do anything to make sure nothing stands in his way. David decides to warn Dr Ferragamo but when he calls him he gets the doctor's answering machine.

At **10:59 A.M.**, Eli comes to the shed. Teri quickly grabs the gun she got from Rick and fires, only to discover all too late that it's out of bullets. Eli grabs her and pulls out his own gun. The two struggle, watched by an anxious Kim, and Teri manages to knock Eli's gun away just as he pulls a knife on her. She seizes his gun and shoots him dead. She shoots him again, coldly explaining to Kim that anyone listening out for shots will be expecting the gun to fire twice.

As Jack drives, he asks Carroll where they are headed. Carroll tells him to drive straight – he's taking him to find his family...

NOTES

- **Who's Who?:** Jenny Gago (Principal) was a semi-regular in the soap operas *General Hospital* and *Knots Landing*, and played Detective Beatrice Zapeda in the sci-fi drama *Alien Nation*.
- **Time Checks:** Drazen gives Gaines just half an hour to fix his failures. Jack tells Cofell that his wife and daughter have been missing since midnight.
- **Death Count:** Ted Cofell (10:35 A.M. of a heart attack) and Eli (10:59 A.M. of a gunshot).
- **Trivia:** David and Sherry first met at elementary school. The registration on Cofell's limo is 4MN0993.

COMMENTS

In the old days, when even the 'Red, White and Blue' was in black and white, us fans had two choices: either pay X amount of pounds to join the 'official' fan club, which would probably offer a quarterly magazine, a badge and maybe a few discounts on other official merchandise; or you could make your own 'fanzine' filled with self-penned articles with Letraset headings on why the show is the bestest thing ever, and illustrate it with biro or felt-tip-inked sketches that might look a little like your favourite stars... immediately after their first face-lift. In either event, unless you were very lucky, neither publication would celebrate its first anniversary. But, as mentioned earlier, the early 1990s welcomed a creation called the world wide web, which made the internet more accessible than it had been for the last 20 years while in the hands of the government. While it would of course revolutionise business and education, one of its unanticipated side effects was that it also made it much easier to be part of a fan community.

At first, people began putting up pages that showed their appreciation of the shows. They included a few scanned-in pictures from *TV Guide* or *Radio Times*, episode guides, cast lists, a short story or two and an expression of love for an actor or actress. In terms of online communities, Usenet was the first port of call for many fans, where you could converse about the socio-political aspect of *Star Trek*, collectively swoon over the latest exploits of *Quantum Leap*'s Sam Beckett or make up rude limericks based on the monsters in *Doctor Who*. What was good about this was that it was largely unmoderated. As it was a free, open service for anyone to use, the producers of these shows couldn't really complain if their shows were popular enough to have a fandom that they couldn't control. Sometimes, you'd even get the producers or stars themselves getting involved (although more often than not, it was some geek from Milwaukee pretending to be Leonard Nimoy who got upset when everyone called his bluff). Then came mailing lists – systems that allow members of a community to send an e-mail to all subscribers on the list – and message boards, where members can enter 'rooms' and post their thoughts, and live chat-rooms where everyone talks at once and invariably someone starts sulking because they're being ignored.

Of course, by this time, the people that owned the shows realised that if they set up their own mailing lists and chat-rooms, they could control the whole ball game (cue maniacal laughter and a clap of thunder).

Cut to 2002. Post 'dotcom' boom, we still have Usenet, though many people have abandoned it because of the trolls (morons whose only joy in life is to post messages designed to cause arguments, upset people or simply irritate everyone reading), and the mailing lists are thriving (though as most of them are owned by one commercial company – whose name begins with 'Y' – the mailing groups tend to get bombarded with adverts). But we also have officially sanctioned versions. Fox has been very astute in creating a dedicated website to ***24*** with weekly updates, character profiles containing information not revealed in the show itself and even a message board where fans can speculate what the heck is going to happen next. When the show came to the UK, BBCi (the online division of the Beeb) provided the same basic content, but split their message boards into 'Spoiler' and 'Non-spoiler' to give fans the chance to decide whether or not they wanted to know what had already been revealed in the US transmissions. And, to support the final few episodes, they even opened up live chat-rooms where everyone could talk at the same time and one person ended up sulking because no-one paid him any attention...

It's easy to get all cynical about the way the TV companies are beginning to exploit the internet ten years after the fans began building their own communities there. But the very fact that they're not only putting effort into developing unique content for the fans but they're ostensibly doing it for free (advertising aside) is something to be celebrated.

QUESTIONS ARISING

- So, where is Jonathan, the assassin, who hasn't been seen or heard of since 8:00 A.M.?
- Drazen has, according to Gaines, been planning his revenge on Bauer for a year. But what was the catalyst that drove him to such extreme measures?
- Is 'Kevin Carroll' just another pseudonym?

0:00 13:41 07:24 22:38 10:09 17:59 09:13 21:01 04:45 14:12 07:57 13:41 07:24 22:38 10:09 17:59 09:13

Production Code 1AFF11

First US Transmission: Tuesday, February 19, 9/8C

Written by Howard Gordon
Directed by Stephen Hopkins

'The following takes place between 11:00 A.M. and 12:00 P.M. on the day of the Californian presidential primary... Events occur in real time.'

Cast: Carlos Bernard (Tony Almeida), Richard Burgi (Kevin Carroll), Michael Massee (Ira Gaines), Tamara Tunie (Alberta Green), Daniel Bess (Rick), Jude Ciccolella (Mike Novick), John Prosky (Dr George Ferragamo), Al Leong (Neill), Jon E. Epstein (Assistant).

EPISODE SUMMARY

While Kevin Carroll directs Jack towards Gaines's compound, Alberta makes another announcement to the CTU staff – that finding and arresting Jack is now their top priority. Surreptitiously, Nina calls Jack to tell him that Alberta's putting pressure on her and Tony to tell her everything. Jack tells her to stand her ground and not reveal a thing until he gives her the signal. In the meantime, he requests satellite pictures of the compound directed to his PDA to enable him to find his way around.

Teri and Kim find a large metal bathtub to hide Eli's body under. Though Teri admits to feeling sick over the murder of the man, Kim says she doesn't feel anything except relief that it's him who's dead and not them. As they cover up the bloodstained floor with straw, they hear a beeping sound. It's Eli's pager, which means that Eli will soon be missed. Teri takes Eli's knife and prepares herself for a fight. Meanwhile, outside the compound, Jack receives Nina's satellite pictures of the area. Nina apologises for them being a few hours out of date, but they still reveal a large armed presence there. Nina tries to persuade him to allow her to tell Alberta what's happening so they can at least send him back-up, but Jack refuses – he's not willing to risk his family's lives by getting CTU involved just yet. Ending the call, he then moves Kevin Carroll, at gunpoint, to the driver's seat of the car and tells him to head towards the main gate of the compound.

David Palmer tells Mike Novick that Carl plans to threaten, perhaps even kill, George Ferragamo. He's also forced to confess to Mike that he tried to warn Ferragamo that his life might be at risk, something Mike is not happy with as that could be seen as evidence of David's part in the conspiracy, which in turn could threaten David's candidacy.

At **11:11 A.M.**, lying low in the rear passenger seat of Carroll's car, Jack threatens Carroll that if he tries to tip anyone off, he'll begin shooting, with Carroll as his first victim. Jack lies down low in the back of the vehicle, while Carroll bluffs his way past the guards on the compound gates. Once inside, Carroll foolishly tries to goad Jack with comments about Teri, suggesting that while he and Teri were separated she must have been sleeping around. Jack silences him by holding the gun to the back of his head. Having travelled a fair distance inside the compound, Carroll points Jack towards a shack where Teri and Kim are likely to be kept. With that, Jack knocks him out cold and leaves him tied up while he begins to make his way through the compound. Back at the main building, Gaines's army are packing up and preparing to leave. Gaines orders Rick to fetch Eli, who hasn't called in for some time.

Ferragamo finally returns Palmer's call at **11:20 A.M.** and accuses Palmer himself of threatening him. Ferragamo refuses to discuss anything with him and hangs up. Although he has another appointment in less than an hour, David insists on seeing Ferragamo in person and instructs his driver to head for the doctor's office.

Teri and Kim hear someone enter their shack from outside. Teri stands poised for attack but when the door opens, it's Jack who enters. He, Teri and Kim collapse into an emotional hug, relieved to be reunited once more. At CTU, Alberta is losing patience. She airs her belief that Nina knows where Jack is and that Tony is probably covering for Nina. She puts them on immediate suspension and sends them to separate holding rooms, warning them that unless they begin to co-operate, she'll bring charges against them for impeding her investigation.

The Bauer reunion is interrupted by Rick, who is startled when Jack grabs him and begins to strangle him. Kim begs him to stop, explaining that Rick has in fact been helping them. Jack wants to head towards the car where he left Kevin Carroll and then drive it to the shack and pick them up, but Teri is unhappy with being separated from him again. Rick then suggests he could steal one of Gaines's vans for them to escape in and offers to drive it over to the shack himself. Jack is persuaded to let him go by Teri and Kim. Gaines calls Rick on his radio to ask where he and Eli have got to. Rick stalls him, saying Eli is busy digging a grave for the women. Rick heads over to the main building and manages to steal a gun and a van, but as he prepares to leave, Gaines finds him and asks him what he's doing. Rick bluffs that Eli asked for the van to move the bodies of the women in. Simultaneously, Neill, one of Gaines's guards, finds Kevin Carroll's unconscious body in the car inside the compound and radios in to Gaines to tell him about it. Gaines commandeers Rick's van and tells him to drive to where they found the car.

At approximately **11:42 A.M.**, Mike advises Palmer not to speak to Ferragamo, but Palmer won't listen. However, when they arrive at Ferragamo's office, they see the place swarming with firemen trying to put out a blaze. Speaking to the officers on the scene, Mike learns that there has been a huge gas explosion decimating the building – there is no way Ferragamo could have got out alive. Palmer tries to head towards the scene, but Mike pulls him back. Even if he isn't involved, rushing in to a possible arson scene will send out all the wrong signals. David is persuaded to return to his car and drive away.

Having given both Tony and Nina all the chances she can, Alberta prepares to suspend them both just as Jack calls her directly. He apologises for not contacting her sooner, but explains that he couldn't risk contacting anyone at CTU. He tells her he has uncovered the people behind the Palmer threat and uses his PDA to transmit his location to her. Alberta reminds him that unless he can prove otherwise, he is also still a suspect. However, she despatches two helicopters to Jack's location. Then she reluctantly tells Nina and Tony about Jack's call and withdraws their suspension.

At about **11:54 A.M.**, Gaines and Rick find Neill with the unconscious Carroll. Gaines rouses Carroll from his sleep and asks him what has happened. Carroll, still dazed, struggles to tell him that Jack Bauer is inside the complex. Rick takes advantage of the distraction and drives off in the van, but Gaines sees him and immediately radios his guards to block the front gates. By the time Gaines and Carroll have reached the shack, Jack, his wife and daughter and Rick have already driven off. Searching the cell, Gaines finds Eli's body hidden under the old bathtub.

Jack drives the van towards the exit, but Gaines's guards shoot out his tyres. The group shelter behind the van as it is pelted with a barrage of bullets. Giving Teri his PDA with the downloaded maps, Jack tells her to take Kim and head for a disused water tower on the edge of a reservoir and wait there for him. As they run off, Jack uses a knife to puncture the van's petrol tank, sending petrol pouring out. He and Rick reach cover, but Rick takes a bullet in the arm. Jack shoots at the van, igniting the petrol and engulfing the vehicle in a huge explosion which momentarily keeps Gaines's men at bay. In the woods, Teri and Kim watch the smoke rising through the trees in horror, while Jack helps a stumbling Rick away from the inferno.

NOTES

- **Who's Who?:** John Prosky (Dr George Ferragamo) played Bart Simon in the medical TV drama *Chicago Hope* and the bellman in *A.I. Artificial Intelligence* (Steven Spielberg, 2001).
- **Time Checks:** Mike reminds David that he is due to deliver a speech on his public healthcare policy in an hour. Alberta gives Tony ten minutes to mull over her warning while she interrogates Nina. Jack gives Rick just five minutes to steal one of Gaines's vans and get it to the shack.
- **Death Count:** Dr George Ferragamo (victim of a 'gas explosion', 11:40 A.M.).

- **Trivia:** Jack refers to 'Waco', the location of the infamous religious cult that committed mass suicide after the FBI threatened to storm their compound.

COMMENTS

What's in a name? With the hero of ***24*** we have some obvious (and some less obvious) connotations with the name 'Jack': 'Jack-of-all-trades', 'Jack-in-the-box', 'jackdaw', 'jack shit' (which, let's face it, describes how much Jack knows for most of the series), 'jack off' (ahem!), 'carjack' and 'Jack of hearts, spades, diamonds and clubs'. But the name 'Bauer' is a little more troublesome. In German, it means 'farmer', while in the 2000 American presidential primaries, Republican candidate Gary Bauer stepped aside to allow George W. Bush to gain the party's candidacy. As we know, though, words have a habit of changing over time. The word 'Bower' (to rhyme with 'flower' or indeed *'bauer'*) has its roots in Elizabethan fables, most notably in Edmund Spenser's six-volume poem *The Faerie Queene*.

The main story of *The Faerie Queene* is a quest, Arthur's search for Gloriana (believed to have been the author's projection of Queen Elizabeth), who appears in other guises (Spenser's women are rarely who they appear to be). Book One depicts the 'knight of holiness' whose mission is to protect Una and free her parents from a dragon. The book is concerned with Christians seduced by false religion and ends triumphant with the assistance of 'truth'. Book Two tells of the adventures of Guion and his voyage to Acrasia's Bower of Bliss. Guion ultimately destroys the bower, a twist that has caused problems for those readers who see Spenser's poetic skill at odds with the moral intention. Had anyone on the ***24*** production team been familiar with Spenser? Perhaps Guion's threat to the Bower might be connected with Gaines's threats to Bauer.

Later books recount stories of estranged lovers, Amoret and Scudamour, and Florimell and Marinell. In Book Five (a political allegory based on events of the time), Artegall, the Knight of Justice, sets out to destroy the giant Grantorto and to rescue Irena, while the final volume concerns the mission of Calidore, the Knight of Courtesy, who sets out to capture the 'blatant beast'. The 'blatant beast' bizarrely escapes from the world of the poem and threatens to destroy Spenser's work.

Feel free to spot any parallels between this and ***24*** at any time.

One other classical reference can be found in the phrase 'bower-woman', which, according to *Brewer's Dictionary*, refers to: 'A lady's maid and companion.' Apparently, the Bower-women were 'admitted to considerable freedom of speech, and were treated with familiarity and kindness'. Here, sadly, my cheap attempt to associate popular culture with centuries-old legends completely unravels. Shame. It was going so well.

QUESTIONS ARISING

- Was Ferragamo's death actually murder, as David believes, or could anything be considered a mere coincidence today?
- Now that Gaines has failed to kill Jack within the time limit, what is Drazen's 'Plan B'?

Production Code 1AFF12

First US Transmission: Tuesday, February 26, 9/8C

Written by Andrea Newman
Directed by Stephen Hopkins

'The following takes place between 12:00 P.M. and 1:00 P.M. on the day of the California presidential primary... Events occur in real time.'

Cast: Penny Johnson Jerald (Sherry Palmer), Carlos Bernard (Tony Almeida), Richard Burgi (Kevin Carroll), Michael Massee (Ira Gaines), Tamara Tunie (Alberta Green), Daniel Bess (Rick), Jude Ciccolella (Mike Novick), Zeljko Ivanek (Andre Drazen), Zach Grenier (Carl), Christine Avila (Erica Vasquez, Jamey's mother), Devika Parikh (Maureen Kingsley), Al Leong (Neill), Ricardo Antonio Chavira (Bundy), Pete Antico (Commando).

EPISODE SUMMARY

Teri and Kim try to follow Jack's directions towards the water tower, not sure whether he and Rick are still alive. Rick thinks (correctly) that he's slowing Jack down, but Jack refuses to leave him behind.

Tony has found the records for the house where Jack's family are being held – it was leased six months ago by a company that doesn't appear to exist. Nina apologises to him for the way she's been behaving since this whole mess kicked off, but Tony tells her they can talk about it later. Alberta warns Tony and Nina that she wants them to question Jamey's mother, who is coming in to collect Jamey's son. They've just inspected her mother's bank account and found $300,000 worth of deposits into the account in the last four months.

Still concerned about the nature of George Ferragamo's death, Palmer argues with Mike Novick, insisting that he wants to tell Maureen Kingsley everything – and then speak to the district attorney. Mike urges him to at least consider all the facts first. At the very least, Mike says, he should discuss this with Sherry.

Andre Drazen contacts Gaines at **12:09 P.M.** and is quickly brought up to date with the news of Jack's arrival at the compound. Drazen congratulates Gaines on earning himself a second chance. Gaines reminds him that his original instructions were to kill Palmer, a mission he still wants to make good before Drazen puts his back-up plan into action. Drazen tells him to kill Bauer first; then they can discuss Palmer. Kevin Carroll tells Gaines that he overheard Jack giving his location to someone and that it can't be long before government troops begin to storm the compound. Perhaps, he suggests, they should cut their losses and escape. But Gaines points out that the Drazens are not the sort of people to let them just walk away. The only chance they have to survive the mess they're in is to kill Bauer.

Jack and Rick reach the water tower and are concerned that Teri and Kim aren't already there waiting for them. Luckily, the bullet that hit Rick's arm passed straight through and it's quite a neat wound so Jack prepares a makeshift tourniquet for him. Meanwhile, cut off from their original route by the arrival of more of Gaines's men, Teri and Kim have tried to find an alternative way, only to end up lost.

At **12:16 P.M.**, Sherry tells David that she agrees with Mike – they can't risk speaking to Maureen about Ferragamo's death. At the moment, David is under the control of the people who have financed his campaign. They have the power to twist things to suit their ends. But once Palmer is President, Sherry believes he'll be in a better position to change the lives of millions of people for the better as well as fight Carl's people on a more even plain. David seems unconvinced, though, the revelations of the last few hours still pricking his conscience.

As he searches for his family once more, Jack calls Alberta at CTU and asks her to confirm that back-up is on its way. He asks her to send them to the water tower where they'll find the wounded Rick. Rick thanks him for helping him and again tries to convince him that he had no idea what trouble he was getting into when this all started. Jack gives him some valuable advice:

> *'You kidnapped my daughter; you're going to have to live with that... Some part of getting a second chance is taking responsibility for the mess you made in the first place.'*

With that, Jack leaves the water tower to find his family.

Teri and Kim hide in an old shack in the grounds of the compound, narrowly avoiding Gaines's man Neill. Just as they think the coast is clear, Neill appears at the back of the shack. He raises his gun to shoot them but is himself shot down by Jack, who has just found the cabin. He steals Neill's radio and the three Bauers make their way cautiously out of the shack towards the water tower.

By **12:29 P.M.**, Jamey's mother, **Erica Vasquez**, has arrived at CTU to collect her grandson. She is understandably distressed and berates Tony and Nina for allowing her daughter to bleed to death. Tony is duty-bound to inform her that Jamey had confessed to being a traitor shortly before she died. He appears uncomfortable with being the one to have to question her, but tells her that as large sums of money have been found in Mrs Vasquez's bank account, she could find herself charged with being an accomplice. She tells them that Jamey had claimed the money was for her son's future should anything happen to her, but that she had never asked her where the money came from.

Gaines co-ordinates the hunt for Bauer via the radios, unaware that, equipped with Neill's radio, Jack can hear everything he says and so evade capture.

Palmer goes to Maureen Kingsley's hotel room to find the reporter packing. He tries to explain to her his reasons for wanting her to go public with her story, but she refuses; she has heard about Ferragamo's death and has herself been threatened by Carl's men into resigning from the network. Now that the evidence against Keith has presumably been destroyed in the fire, she doesn't have a case any more. Palmer tries to apologise for what she's been put through but Maureen doesn't want to discuss it. But as a friend, she warns him against the people he's involved with who, she predicts, will stop at nothing to get what they want.

By **12:35 P.M.**, Gaines has found the body of Neill and realises that Jack has taken his radio. Meanwhile, Tony and Nina have traced the money in Mrs Vasquez's account to Luca Univox, an offshore holding company in Belgrade. Nina recalls that Jack was interested in any connections to Belgrade and that it had something to do with one of his previous missions.

The Bauers reach the lake by the water tower. Though both Jack and Teri insist on staying hidden in the bushes until CTU arrive, Kim is determined to make sure Rick is OK and breaks cover. She takes just a few steps before she comes under fire from a sniper hidden in the woods. Her father pulls her back under cover. Jack decides to draw the fire of the sniper. Heading up through the woods, and using the trees as cover, he identifies where the shots are coming from – Gaines and Carroll are located just up ahead. Carroll begins to move to one side to cut Jack's escape route off while Gaines uses his sniper rifle to keep Jack hemmed in. Jack, meanwhile, finds an old sheet of twisted metal. Shining it up, he uses the metal to shine sunlight direct into Gaines's viewfinder, blinding him for a second and providing himself with the opportunity to escape. As he runs off, Jack manages to shoot Gaines in the arm. Suddenly the hunter becomes the hunted as Gaines is forced to flee. Just then, the CTU helicopter flies overhead, prompting Carroll to give up on Jack and try to escape.

Palmer goes to see the district attorney but finds Carl waiting for him. Palmer is furious with Carl's handling of the situation and threatens to expose his part in the whole affair. But when Carl hints that Palmer's disobedience could incriminate Keith in a charge of arson, Palmer realises that he is in no position to make demands. Carl walks away smugly, leaving Palmer to tell Mike to cancel his appointment with the district attorney. As he leaves, Palmer tells Mike with determination that he intends to run for president and win.

At around **12:51 P.M.**, the CTU helicopter comes in to land near to the water tower. Under the protection of the CTU operatives, Kim runs towards the water tower and is dismayed to find Rick has bolted. She makes to go after him, but Teri begs her not to. Right now she needs her daughter to be there for her, and they both need to be there for Jack. Reluctantly, Kim agrees. Unbeknownst to anyone, Rick has managed to escape from the compound and is making his way along one of the back roads.

Jack, meanwhile, is stalking Gaines, following the trail of blood from his arm. Speaking to him over his radio, Jack asks him what the connection is with Belgrade. At first, Gaines taunts him, telling him, 'You should know,' before admitting that he hasn't actually been told what the connection is. All he does know is that his employers want to make this personal. As Gaines gloats, he fails to hear Jack creeping up behind him. Keeping him covered with his gun, Jack tells Gaines to drop his weapon and says that in exchange for help, he'll help Gaines gain immunity. But Gaines has already decided his only way out. With the words 'good luck', Gaines lifts his gun, but Jack fires first and shoots him dead. The CTU operatives arrive at the scene and arrest Jack as per their instructions, taking him to the helicopter with his family. As the chopper lifts off, Teri winces, alarming Jack, but she tells him it's just a cramp.

Rick, meanwhile, finds a bus stop and climbs onto a bus, shielding his bloodied arm from the other passengers. He sits at the back of the bus, relieved to have escaped alive.

At **12:59 P.M.**, Alberta informs Nina and Tony that the Bauers have been saved from the compound and are now on their way to CTU. But Nina has news for Alberta. It seems that the photographer, Martin Balkin, was not alone – a second assassin has been hired. He flew out from Yugoslavia that morning and has already reached Los Angeles...

NOTES

- **Who's Who?:** Christine Avila (Erica Vasquez) played Lupe Guerrero in the US TV series *Dangerous Minds*, Ricardo Antonio Chavira (Bundy) is a recurring performer in the second series of grim HBO drama *Six Feet Under*.

- **Time Checks:** The second assassin left Yugoslavia some time after midnight and is already in L.A.. The CTU back-up squad took over 50 minutes to reach the compound. In one of the time checks, as the show breaks to commercials, the clock ticking stops at '12:24:48', all multiples of 12.
- **Death Count:** Ira Gaines (shot by Jack at 12:56 P.M.).
- **Trivia:** Jamey's mother Erica currently earns $45,000 a year. Maureen's room number at the hotel was 914.

COMMENTS

Had ***24*** not been commissioned for a full series, this is where it would have finished – episode 13. And although it falls short of the promised full day of action, it at least ties up a lot of the loose ends: the Bauers have been reunited; the villainous Ira Gaines has been shot dead by the courageous Jack; Palmer has decided to proceed with the presidential bid; and Jack is hopefully on the verge of being exonerated after a brief suspension. OK, so the assassin Jonathan, the reluctant kidnapper Rick and the fake 'Alan York', Kevin Carroll, have escaped justice, and Palmer still faces a fight within his own ranks against the corruptive blackmailing influences of Carl and his friends, but at least he's alive and well and able to carry on with his campaign. But of course the show was a huge hit and an additional 11 episodes were hastily fast-tracked into production – hence the somewhat implausible 'second assassin' plot line.

Fan reaction to this seems to be mixed. On the one hand – *great!* More ***24***, more action, more twists than a convention of Dickensian orphans. But on the other hand, even the most ardent of the programme's supporters confessed to feeling a little disappointed by this one episode. For the first time since the big clock started ticking, it was a little... dull, frankly. With so many of the main plot strands apparently tidied up, and with the general understanding that the show would reach that 24th episode milestone, rebooting the story with another rogue assassin on his way to L.A., just as we'd seen 12 hours previously, was just a bit of a cheat. Bearing in mind how long it takes to reach California from Europe (at least 11 hours), this would indicate that the Drazens had always expected Gaines and his team to fail. If they had such little faith in Gaines, why did they hire him in the first place? The flippant answer is, of course, to pad out the first 12 episodes, though that's neither fair nor accurate. But it does beg the question – if the mind-boggling, disturbing, compelling first half of the series was just treading water, what in hell's name could the second half offer?

Well, let's see, shall we?

QUESTIONS ARISING

- When they were hiding in the woods, why didn't Teri give Kim her grey cardigan to cover up her bright red top?
- How much did Gaines really know?
- Now that Rick has escaped, what will he do?
- Who is the new assassin and where did he get those rather nice shades?

Production Code 1AFF13

First US Transmission: Tuesday, March 5, 9/8C

Written by Joel Surnow & Michael Loceff
Directed by Jon Cassar

'The following takes place between 1:00 P.M. and 2:00 P.M. on the day of the California presidential primary... Events occur in real time.'

Cast: Penny Johnson Jerald (Sherry Palmer), Carlos Bernard (Tony Almeida), Richard Burgi (Kevin Carroll), Tamara Tunie (Alberta Green), Zeljko Ivanek (Andre Drazen), Vicellous Shannon (Keith Palmer), Jude Ciccolella (Mike Novick), Misha Collins (Alexis Drazen), Paul Schulze (Ryan Chappelle), Kara Zediker (Elizabeth Nash), Tanya Wright (Patty Brooks), Eric Balfour (Milo Pressman), Judith Scott (Dr Kent), Mina Badie (Agent Holmes), Jon H. Epstein (Al), Angelo Pagan (CTU Agent).

EPISODE SUMMARY

The helicopter carrying the Bauer family arrives at CTU where Alberta Green and Nina Myers are waiting for Jack. As she steps from the helicopter, Teri suffers another bout of stomach pains which she explains away to a concerned Jack as just the after-effects of the stress she's been under all day. Thankfully, an ambulance is waiting to take them to a clinic for a check-up. Although he obviously wants to stay with his family, Jack knows that he will not be allowed to. As Alberta approaches the party, he makes a point of introducing her to his wife and daughter and Alberta tactfully avoids mentioning how much trouble he is in while they are present. Jack thanks Nina for helping him and Teri notices something between the two of them but doesn't say anything. Jack sees his family to the ambulance and, saying his goodbyes, explains that he needs to be debriefed before he can come with them. But once they are out of earshot, Alberta tells him that she will be doing more than just debriefing him; he will be kept under arrest at CTU for questioning before being handed over to the FBI. As they all head back into CTU, Jack quietly begs Nina to look after his family. She explains that Alberta has got her tying up loose ends after the operation. Jack tells her to leave Tony to do that – he wants his family looked after by someone he can trust. With that, Jack is led to a holding room.

Nina asks Alberta for an hour off to clean herself up after being on duty for 13 hours straight. Alberta refuses, telling her she can spot that she's lying about why she needs the time off. Nina confesses that Jack asked her to look after his family. Satisfied that Nina's telling the truth, she notes the irony of Jack's ex-mistress being sent to look after his wife – but relents and grants her the time off.

It's **1:07 P.M.** and back at the campaign suite at his hotel, David checks the poll projections with his aide, **Elizabeth Nash**, before tackling the more difficult issue of his wife. Sherry warns him that he must make all of his public appearances today with his best face on – no mention of Keith or Dr Ferragamo. To her massive relief, David tells her he's dropping his investigations into Ferragamo's death, but then he reveals that it's only because he's being blackmailed by the very people who've been financing his campaign. According to Carl – who Sherry had used to cover up Keith's involvement in Lyle Gibson's death – his backers have planted evidence to implicate Keith in Ferragamo's murder. Bitterly, he tells her: 'This is what happens when you cover things up.' Sherry is in no mood for a lecture, but can see that she is partly to blame for this entire mess. She asks David whether Keith knows what has happened yet. David tells her he doesn't – and that's how he wants it to stay!

At the clinic, Teri and Kim are met by **Dr Kent**. She tells Teri she has booked her in for an ultrasound because of her abdominal pains, and asks if there are any other problems she should know about. Teri says no, but Kim gives her mother a look that tells Dr Kent that something has happened. Teri signals to a nurse to take Kim into the next room and only then does she tell the doctor that she was raped during her ordeal. She asks the doctor to keep this confidential from her husband.

At **1:15 P.M.** Mike Novick encourages David to ally himself with **Senators Blaylock** and **Gleeson**; despite David's reservations, being seen to associate with them could win him their states during the presidential election. Mike tells him the situation with Ferragamo worries him. Unfortunately, Keith overhears them talking and David is forced to tell him that his psychiatrist has been killed in a gas explosion. Keith is confused, but then suddenly realises that Ferragamo must have been the link between his involvement in the death of Lyle Gibson and Maureen Kingsley's allegations. Ferragamo must have told her some of the things Keith had told him during his sessions with him. David tries to assure him that Ferragamo's death was an accident, but Keith is not convinced. Ferragamo was there for him when he was in agony over his sister's rape and the subsequent death of Gibson. He wants someone to pay for Ferragamo's death and, with tears in his eyes, insists his father takes their case to the police. David tells him that he is doing the best he can for his son, but the strain on both of them is too much and, hugging, they both begin to weep.

Seeing regional director Ryan Chappelle arrive at CTU, Milo and Tony speculate on what this will mean for Jack. 'They're not going to name a street after him,' Tony quips bleakly. Chappelle is led to the room where Jack is being kept and greets him warmly:

> *'I've got five priority cases on my desk this morning. Your name is on each one of them.'*

Jack is relieved to see him, but is disappointed to note that Chappelle is recording their conversation. The 'cheery reunion' is to be a formal interview. Jack wearily begins to tell him about the events of the last 13 hours.

At the clinic, Nina goes to see how Teri's doing only to find her room empty apart from a man from the FBI who's using the phone. He tells her he's waiting for his debrief team who are coming to interview the injured prisoners from the raid on the compound earlier that morning. Nina finds Teri and Kim up the corridor and properly introduces herself. She tells Teri that Jack is being questioned over 'a few laws' he broke in the process of rescuing her and Kim, but says she's confident he'll be OK. She tells the women they will be kept in the clinic for a while; until they can determine what happened, they want to take every precaution to keep them safe. Nina has already sent someone to their house to fetch them some clean clothes. Before Nina leaves, Teri takes the opportunity to thank her – if it wasn't for her, they might not be alive.

Nina returns to the room where the FBI agent had been, only to find it empty. She meets two other FBI agents down the corridor and learns that they are the only agents assigned to the hospital – clearly the other man was not who he had claimed to be. Alarmed, Nina runs back to Teri and Kim.

By **1:29 P.M.**, Jack has finished explaining his motivation for breaching protocol over the course of recent events. Chappelle is convinced that Jack has done what any loving father would do, but tells him he still can't reinstate him. An incredulous Jack reminds him that although he broke the rules to protect his family, he never deviated from his original mission, to protect Senator Palmer. With his knowledge of the people involved in the attempt on Palmer's life, Jack insists he is in a unique position to protect him. Chappelle tells him that this will possibly prevent him from going to prison but it's not his decision. He is happy to defer to Alberta Green but Jack is not impressed, reminding him that she has only been on the case for four hours, whereas he can personally identify some of the people responsible. They are interrupted by a call for Jack. It's Nina, who has clearance to speak to Jack, so Chappelle terminates the interview and leaves. Jack tells Nina that he's being handed over to the Justice Department (which he thinks has something to do with Alberta trying to advance her career at his expense). Nina asks him if he thinks someone else within the division might have been working alongside Jamey. Jack agrees it's a possibility – after all, someone had to have recruited her. Nina decides not to trouble Jack with her suspicions about the fake FBI agent and reassures him that his family are safe.

Alberta comes to Tony for an update on the back-up assassin they learned about half an hour ago. Their information seems to match the division's database: three shooters, probably hired as a contingency should the breakfast assassination attempt fail; two of them, **Jovan Myovic**, who entered the country two days ago, and **Mishko Suba**, who came into the US via Florida, are from the Balkans, while a third assassin remains unidentified.

The third assassin is, as of **1:33 P.M.**, staking out a transfer point in the desert where Kevin Carroll and the remnants of Gaines's men have just arrived. Carroll calls **Alexis Drazen** to tell him that Gaines is dead and that, having had some experience of similar operations, he is confident he can fix Gaines's mistakes. However, Drazen tells him smugly that 'Plan B is already in effect' and hangs up. Carroll is immediately worried. In the dunes that surround the transfer point, Carroll spies the third assassin and makes his way towards him, gun in hand. He's walked but a few feet when, behind him, the transfer point is ripped apart by a massive explosion which sends him sprawling to the ground. As Carroll lies dazed, the assassin strolls over to him and shoots him at point-blank range.

Tony advises Alberta that in his opinion the threat against Palmer is so great that he should leave L.A. immediately. Off the record, Alberta asks him if he's considered his position at CTU – it's clear to her that Tony is being kept back by Nina and Jack, and as he will soon be interviewed by Chappelle as part of the investigation against Jack, he might consider informing Chappelle that there were other ways Jack might have proceeded with his mission.

At **1.42 P.M.**, Alberta comes to Jack to debrief him, telling him she feels a little uncomfortable stepping into his 'turf'. Jack asks her to allow him to speak to his family to tell them what's happening and when Alberta refuses, Jack tells her to drop the 'friendly' approach and talk straight with him. Alberta begins recording their conversation so he tells her to speak to one of their contacts, Langley, and ask him to open up his database on Balkan terrorists – the people trying to kill Palmer were being financed by Ted Cofell, who had family connections to the Balkans, though he is, of course, now dead.

Nina calls Tony to send someone over to the clinic to dust the phone for fingerprints – she tells him about the bogus FBI agent she saw using the phone in Teri's room earlier and expresses her concern.

While Sherry and David's aide **Patty** select a photograph for an article due to appear in *Time* magazine, Keith interrupts. He tells his mother that he wants to tell the police about George Ferragamo's murder. Sherry is furious and tells him that he does not have the right to make a decision that could put his family at risk.

> *'Nothing is simple in life. Sometimes you just have to make a decision. That is what we did and you will respect that, you understand?'*

Their discussion is cut short by David, who tells them to gather their things and prepare to leave the state immediately for Dallas Airforce Base in Nevada. The threat assessment suggests that there are others apart from Jack Bauer who may be involved.

Tony is finally called in to give evidence to Chappelle. Tony's testimony might well decide Jack's fate as, in Chappelle's opinion, Tony appears to be 'the most impartial observer' of the events of the last few hours. Tony freely admits that he is not Jack's biggest fan but with regard to the period in question – since midnight last night – Tony refuses to disapprove of any of Jack's actions.

En route to the airport, Mike Novick gets a call from the Pentagon. It seems that the agent implicated in the incident at the breakfast, Jack Bauer, was once in Special Forces. He was on a mission to Kosovo – 'the

Drazen mission' – from which only he survived. On hearing this, David is convinced Bauer's actions must be revenge motivated; he must blame David for the deaths of his men.

Palmer's team prepare to evacuate the campaign suite. Elizabeth gives Patty a bag that she claims Mrs Palmer left behind and tells her that she'll be joining the team later as she has to visit a sick aunt who's in a nursing home. But instead of leaving the hotel, she catches the lift down a few floors and goes to a hotel room to meet up with her lover – the mysterious assassin who killed Kevin Carroll. The couple begin tearing each other's clothes off and kissing passionately.

By **1.56 P.M.**, Nina has been joined at the hospital by a CTU forensics expert who dusts the phone in Teri's room for fingerprints. Sadly, he can't find any. Nina is puzzled because the room hasn't been visited by cleaners in all the time she's been there, but the expert clarifies that the phone doesn't have a single fingerprint on it – it's been cleaned by a professional. She calls Alberta to get authorisation to move Teri and Kim to a safe house.

Dr Kent tells Teri that the initial ultrasound has revealed she has a small benign cyst on one of her ovaries that has burst. She tells her she wants to do a pregnancy test, just to rule it out. Just then, Nina enters the room to tell Teri that she's moving her and Kim to a safe house because the women are not as well contained there as she would like. Teri tells Kim to grab her things immediately. As they leave, Dr Kent slips her a home pregnancy test. Nina escorts the Bauers to a CTU vehicle waiting by the exit. From a window a few floors above them, the fake FBI agent calls someone to let them know the Bauers are leaving.

At just a few seconds before **2.00 P.M.**, David Palmer and his security guards stride into CTU. Tony Almeida greets the Senator nervously and David tells him he's come to see Jack Bauer...

NOTES

- **Who's Who?:** Misha Collins (Alexis Drazen) – born Misha Collins Krushnic – popped up briefly in *Girl Interrupted* (dir. James Mangold, 2000). Paul Schulze (Ryan Chappelle) memorably played Father Phil in the HBO series *The Sopranos* and recently played a cop in the thriller *The Panic Room* (dir. David Fincher, 2002). Judith Scott (Dr Kent) has been a regular in both *L.A. Doctors* and *CSI: Crime Scene Investigation*. Jon H. Epstein (Al) was David Duchovny's stunt double in *The X-Files*.
- **Time Checks:** Despite having taken over 50 minutes to reach the compound, the helicopters are able to bring Jack and his family back to CTU in just over ten minutes. Nina asks Alberta for one hour off to check in on Teri and Nina at the clinic. David tells Keith that Ferragamo died about an hour ago (although he might as well have said 'two episodes back'). Tony mentions that they got information half an hour ago on the other assassin. Jack tells Alberta that Ted Cofell died three hours ago.
- **Death Count:** Kevin Carroll, AKA 'Alan York' (shot by the third assassin at around 1:36 P.M.).
- **Trivia:** Kevin Carroll boasts to Drazen that he worked for the D.E.A. (Drug Enforcement Agency) in Florida where he once managed to get to a witness that no-one else could find. Alexis is staying in room 1243 in the same hotel as Palmer and his team.

COMMENTS

Before it had even finished its run, ***24*** had been honoured by a number of organisations. At the 2002 Golden Globes, Kiefer Sutherland won Best Performance by an Actor in a Television Series (Drama), beating

Simon Baker of *The Guardian*, Peter Krause of *Six Feet Under*, James Gandolfini of *The Sopranos* and Martin Sheen from *The West Wing*. It was also nominated for Best Television Series (Drama) alongside *Alias*, *CSI: Crime Scene Investigation*, *The Sopranos* and *The West Wing* (the winner was *Six Feet Under*). The show also pulled in Best Television Series at the Golden Satellite Awards while Best Performance by an Actor in a Series (Drama) again went to Kiefer. Editor Chris Willingham's work on episode '4:00 A.M. – 5:00 A.M.' was nominated for Best Edited One-Hour Series for Television at the 'Eddies' (the American Cinema Editors awards).

The pilot episode has, understandably, received the most attention. At the American Society of Cinematographers (ASCs), Peter Levy's work on the pilot bagged him the Outstanding Achievement in Cinematography in Movies of the Week/Mini-Series/Pilot for Network or Basic Broadcast TV, while the same episode won Stephen Hopkins the Directors Guild of America's trophy for Outstanding Directorial Achievement in Dramatic Series (Night). The Society of Motion Picture and Television Art award for 'Excellence in Production Design (Television – Episode of a Single-Camera Series)' went to Carlos Barbosa and the show won Best Sound Editing in Television (Dialogue and A.D.R., Episodic) at the Motion Picture Sound Editors' Golden Reel Awards.

At the time of writing, the Emmy nominations have yet to be announced. I don't think it's too presumptuous to suggest that ***24*** will appear in at least a couple of categories. But it would be nice if the very talented female cast received some recognition. I'd hope, at the very least, Penny Johnson Jerald and Leslie Hope get the chance to dress up in nice spangly frocks for the occasion.

QUESTIONS ARISING

- So, what was the Drazen mission and why did it go so badly for Jack's team?
- Who is the fake FBI agent?
- What is his connection between the assassin and Palmer's aide Elizabeth? Does she know who he is?
- Should Patty be worried about the bag that Elizabeth gave her?
- Are Teri and Kim still in danger?
- Will Chappelle reinstate Jack after all?
- Is Alberta playing a dangerous game of career advancement?
- Is Tony still acting out of loyalty to Nina or does he truly believe Jack acted in the best interests of his mission?

3:00 13:41 07:24 22:38 10:09 17:59 09:13 21:01 04:45 14:12 07:57 13:41 07:24 22:38 10:09 17:59 09:13

3:00 P.M.

Production Code 1AFF14

First US Transmission: Tuesday, March 12, 9/8C

Written by Michael Chernuchin
Directed by Jon Cassar

'The following takes place between 2:00 P.M. and 3:00 P.M. on the day of the California presidential primary... Events occur in real time.'

Cast: Penny Johnson Jerald (Sherry Palmer), Carlos Bernard (Tony Almeida), Tamara Tunie (Alberta Green), Zeljko Ivanek (Andre Drazen), Daniel Bess (Rick), Misha Collins (Alexis Drazen), Paul Schulze (Ryan Chappelle), Kara Zediker (Elizabeth Nash), Eric Balfour (Milo Pressman), Wade Andrew Williams (Robert Ellis), Kevin Ramsey (Agent Ted Paulson), Logan Alexander (Lenny), Nina Landey (Amanda), Sam Ayres (Agent Breeher).

EPISODE SUMMARY

Elizabeth and her boyfriend make love in the hotel room. Meanwhile, at CTU, David Palmer threatens to go over Tony's head to get to Jack. Tony informs him that district director Ryan Chappelle is working on his clearance, though it might help them if he could reveal why he has come to CTU. Palmer tells him bluntly that all he needs to know is that he needs to speak with Bauer immediately. Tony leaves him stewing while he goes to call Chappelle (who has taken over Jack's office). Chappelle is unwilling to allow Palmer and Bauer to meet until he knows more. Milo tells Tony that he has managed to identify the third assassin – Alexis Drazen, who is connected to the other shooters. The evidence suggests he stopped off at Washington before reaching LAX airport on Saturday, three days earlier. He's sent a report to Nina so Tony asks him to pass a copy onto him.

Nina accompanies Teri and Kim to the safe-house, claiming that although they're not in danger, a small controlled environment is the best place for both of them. Teri asks her if Jack knows about them being moved and Nina claims that he does. Kim asks her mother about the results of the doctor's tests. Teri tells her it was just a burst cyst but claims it's all fine and refuses to be drawn into a discussion about it.

Alberta is still questioning Jack. He requests a break and asks her to find out how his wife and daughter are doing at the clinic. Alberta coolly informs him that Teri and Kim have been moved from the clinic to a safe house. Jack is furious that she didn't tell him about this sooner and refuses to speak to her any longer. He orders her to fetch Chappelle.

Elizabeth reveals that she was surprised but pleased when Alexis called her the previous night. After their date in Washington, Elizabeth didn't think she'd see him again. He asks her if she'll be able to see him later in the day, but she says she has to follow Palmer's team up to Nevada. He asks her if she'll get some free time in Nevada and she's overjoyed that he'd consider travelling out to see her. While she takes a quick shower, Alexis goes through her bag and reads her schedule.

Growing impatient with the delays at CTU, David Palmer calls a contact, Alan, at the Defence Department and has him hurry things along for him. Ryan Chappelle finally comes to see David in person and apologises for keeping him waiting. He explains that when an agent is under internal investigation, the procedure is to keep him isolated until after he's been interrogated. David asks him if this would extend to a senator that might be able to help in their investigation, but before Chappelle can answer, Tony Almeida interrupts to inform him there's a call from Alan from the Pentagon. Palmer can barely hide a smirk as Alan tells Chappelle to give the Senator whatever he needs. Chappelle orders Tony to fetch Jack. Chappelle obsequiously thanks Palmer for helping him 'cut through the red tape'. Palmer tells him he wants all surveillance cameras and microphones in the room to be shut down; this will be 'a private conversation'.

Tony goes to the holding room to take Jack to the conference room where Chappelle is waiting for him. He tells Jack that Nina called to say his wife and daughter are safe and that **Agents Paulson** and **Breeher** are guarding the safe house. As he walks, under guard, through CTU, Jack grabs an opportunity to apologise to Milo for switching the cards on him but explains that he had no choice. Milo tells him he understands. With the whole of his staff watching, Jack walks into the conference room. To his surprise, it is Senator Palmer and not Chappelle who is waiting for him. Palmer orders the guards to leave them alone and close the door. Coming straight to the point, Palmer asks Jack who he is working with. For the moment baffled by the question, Jack asks him what he means and assumes his enemies within CTU have primed Palmer. Palmer has no time for games and accuses Jack of wanting him dead because of the events in Kosovo two years ago. His mention of the Kosovo mission surprises Jack, unaware that Palmer would know anything about 'Operation Nightfall', but Palmer points out that it was he who authorised the mission. He knows that Jack lost six men while in the process of taking out Victor Drazen and accuses Jack of wanting revenge. Jack loses his temper and tells Palmer that he has risked his life today to protect him. When Palmer challenges him to justify his actions at the breakfast, Jack is forced to let him know about the kidnapping of his family, the plot to make him appear involved in the assassination and his attempt to cause Palmer to be evacuated without giving himself away to Gaines. Palmer's shocked expression tells Jack that no-one had told him any of this. Jack assures him that all he has told him is true.

At **2:16 P.M.**, Nina, Teri and Kim arrive at the safe house and are met by Agents Paulson and Breeher. Kim asks Nina how long they'll have to stay at the house; Nina deflects the question, telling her they can discuss that after she debriefs them both. Teri tells Nina she needs to use the bathroom and, once alone, pulls out the home pregnancy kit that Dr Kent gave her.

Palmer tells Jack that three years ago he was the head of the Special Defence Appropriations committee in the senate. CIA had shown him evidence of 'ethnic cleansing' atrocities – massacres committed by Victor Drazen in Kosovo. Palmer tried to go through official channels to put a stop to Drazen's regime but was making no progress. So instead he contacted someone that he could count on to get the job done and have Drazen terminated – **Robert Ellis**, Jack's superior at the time. Jack speculates that if someone has made the connection between the hit on Drazen and both Palmer and Bauer, they've more than likely made the connection to Robert Ellis too.

Ellis is in a bar in New Orleans when Palmer calls him on his cellphone. Ellis is not pleased to learn that Palmer is with Jack Bauer, and reminds him that he went to a lot of trouble to make sure he and Bauer never met. Palmer tells Ellis about their belief that someone connected to Drazen is hunting himself and Bauer today, on the second anniversary of 'Nightfall'. Ellis argues that he was the only person who knew that Jack and David had anything to do with that operation, but David points out, rightly, that this is evidently not the case. If their connection is known, then Ellis's life could also be at risk. Ellis asks to speak to Jack and suggests that they pool their resources to solve the problem. Jack tells Ellis that, thanks to his actions over the last day, he's under investigation and unable to act. Ellis suggests that Palmer can pull some strings to get him released. Jack is certain that no-one on his team knew anything about Palmer's involvement with 'Nightfall', which leaves only Drazen's group. Ellis offers to send him the closed file on the operation which contains details on all of Drazen's known associates. In the meantime, he recommends Jack follows the trail on the money behind the plot – Ellis bets it will all lead to Belgium. They agree to compare possible leads shortly and Ellis hangs up.

At the safe house, Teri's home test kit reveals she is pregnant. It is now **2:22 P.M.**

Elizabeth is called back to the campaign suite to meet with Sherry Palmer, who has returned to the hotel. She tells Elizabeth that they won't be going to Nevada after all as David has decided to keep the campaign team in Los Angeles so he can 'take care of something'. Elizabeth calls Alexis to tell him about the change of plan. She promises to call him later. Alexis is sitting with his brother Andre in a restaurant. Andre is pleased to hear that Palmer will be staying in town after all – it makes things easier for them. He asks Alexis if he disposed of Gaines's men and Alexis voices his opinion that Andre shouldn't have used Gaines in the first place. Andre sees a waitress who reminds him of their sister, Martina, but Alexis reminds him that she is dead. He confirms to Andre that the other two shooters have found their targets and that Palmer will be dead by midnight.

Kim comes to Teri's bathroom to borrow some toothpaste and notices the pregnancy kit. At first, Teri tries to pass it off as just a precaution on the advice of the doctor, but then decides to confide in her daughter that she is indeed pregnant. Thinking this to be the result of her mother's rape, Kim is confused until Teri explains that, of course, it's Kim's father's. Kim selfishly criticises her mother for not even consulting her about planning for another child. Teri tells her that this has come as a shock to her too:

> *'I'm not asking for your permission, Kimberly. Once in a while you have to think about what another person is going through. Honey, I've just found out I'm pregnant. You don't think that terrifies me? ... Well, it does.'*

Realising her mistake, Kim tries to apologise but Teri returns to her room and shuts the door, not wanting to be disturbed.

At **2:31 P.M.**, Milo is called to the conference room. Jack is speaking on a conference call to Ellis (who is still in the bar in New Orleans) while Palmer checks printouts of Drazen's associates. Jack tells Ellis that Milo has joined them and Ellis reveals that he already knows something of Milo's history, specifically his hacking into MI5 files. On Jack's insistence, Milo gives Ellis his log-in name and password and Ellis begins to search through a set of files. Within seconds he's identified that one of the files is missing.

As Ellis looks through the data, he sees a man walk into the bar. Immediately suspicious of him, Ellis hides his gun under his coat but within easy reach. He tells Milo that he's about to send a file to his server and suggests Milo prints out hard copies of it for Jack and David.

Kim and Teri enjoy their first meal together in some time. Kim again apologises for being so selfish and asks Teri when she plans on telling her dad about the pregnancy. Teri decides to do it straight away and calls him at CTU. Unfortunately, she gets through to Tony who tells her that Jack's too busy to come to the phone. He promises to tell Jack that she called though. Nina comes to see the women to begin the debrief. She asks to speak to Teri first so Kimberly decides to go to her room – and takes Nina's phone with her. Nina sits Teri down in front of a video camera, which she says is standard procedure.

Kim digs into her belongings and finds Rick's phone number. When she calls him she's relieved to hear he got away OK but is concerned that he sounds quite ill. He tells her he lost quite a lot of blood but refuses to go to a doctor in case he gets arrested. Kim agrees to help him by telling Nina that he was bullied into getting involved by his friend Dan. Rick points out that he's not as lucky as Kim; he doesn't come from such a good family and suspects that the system won't look on him so favourably. If he gives himself up he could face a lifetime in prison for kidnapping. With that, he hangs up.

Palmer confesses to Jack that he finds it hard to believe that the plot against him has nothing to do with his presidential bid or the fact that he's black; it's just revenge for being a part of the termination of Victor Drazen. Sherry calls him and asks him where he is. He tells her that he's helping with the investigation into the conspiracy, and that he'll speak to her later. Jack tells David that he's sorry for what he's had to go through. David is surprised that after all Jack's endured so far today, he still has enough compassion to worry about someone else's problems. He confides in Jack that the call from his wife was about their son, not the election. He's realised today that he hasn't always been there for him when he should have been. David asks if Jack's family are OK now. Jack replies honestly that although he hopes so, he doesn't know.

By **2:43 P.M.**, the printouts of Ellis's report have come through via Milo. As Jack and David begin to study all the documents, David finds a report that states that Drazen's wife and daughter were also in the bunker that Jack's team bombed during the operation to kill Drazen himself. The kidnapping of Jack's family was a direct eye-for-an-eye payback for what happened to Drazen's family. Palmer immediately orders Chappelle to step up the security on Teri and Kim.

Nina questions Teri about the events at the compound, specifically about Rick and his involvement with Ira Gaines. Teri tells her honestly that she doesn't know much about Rick, except hat he had met Kimberly through her friend Janet York. Nina lets slip that Jack has spoken about Kim, which strikes Teri as odd. She'd never pictured him gossiping with his workmates about his family. Nina tries to cover up her error, but Teri has already picked up something in the way Nina looked at Jack when he and his family stepped off the helicopter. She tells Nina that when she and Jack got together again after their separation, he'd told her he'd been with someone else. She now knows that it was Nina. Nina tells Teri that their affair started after he left Teri and was over long before he went back to her. He'd realised their relationship was a mistake and that he wanted to return to his wife. Teri insists she needs a break and leaves the room.

Having spoken with Mike Novick, David tells Jack that he'll have to return to the campaign shortly. Jack tells him that as he's still under arrest, he won't be allowed to work on the case on his own. David asks Jack to follow him and then walks out into the CTU office and orders Ryan

Chappelle to reinstate Jack to his previous position, effective immediately, insisting that the current crisis must supersede any charges against him. Alberta Green intervenes and informs the Senator that he has no authority to make such a demand. Chappelle agrees, claiming that Jack cannot be reinstated without a hearing. Jack tells Chappelle that he could simply give him temporary status to allow him to continue the investigation until the end of the day, after which time he can be taken back into custody. Reluctantly, Chappelle concedes and tells Jack that he will work within CTU and report directly to him. In private, David tells Jack that he wants to ignore Secret Service's advice to leave the state and stay put to help flush Drazen's men into the open. Before he leaves, he apologises to Jack for misjudging him and shakes Jack by the hand.

It's **2:55 P.M.**, and Nina is questioning Kimberly, who claims that Rick was just as much the captive of Dan as she was. They are interrupted by Nina's cellphone. It's Jack calling to let her know that, thanks to Palmer, he's been provisionally reinstated, and that two more teams will be coming to look after his family because they've discovered that Teri and Kim were actual targets too (he insists that this is not something his family need to know just now). He asks to speak to Teri. Nina takes the cellphone to Teri and tactfully leaves her alone. Jack got Tony's message that Teri needed to speak to him urgently, but after learning about his affair with Nina, Teri doesn't want to tell him about her news. Holding back the tears, she tells him it was nothing and that she's just tired. She hangs up and heads for the kitchen. Kim excuses herself from Nina for a moment and asks how her dad took the news about the pregnancy, but Teri tells her she decided it wasn't the right time to tell him and suggests she returns to Nina to finish off her debriefing.

Ellis calls Jack from the bathroom of the bar to tell him that he still can't locate the missing file, which leads him to believe it was removed deliberately because it contained exactly what they're looking for. Jack asks Ellis to give him an estimate of when the file was stolen, but Ellis's reply is cut short – an assailant attacks Ellis from behind and chokes him to death with a garrotte.

Unable to sleep, Teri lies on the end of a bed in the safe house, considering what to do next...

NOTES

- **Who's Who?:** Wade Andrew Williams (Robert Ellis) had small roles in *Erin Brockovich* (dir. Steven Soderbergh, 2000) and *Ali* (Michael Mann, 2001). Sam Ayres (Agent Breeher) appears as Sam the Sweeper in *The Pretender*.
- **Time Checks:** Elizabeth tells Alexis that she'll know for certain within an hour whether or not she and Palmer's team will be leaving the hotel. Alexis boasts that Palmer will be dead by midnight. We sit with Teri as she waits for the result of her pregnancy test, a long minute that is a welcome break, made all the better by Teri's visible happiness at the news of her impending arrival in nine months.
- **Music:** In the background at the New Orleans bar where we meet Ellis, we hear 'I'm On The Wonder' by Clifton Chenier, 'I'm A Doggy' by Marvin Pontiac and Clifton Chenier's 'Barely Available'. Ellis dies to the sound of the 'Louisiana Two-Step'. When Kim phones Rick, she listens to 'Clocks Grow Old' by I Am Spoonbender.
- **Death Count:** Robert Ellis (strangled at 2:59 P.M.).
- **Trivia:** Milo's log-in name for the CTU system is LFN, while his password is 'foothill94022'.

COMMENTS

Political intrigue, a presidential candidate at risk because of what he believes in, a web of conspiracy that might involve government officials, maybe even entire departments. This show's not really asking anyone to suspend their disbelief, now, is it? That all of this is part of the day-to-day political machine is public knowledge. And it all comes down to JFK again, I'm afraid. The most viewed assassination in world history showed America and its neighbours in the global village just how vulnerable we all are. Remember, this is the man who was an unlikely president; he was young, attractive, energetic and (most unusual of all) Catholic. He rose to the White House thanks to a strong campaign and a savvy awareness of the power of television; in a live debate with Nixon, Kennedy looked fresh-faced and honest compared to his five-o'clock-shadowed adversary and the voters knew precisely who they could trust (and when, some years later, they forgot how they'd felt about Nixon, the man gave them a helping hand by offering them Watergate on a plate). But just as television made Kennedy, so it helped erase everything he'd ever done. As far as current generations remember it, Kennedy was not the man who fought his government to avoid war with Cuba and Vietnam, he was the one whose death was captured on home-movie footage and replayed (back and to the left, back and to the left), over and over again. By the time the paranoid theorists got hold of the case, Kennedy was no longer a star president; he was just the man who gave his name to the biggest conspiracy theory in human existence.

The after-effects of the assassination of that particular president were immense. Lee Harvey Oswald may have been the one who pulled the trigger, but everyone from Oliver Stone to *Quantum Leap*'s Sam Beckett and even the crew of the BBC comedy *Red Dwarf* have speculated as to who loaded the gun. Political thrillers could no longer be about the lone saboteurs or crime syndicates that had fuelled the films of Hitchcock or Warner Bros. As soon as it was suggested that Kennedy's assassination might have been government-sponsored (which accounts for one of the theories District Attorney Jim Garrison uncovered in his investigations over the years), the healthy mistrust that the American people had for their government was magnified to a frightening degree. What doesn't help matters is the speed with which conspiracy theorists are discredited. To take a fairly recent example, Oliver Stone's 1991 film *JFK* suffered a smear campaign from the American media before it had even been released, one that lasted over a year after its theatrical run. The *Chicago Tribune* and *Washington Post* both printed articles claiming the movie was factually inaccurate, while David Belin, the former assistant counsel to the Warren Commission and author of two books about the assassination, took out an ad in *Variety* magazine which some have speculated spoiled Stone's chances at that year's Oscars. As Hitchcock used to say, it's only a movie...

Two years after the release of *JFK*, *The X-Files* aired for the first time. Though it was mainly about the existence of extra-terrestrial life on our planet, it also concerned itself with the wider issue of government cover-ups: men in suits hiding in shadowy offices ensuring that the public never learn of the top-level operation involved in keeping the truth from the public. It doesn't take a genius to see why the viewers were so ready to believe in a corrupt government. After all, they'd already known about it for 30 years.

QUESTIONS ARISING

- When will Elizabeth realise that careless talk costs lives?
- Are Alberta and Chappelle deliberately hindering the investigation, or are their concerns about Jack genuine?

- Does Nina really still care for Jack? Did she confess all to Teri out of malice?
- What is in that missing file that Ellis identified?

07:24 22:38 10:09 17:59 09:13 21:01 04:45 14:12 07:57 13:41 07:24 22:38 10:09 17:59 09:13 19:47 05:20

Production Code 1AFF15

First US Transmission: Tuesday, March 19, 9/8C

Written by Robert Cochran & Howard Gordon
Directed by Stephen Hopkins

'The following takes place between 3:00 P.M. and 4:00 P.M. on the day of the California presidential primary... Events occur in real time.'

Cast: Penny Johnson Jerald (Sherry Palmer), Zeljko Ivanek (Andre Drazen), Vicellous Shannon (Keith Palmer), Xander Berkeley (George Mason), Daniel Bess (Rick), Zach Grenier (Carl), Misha Collins (Alexis Drazen), Henri Lubatti (Jovan Myovic), Megalyn Echikunwoke (Nicole Palmer), Kara Zediker (Elizabeth Nash), Kevin Ramsey (Agent Paulson), Eric Balfour (Milo Pressman), Glenn Morshower (Agent Aaron Pierce), Pauley Perrette (Tanya, the driver who picks up Teri), Navi Rawat (Melanie, Rick's friend), Sam Ayres (Agent Breeher).

EPISODE SUMMARY

As Jack calls out to Ellis, Ellis's killer searches through his belongings to whatever he can find before switching off Ellis's cellphone and leaving his corpse on the restroom floor. While Jack tries to come to terms with what has just happened, Milo comes to him with information on the three shooters. One of them, Alexis Drazen, is the son of Victor Drazen. Jack notes with interest that he was trained in the Belgrade Special Forces.

Elizabeth calls Alexis, still unaware that he is behind the plot against her employer, and tells him that Palmer will be staying in L.A. along with his entire campaign team. He tells her he'll be able to be back at the hotel by around 4.30 P.M.

The safe house is surrounded by CTU agents posing as workmen. Inside the house, Teri receives a call from Jack, who was worried by his earlier conversation with her. Teri is still upset with Jack, having only just learned about his affair with Nina, but she refuses to reveal anything to Jack about how she feels.

Agent Pierce briefs Palmer's team about the threats against the Senator. Having received information from CTU, he is able to show them pictures of the three assassins believed to be currently targeting Palmer and stresses that if any one of them sees someone who looks like these men, they should let an agent know immediately. Of course, when he shows Alexis Drazen's picture to the team, Elizabeth cannot believe what she has seen and runs out, distressed. David follows her and asks her what the matter is.

Nina continues her debriefing of Kim but when she again defends Rick's actions, Nina tactfully suggests that it's not unusual for kidnap victims to form a bond with their captors. Kim insists that Rick was not a kidnapper and that she doesn't know where he is. She storms out just as Teri returns to the room. Teri agrees to complete her own debriefing with Nina. Having considered all the facts as she understands them, she accepts that she and Jack were separated when Nina slept with him and so she's decided not to hold that against Nina. Nina asks Teri about Kim's relationship with Rick and suggests that she is covering up for the boy. Teri admits that she suspects there was an attraction between Kim and Rick, but tells her that she's sure Kimberly would tell her if she knew anything. Nina questions her further only for Teri to curtly suggest that she thinks she knows her own daughter better than Nina might.

Palmer contacts Jack at around **3:10 P.M.** to let him know that Elizabeth Nash has compromised her position on his staff by having an intimate affair with Alexis, one of the suspects in the assassination attempt. Jack immediately dispatches a helicopter to collect her for questioning. Jack then tells David about the call from Ellis and admits that they should assume Ellis to be dead.

At **3:15 P.M.,** Kim calls Rick once again to reassure him that she has lied to Nina on his behalf to cover for him. Rick is still apprehensive, worried that Nina might be able to prove that he was directly involved with the kidnapping. He thanks her for all that she's done for him, but says that he doesn't want her calling him for a while. Kim asks her how long she should wait but Rick hangs up as a girl has just walked into his room. She asks who he was speaking to on the phone and he tells her it was a wrong number. Rick moves over to his bed, exhausted, so the girl leaves him alone to sleep.

Nina continues her debriefing of Teri. She asks her if there is anything more she can tell them about Gaines. Teri doesn't seem to know who Gaines is and Nina impatiently reminds her that Ira Gaines was the leader of the group that kidnapped her. Teri is finding it hard to think and tells Nina apologetically that she can't remain calm and rational about everything that has happened. Nina tells her she needn't apologise and suggests that Agent Paulson can finish the debriefing. With that, Nina switches off the video camera and walks out.

Deputy director George Mason returns to CTU to tell Jack that he is now his 'new quarterback'. After the incident with David Palmer, both Ryan Chappelle and Alberta Green have been sent back to District and from his description of Green as a 'sociopath', it's obvious Mason dislikes her almost as much as Jack does. Jack updates Mason on all that he has learned in the last hour: Palmer's connection to 'Nightfall'; that Robert Ellis, who Mason knows was in charge of that mission, is believed to have been murdered; the connection between 'Nightfall''s target, Victor Drazen, and his sons, Alexis and Andre Drazen, who have mounted this whole operation as revenge for the death of their father; and the relationship between Alexis Drazen and Elizabeth. Mason recommends that they simply arrest Alexis but Jack is not so sure that would be the right course of action. If they can interview Elizabeth Nash first, they might be able to persuade her to lure Alexis out into the open.

At **3:20 P.M.**, David decides to speak to his son, Keith. David acknowledges that things have been strained between them recently. Keith tells him as far as he is concerned everything is now fine between them, but David admits that they have all been under tremendous pressure this last day. He confesses that he has been thinking over what Keith said to him a few hours earlier, that Ferragamo had been there for him when David himself had not. He tells his son that everything is going to change from now on, that he knows he can't expect to win his trust overnight, but that he intends to make sure he's always there for him. Keith is relieved to hear this and shakes his father's hand. He then asks his father if the police told him anything about Dr Ferragamo's death. David is angered by his son challenging his loyalty like this, but Keith tells him that now is when he needs him most, to show him that he's prepared to do the right thing.

'Keith, I will do the right thing... at the right time.'

Disappointed that his father appears to be putting his career before his family again, after everything he's just said, Keith walks out.

A telephone maintenance vehicle manned by CTU agents is still positioned outside the Bauer safe house. Sitting in the passenger seat of the vehicle is the fake FBI agent – in reality one of Drazen's assassins, **Jovan Myovic**. He has propped the dead body of one of the agents in the driver's seat and hidden another in the crane on the top of the vehicle. Myovic calls Andre Drazen to inform him that he has now found the safe house holding the Bauer women. He assures Drazen that he will be able to handle the remaining security forces and that 'the women will be dead soon'.

3:28 P.M. Having downloaded all his files to one of the terminals, Jack finds that he can't access the CTU network and comes to Milo for help. Milo is embarrassed to be the one to tell Jack that his security rating has been downgraded, meaning his access to the network is now locked out. He manages to grant Jack limited temporary access to the network. Mindful of what Nina suggested to him a few hours ago, Jack asks Milo if he's noticed anyone trying to access anything unusual through the servers. Milo tells him he hasn't, but admits that he hasn't actually been looking for it either. He realises that Jack believes that Jamey was not the only traitor working at CTU.

Nicole overhears Keith talking angrily to someone on the telephone but then hangs up when he notices Nicole listening in. At first, Keith refuses to tell her who he was speaking to, and when he finally tells her it was Carl she asks him why:

'Because I don't wanna spend the rest of my life with the same regret I've been living with the past seven years.'

He explains that although he didn't kill Gibson intentionally, he feels it's not too late to put things right. He tells her that he needs her to help him sneak out of the suite past the Secret Service agent guarding the door. Although she thinks Keith is probably doing the wrong thing, she agrees to help him. She calls the Secret Service agent to one side, telling him she heard a suspicious click on the phone, and while the agent is distracted, Keith makes his way out of the suite.

Elizabeth Nash arrives at CTU. George Mason introduces her to Jack and Elizabeth tells him that Senator Palmer has told her to do exactly what Jack says. In turn, Jack thanks her for helping them and states for the record that she is not considered a suspect and is just there to help them with a few questions, though she is entitled to a lawyer at any time. She declines the offer of legal assistance, telling him she wants to help in any way she can. George begins by asking her how she and Alexis Drazen got to know each other. She explains that she first met him about a month ago in a bar in Washington D.C., where he told her he worked for an import company. Working full-time on a campaign like Palmer's, she says, means that people like her have to put their lives on hold for over a year at a time. She just felt lonely and then he came along. Aware that she's due to meet up with Drazen within the hour, Jack tells her they want her to help them put a tracking device on Alexis. He assures Elizabeth that she'll be safe, but she doesn't like the idea of meeting him again, and tells them she won't do it. George Mason tactfully backs off and suggests Jack heads over to the hotel himself. But then Elizabeth has a change of heart. She realises that by helping them she will protect the Senator. If these people could get to her, then they could easily get to someone else, and if something should then happen to Palmer that she might have helped prevent, she says she could never forgive herself. She agrees to help them.

Agent Paulson begins showing Teri and Kim some photos of some of Gaines's men. Teri thinks she recognises one of them as a man called 'Jenson' though when Paulson shows them a picture of Eli, the man who raped Teri, he notices Mrs Bauer tense up. Kim tells him she thinks she recognises him but can't tell him anything about the man. As they continue to look through the mugshots, Jovan Myovic quietly breaks into the house through the back door. He shoots one of the agents with a dart and then makes his way through the house.

Kim realises that her mother is distressed after seeing the mugshot of Eli and suggests to Agent Paulson that they should take a break. Paulson goes to the kitchen to make some coffee and only then does he notice that he can't see any of the other CTU agents. Immediately concerned, Paulson returns to the living room and tells the women to follow him. He leads them to one of the bedrooms and closes the door behind them. He then makes his way through the house, searching every room. Eventually, he finds Myovic hiding in a closet and tells him to step out with his hands up. Myovic surrenders just as Mishko Suba sneaks up behind Paulson and attacks him from behind.

Hearing the noise, Teri and Kim escape to the garage and drive off in the car. The assassins run after the women – Paulson shoots Suba but then he himself is shot by Myovic, who runs to his own car and follows the women.

Jack tells Elizabeth that she will meet his team at the hotel and that he'll be with her every step of the way. As he goes to leave, Milo calls him over urgently. Robert Ellis's body has been found in the men's room of a bar in New Orleans. Before this can sink in, Jack is surprised to see Nina returning to CTU. He asks her why she's not with his wife and daughter as he had asked. Nina tells him that they are safe and no longer need her. She chooses not to mention her disagreement with Teri.

Myovic chases Teri and Kim high into the hills overlooking Los Angeles. Taking advantage of the tight bends of the roads, Teri leaves the main route and turns down a dirt road. Once she's sure they've lost their pursuer, Teri pulls over by the side of a hill and, leaving Kim in the car, walks back along the road to check that they haven't been followed. Just then the edge of the hill begins to crumble underneath the weight of the car. Teri turns round to see the car toppling over the edge of the embankment; by the time she's run back the car is engulfed in a ball of flames. Aghast by the possibility of losing her daughter in such a horrific way, Teri collapses into a faint.

By **3:52 P.M.**, Keith has gone to the Griffith Observatory where he meets Carl, as arranged. Keith blames him for the death of Dr Ferragamo and tells him that the doctor was the only person who was around for him when he needed help. Carl points out that the doctor also betrayed his confidence by speaking to Maureen Kingsley. He then suggests that people might be suspicious if they hear that right after Keith paid Lyle Gibson a visit the boy ended up dead, and that a further accusation of being responsible for the death by arson of Ferragamo might not go down too well either. Keith clarifies the situation to see if he's got Carl right: if he goes public about the truth over Ferragamo's death, Carl will go public with a *lie* about Gibson's. Keith warns him that this means there are now two cover-ups that Carl is involved in and that he should be careful they don't come back to haunt him. Carl boasts that he can look after himself, especially because they've planted evidence at Ferragamo's office that could incriminate Keith and frame him for the doctor's murder. He'll do whatever it takes, which is why he's confident that both David and Keith will back off. Carl leaves feeling triumphant, unaware that Keith has taped their entire conversation...

Teri wakes up on the side of the road. Dazed and disorientated, she walks back towards the main road. A woman drives towards her and, seeing Teri walking aimlessly, pulls over. She asks Teri if she's OK but Teri can't even remember her name or what has happened. The woman offers Teri a ride so Teri gets in her car. Further up the road, Myovic abandons his search for the women.

Kim wakes up at the bottom of the embankment, grazed but otherwise unharmed. She climbs to the top of the slope and calls out for her mother in vain...

NOTES

- **Who's Who?:** Pauley Perrette (Tanya) played groupie Alice Wisdom in *Almost Famous* (dir. Cameron Crowe, 2000).
- **Time Checks:** Alexis and Elizabeth arrange to meet up at 4:30 P.M.
- **Music:** When the girl enters Rick's room, we hear 'Who's That Kat?' by The Salads coming in from the next room.
- **Death Count:** Daniels, plus two other unidentified CTU agents (killed by Myovic some time before 3:23 P.M.), Agent Breeher (killed by Myovic, 3:36 P.M.), Mishko Suba (shot by Paulson) and Agent Paulson (shot by Myovic, both 3:41 P.M.).
- **Trivia:** The full name of the man who raped Teri is Elija Stram. His arrest photo carries a Compton Police Department number – 38594. The Griffin Observatory where Keith meets Carl also appears in the films *Rebel Without a Cause* (dir. Nicolas Ray, 1956) and *Terminator 2: Judgement Day* (dir. James Cameron, 1991).

COMMENTS

As she interviews Kim, Nina becomes aware that the girl is possibly covering up for Rick and that she may have formed an emotional attachment with her would-be kidnapper. This kind of co-dependent relationship between captor and hostage is often referred to as 'Stockholm Syndrome' after an incident on August 23 1973 where four people were taken hostage by two men during a bank robbery. In just six days, the captives had formed such a close emotional bond with the robbers that they actively resisted being rescued. After the robbers were arrested, the hostages refused to testify against them and indeed contributed money towards their defence. Some reports even claim that one of the women later became engaged to one of the robbers.

In the United States, the most famous example of this kind of behaviour is the case of Patty Hearst, the heiress who was kidnapped by members of the Symbionese Liberation Army but years later was discovered to have joined their ranks (having changed her name to 'Tania') and was finally caught attempting to rob a bank for their cause.

Psychologists have identified certain conditions that can lead to Stockholm Syndrome. The hostage must be convinced that their captor will kill them; they must believe that escape is impossible unless the captor allows it; they must be isolated from any perspectives other than those of their captor; and lastly, the captor must reward them with small kindnesses which then begin to work on the hostage's mind. In these conditions, the hostage is reliant on the captor for their life, just as the captor is dependent on his hostage not dying (otherwise the purpose of keeping them hostage is lost). As a basic form of survival, the hostage develops a pattern of trying to keep their captor happy in whatever way they can. When this tactic begins to work, the relief the victim feels over not dying becomes gratitude towards the captor for not killing them. What begins as simply a method of staying alive soon grows towards obsession where the primary drive switches from self-preservation to selfless attempts to please their captor as their need to survive becomes greater than their instinct to hate the person who has caused this situation. The result is that the victim's mind becomes slowly conditioned to sympathise with their captor and possibly even consider them their 'saviour' rather than their tormentor. Note how Kim was prepared to abandon her parents in the compound just to make sure Rick was safe?

Now, as Nina should know, this kind of behaviour tends to occur over three or four days, not hours, but given that Kim was already developing an emotional bond with Rick when they first met, it's not too much of a stretch of the imagination to see why she might want to keep her ties with Rick long after she has escaped from him and his employers...

QUESTIONS ARISING

- Is Jack right to suspect another traitor within CTU?
- Why didn't Mason tell Jack that his security status had been downgraded?
- Who in their right mind parks a car on the edge of a cliff?

5:00 P.M.

Production Code 1AFF16

First US Transmission: Tuesday, March 26, 9/8C

Written by Michael Chernuchin
Directed by Stephen Hopkins

'The following takes place between 4:00 P.M. and 5:00 P.M. on the day of the California presidential primary... Events occur in real time.'

Cast: Carlos Bernard (Tony Almeida), Zeljko Ivanek (Andre Drazen), Vicellous Shannon (Keith Palmer), Xander Berkeley (George Mason), Daniel Bess (Rick), Misha Collins (Alexis Drazen), Vincent Angell (Dr Phil Parslow), Kara Zediker (Elizabeth Nash), Pauley Perrette (Tanya), Glenn Morshower (Agent Aaron Pierce), Navi Rawat (Melanie), Andre Canty (Henry Martin), David Franco (Man), John Tague (First Waiter).

EPISODE SUMMARY

Kimberly looks around for her mother, unaware that she is currently being driven away from the scene of the accident by a woman who introduces herself as Tanya. The woman comments on Teri's wedding ring but Teri claims not to remember if she has a husband or not.

Jack and Nina accompany Elizabeth back to the hotel where they are greeted by Special Agent Pierce. Pierce tells Jack that they have gained access to Drazen's room and the room across the hall. They have less than 30 minutes to set up cameras and microphones in the room. In the meantime, every access to the hotel is covered by Pierce's team.

At **4:05 P.M.**, Tanya drives past a restaurant that Teri recognises. They pull over and Teri rushes in and asks to speak to the manager in the hope he might recognise her. She is told that the manager, Mr Martin, isn't due back for another 20 minutes. Teri decides to wait but tells Tanya that she doesn't have to stay with her. She takes Tanya's address so she can send her something when she gets better and Tanya gives her $10 for her cab fare to the hospital.

Nina briefs Elizabeth, reminding her to behave in front of Drazen the way she always has – but without compromising herself. Meanwhile, Palmer reprimands Jack for putting Elizabeth in danger and airs his concern that Jack is allowing his desire for revenge to cloud his judgement. Jack convinces the Senator that getting Elizabeth to plant a trace on Alexis is the best way to trace his fellow conspirators and put an end to the affair. David tells Jack that he is a friend of Elizabeth and has known her since she was born. Should anything happen to her, he will hold Jack responsible.

Having walked quite a distance, Kim eventually finds a payphone and at **4:15 P.M.**, she calls CTU. With Jack and Nina out of the office, she is left with no choice but to tell Tony that the safe house has been attacked, their guards have been killed and she suspects her mother has been kidnapped. Tony asks her to tell him where she is so he can send someone for her, but Kim is unwilling to trust anyone but her father and Nina so she hangs up. Tony informs Mason about Kim's call and he sends a team to investigate the safe house. Tony asks if they should notify Jack about what has happened, but Mason tells him that it will only distract him from his current duties with Elizabeth Nash. He will explain to Jack what's happened once the situation is under control.

Nina tells Jack she's not sure Elizabeth is up to the task ahead and asks him if he's sure they're doing the right thing. Jack is confident that it's their best chance, and even if Elizabeth fails, they can still arrest Drazen. Nina can tell he's distracted and he admits that he's still worried about Teri and Kim; only a few hours ago, Kim was convinced she was going to die and he's worried that the strain will have been too much for them both. Nina reassures him that they both seemed fine while she was there, and that the doctor had said they were only suffering from cuts and bruises.

Kim calls Rick, despite him telling her not to earlier. She tells him that the safe house they were in has been busted and that her mother has been kidnapped again so she needs to come to stay at his house. Rick tells her she can't but Kim warns him that if he doesn't help her, she will tell the police about his involvement with Gaines. He gives her his address and she tells him she'll be there as soon as she can. As Rick hangs up, his girlfriend, **Melanie**, asks him incredulously if the person on the phone was another wrong number.

Keith comes to his father to apologise for accusing him of only thinking of his campaign and tells him he now knows that he was only protecting him from being accused of the murder of Ferragamo. David asks him if his mother told him, but Keith plays him the tape recording of his conversation with Carl. Keith asks him if he'll give the tape to the police and David tells him he'll have to trust him.

Driving to the hotel, Alexis calls Andre to tell him that Elizabeth mentioned that Palmer is now staying in L.A., Andre grows suspicious. He suggests that once he has finished getting information from Elizabeth, Alexis should kill her.

Elizabeth receives her final instructions. She should place the tracking device inside Alexis's wallet. Once it's in position, Jack will call her cellphone and she can make her excuses. Should she feel uncomfortable at any time, she is to say the phrase 'I hope I'm not getting a cold' aloud.

Henry Martin, the owner of the restaurant, finally shows up for work. When he sees Teri he clearly knows her by name and asks her if her usual dining companion, **Dr Parslow**, will be joining her. Teri explains that she has lost her memory and only came to the restaurant because she recognised it somehow. Henry decides to call Dr Parslow for her.

Jack has picked up something about Nina's manner this afternoon and asks her if anything is wrong. She tells him about her confrontation with Teri earlier and how Teri now knows about their affair. She apologises, but Jack tells her it's his fault. Just then, the call comes through – Alexis Drazen is in the building. Jack and Nina watch Alexis enter his room and work out that his wallet is either in his trouser pocket or in his jacket, which he has placed on the bed. With understandable trepidation, Elizabeth makes her way to his room. She hesitates at the door, then knocks. Alexis lets her into his room and kisses her, but she hugs him so he cannot kiss her face. He notices how tense she appears and she passes it off as last-minute nerves due to the polls closing in less than an hour. He asks her seductively if he might be able to do something to make her relax, and she suggests a vodka. While he is making the drink, Elizabeth searches the room for his wallet. She manages to get it from his jacket, but then she drops the transmitter and by the time she's got it and the wallet together, Alexis has returned with the drinks so she's forced to slip the wallet into her own pocket. Jack and Nina watch anxiously as Alexis places the drinks to one side and begins to embrace her again – sooner or later, he is bound to feel the wallet in her pocket. But Elizabeth plays the scene skilfully, mounting him on the bed and holding his hands down, then manoeuvring around and behind him so he can't see her face. Alexis casually asks her why she's been kept back in L.A. and then quizzes her about the election. She asks him why he's suddenly so interested in her job, but then apologises for being in such a foul mood and puts it down to the fact that she's not been able to grab anything to eat. She suggests he should order them some food, and while he's out of the room, she manages to get the wallet back in his jacket pocket at last. Jack gives the order for the team to clear the corridor outside and begins dialling Elizabeth's cellphone as arranged. But just then, Alexis surprises Elizabeth by telling her that he loves her. This declaration is clearly unexpected. Hearing her phone ring, she crosses the room to pick it up, but instead of answering it as planned, she switches it off. She asks Alexis to repeat what he has just said and again he tells her he loves her. On the surveillance monitor, Jack sees Elizabeth pick up a knife – he realises all too late what she is planning to do. Nina orders a SWAT team to head down to the room while Jack kicks down the door just in time to see Elizabeth stab Alexis in the stomach. Jack pulls Alexis away from her and Alexis collapses across the bed. As the SWAT team storm the room, Jack tries to keep Alexis alive.

Kim gets a cab to Rick's house. She asks the driver to wait for her and heads on up the path. Kim is a little taken aback when the door is opened by Melanie, who quickly works out that Kim was the person Rick was speaking to on the phone. Rick hadn't told Melanie that Kim was on her way and quickly makes up a story about a problem with a friend of Dan's who shot him, which was how his arm came to be wounded. Melanie says that he told her he caught his arm on a fence. Kim can see that by being there she's causing trouble for Rick and his girlfriend and tells Melanie that she just wants to find the people who Dan was with, so she needs to look in his room to see if he's left any contact details for them. Behind them, the cab driver honks his horn and, embarrassed, Kim asks if she can borrow some money for the cab fare.

Dr Parslow gets to the restaurant at **4:57 P.M.** and asks Teri if she remembers him. She recalls that his first name is 'Phil' and asks if he is her doctor. Embarrassed, Phil tells her he's not, but that he'll help her figure out what has happened and get her well again.

Jack calls Mason to explain to him just what went wrong and that Drazen might not survive the attack. Mason accuses Jack of allowing his emotions to cloud his vision. Just then David Palmer comes into the room, having heard what happened, and Jack has to inform him that Elizabeth has been taken into custody. Palmer blames Jack and insists that he shouldn't have allowed the plan to go ahead, but Jack tells him that it was Elizabeth's fault for not following instructions. David goes to find Elizabeth, who claims she doesn't know what happened. David orders her not to say anything until he has found her a lawyer. Jack requests that David lets them handle this, but David refuses to listen and Jack quietly tells him that he is not helping matters. Jack is interrupted by Nina who hands him Alexis's phone. It is ringing. Taking a chance, Jack answers it. Thinking it is Alexis, a man with an American accent reminds him that he should bring the money as arranged to a place called Connie's. The man tells him he will be wearing a red baseball cap. With that, he hangs up...

NOTES

- **Who's Who?:** Vincent Angell (Phil Parslow) can be seen in Al Pacino's 1996 examination into Shakespeare's *Richard III*, *Looking For Richard*, and the recent Vietnam film *We Were Soldiers* (dir. Randall Wallace, 2002).
- **Time Checks:** Jack and Elizabeth arrive at the hotel with just 30 minutes to spare before Drazen returns. When Teri arrives at the restaurant, she's told that the manager won't be there for another 20 minutes. Elizabeth notes that the polls will be closing in less than an hour.
- **Music:** When Kim tells Rick she is coming over we hear 'Saturday' by Yo La Tengo. When she finally gets there, Rick's listening to 'Cataract' by Trephines.
- **Trivia:** Rick lives at 1804 Glade, Echo Park.

COMMENTS

> *'Day 18 – the housemates of the Big Brother house face their second nomination day. Elizabeth, Jack and Nina have nominated Alexis; Andre and Alexis have nominated Elizabeth, meaning Alexis and Elizabeth are up for eviction. Who goes? You decide!'*

OK, so it's an obvious comparison: multiple camera angles that give us a unique aspect on the lives of the lead characters; insight into the characters' thoughts and motivations; the best possible position to see everything at once; and regular evictions from the cast. Just like ***24***, *Big Brother* offers the excitement of watching people squirm under pressure and try to cope with the intense scrutiny of everyone around them. Who can they trust, if anyone? The steady growth of supposed 'reality' TV shows such as *Big Brother*, *Survivor* and MTV's *The Real World* over the last few years reveals more about their audiences than the stars themselves. We're becoming a nation of voyeurs, motivated by gossip and paranoia about what other people think about us, and these shows allow us to believe we're seeing everything the time slot will possibly allow.

The multi-camera aspect of ***24*** is nothing new either, though. The idea of the split screen dates right back to the old serial films such as *Flash Gordon* and *Buck Rogers*, while later movies would show both parties in a telephone call on either side of the screen, separated by that artificial divide. In a way, these pictures have mirrored the effect that comic books have always had of depicting scenes in panels, allowing two completely different locations side by side, joined by a 'Meanwhile, across town...' caption.

As editing techniques have improved, so directors have employed various ways to show as much action at once as they can: Brian De Palma's *Snake Eyes* was celebrated for its use of split screen to show different angles of the same screen (and, like ***24***, it consisted of numerous plot twists leading towards a very convoluted conclusion); Mike Figgis's *Timecode* (which coincidentally starred ***24***'s Xander Berkeley – was a film in which the screen was divided into four throughout, with four characters occupying a quarter each; and of course *Series 7: The Contenders* (dir. Daniel Minahan, 2001), *Ed TV* (directed by Imagine's Ron Howard, 1999) and *The Truman Show* (dir. Peter Weir, 1998) spoofed reality TV shows like *Big Brother* by asking just how far TV companies will eventually go in the name of 'entertainment'. *Big Brother* still has the edge in terms of depicting 'reality' as it happens; we're already 16 hours into ***24*** and not one person has stopped to go to the toilet. It's a serious issue that should be addressed in the second series or the DVD release of the series... though they're free to skip the optional multi-angle selections and a commentary if they wish.

QUESTIONS ARISING

- Will Teri remember who she is any time soon?
- Who is the girl in Rick's apartment, and can Rick be trusted?
- Has Elizabeth killed Alexis, and what will happen to her now?

5:00 P.M.

7:24 22:38 10:09 17:59 09:13 21:01 04:45 14:12 07:57 13:41 07:24 22:38 10:09 17:59 09:13 19:47 05:20

Production Code 1AFF17

First US Transmission: Tuesday, April 2, 9/8C

Written by Maurice Hurley
Directed by Fred Keller

'The following takes place between 5:00 P.M. and 6:00 P.M. on the day of the California presidential primary... Events occur in real time.'

Cast: Penny Johnson Jerald (Sherry Palmer), Carlos Bernard (Tony Almeida), Zeljko Ivanek (Andre Drazen), Vicellous Shannon (Keith Palmer), Xander Berkeley (George Mason), Daniel Bess (Rick), Jude Ciccolella (Mike Novick), Edoardo Ballerini (Frank), Tanya Wright (Patty Brooks), Vincent Angell (Dr Phil Parslow), Henri Lubatti (Jovan Myovic), Kirk Baltz (Agent Teddy Hanlin), Navi Rawat (Melanie), David Franco (Alan Morgan).

EPISODE SUMMARY

Having just learned about Alexis's role in the arranged drop-off, Jack orders his team to scour the hotel room for large quantities of money. David Palmer tells him he holds him responsible for what just happened but Jack points out that they have a videotape of Elizabeth plunging the knife into Alexis's stomach. He does concede that he seriously misjudged her ability to cope with the stress of the operation. He implores David to make sure he has as much security around him as he can cope with and to let them do their job. Nina finds a large amount of bonds, which must be the purpose of the drop-off. Swapping his blood-stained shirt for the shirt of another agent, Jack gets ready to head off to Connie's in California Plaza.

Tony tells Mason that Bauer's wife and daughter are still missing and that initial forensic tests on the house suggest that the CTU agents were killed trying to protect the women. Mason reminds Tony not to say a word to Jack about the situation; if Jack should call and ask, Mason tells him to put the call through to him.

Rick and Kim search Dan's room for clues about Gaines. Melanie mockingly asks Kim what she's looking for and Kim tells her that she wants to find anything that can tell her where her mother might be – and once she's found what she's looking for she'll go straight to the police. Melanie tells Rick that Dan will not be happy to see they've gone through his things and walks out. Rick tells Kim he hasn't told Melanie about Dan's death because he doesn't want to freak her out, and as Dan's brother **Frank** is expected any minute he doesn't want Kim to mention Dan to him either.

At **5:06 P.M.**, Dr Parslow tries to get Teri to remember that she is married and has a teenage daughter. He tells her that she separated from her husband about six months ago, which was when the doctor met her. Though he had wanted to take things further, she had told him she didn't want a relationship, and eventually she asked him to stop calling her as she wanted a reconciliation with her husband. He suggests he should get her to a hospital but for reasons unknown to Teri she is set against the idea. She consents to letting the doctor examine her at the restaurant instead.

David plays Keith's tape to Mike and Sherry, pleased at last to have the upper hand on Carl Webb. Mike and Sherry are less convinced. Mike points out that unless Keith was primed by a court of law to record that conversation the tape cannot be used as evidence. David suggests that if the media get hold of the tape, they will be exonerated, but Sherry refuses to even consider it:

> *'Today can't be about two things, David. It's either about winning the primary, securing the party nomination, or it's about a political scandal, but it can't be about both.'*

Sherry tells David to destroy the tape. She is confident that he will win the primary, so the evidence of that tape won't just destroy him, it will destroy the party that he represents. David insists that he doesn't consider telling the truth the same as self-destruction. Mike reveals that he has been aware of much worse scandals being kept secret. Mike disagrees with Sherry about destroying the tape. Instead he suggests they should keep the tape a secret. Once David is in the White House, he will then have evidence against some of the most powerful men in America and they will no longer be able to exert control over him.

As he leaves the hotel for his dangerous rendezvous, Jack calls Tony to ask after his family. As instructed, Tony puts him through to George Mason. Jack tells Mason about the meet with one of Alexis's contacts and convinces him it's their best chance to stay on top of the conspirators. Mason grants him permission and agrees to send him back-up. But when Jack asks for the number of the safe house so he can check on his family, Mason tells him that he has just spoken to Paulson and that the women are asleep. Jack asks him to make sure they call him when they wake. The time now is **5:12 P.M.**.

As Jack and Nina drive over to California Plaza, Nina explains that Teri became unresponsive to questioning after learning of Jack and Nina's affair. She left things with Paulson but felt that was a mistake. Jack reassures her that she did the right thing, and that he feels he should have told Teri himself. Jack suggests she give Paulson a call at the safe house, but when she finds she can't get connected to the house number she puts it down to being in a bad reception area. Jack asks her to try again when they get to the Plaza.

Tony asks Mason for some help tracking down Teri and Kim as with Nina gone he is a little short-handed. Mason refuses, saying that Nina didn't have to go off with Jack and implies that he suspects the pair are still having an affair. Mason asks Tony how he feels about that and Tony refuses to listen, telling him to stay out of his personal business. Mason cautions him that in his opinion the whole of CTU is being dragged down by 'personal business' and Nina would appear to be at the centre of it. She seems to back everyone who breaks protocol, and everyone who breaks protocol covers for her.

David speaks with Keith about the tape. He spells out to him the consequences of going public with their allegation. Keith will face accusations of a crime that he did not commit and David asks his son if he is really prepared to endure that. Keith admits that the only reason he didn't come forward with the truth seven years ago was that he was scared. He realises now that he accused his father of not being there for him so he didn't have to blame himself for his own mistakes, but David has also realised that his son was right to criticise him; he wasn't always there for him – but he is now.

Unable to get through to Alexis, Andre calls Jovan Myovic to check whether he has heard from his brother. Myovic tells him he has his own problems – he has lost the Bauer women.

Kim has called everyone she can think of but no-one has seen or heard from her mother. Melanie tells Rick that Kim has to go – Dan's brother Frank is coming round and Melanie thinks Kim's presence will only make matters worse. Kim agrees to leave, telling Rick she's going to go to a park where her parents once told her to go in the event of an earthquake. Rick asks why she doesn't just go home, but Kim suspects that the people who are after them probably know where they live, so as long as her mother is OK that's the last place she'd go. Rick gives her some money to catch a cab and Kim asks him if he can come with her. After the events of the last few hours, Rick thinks he should just lie low. Kim tries again to get him to go to the police, but Rick says that he is on probation and would almost certainly face jail. Kim thanks him for everything – she believes she wouldn't be alive if it hadn't been for him, though Rick notes that she probably wouldn't have been in trouble without him. Kim argues that if it hadn't been him they'd hired to kidnap her, it would have been someone else. She kisses him, but their embrace is interrupted by the arrival of Dan's brother Frank. Rick nervously tells Frank that Dan has his money, but that he's not home yet. The presence of Kim, a stranger, makes Frank edgy, especially as he has some business taking place there in just half an hour. Kim makes to leave but Frank blocks her way, telling her nobody's going anywhere just yet.

Jack and Nina reach the plaza at around **5:31 P.M.** Mason calls Jack to give him prior warning – the back-up that District have assigned him is **Agent Teddy Hanlin**, the partner of one of the agents Jack reported for corruption the previous year. From the moment they meet with Hanlin it's clear he still holds a lot of resentment about what happened and wastes no time in gloating about Jack's 'screw-up' earlier today. Jack tries to ignore him and begins to brief him about the assignment but Hanlin continues with his barbed comments, warning Jack to be careful as he'd hate to get confused and shoot one of the 'good guys' by mistake. Jack warns Hanlin that he doesn't want him to cause him a problem and then heads off to try to find the red-capped contact.

Tony informs Mason that a woman matching Teri's description was seen wandering around Griffith Park but subsequently disappeared. Mason decides to get onto the satellite division while Tony tells him that he's sent **Agent Williams** over to the Bauer house, just in case.

Phil Parslow concludes his examination of Teri. Apart from a few cuts and bruises, he can't see anything physically wrong with her, so he asks her if she feels any pain. She tells him she's been feeling sore in her abdomen. Phil diagnoses disassociative amnesia – a condition that can occur if someone suffers an intense emotional trauma. He again suggests that she should go to a hospital but Teri somehow links hospitals with immense danger and begs him to take her home.

While Sherry Palmer is on the phone getting the exciting news about the exit polls, she sees David hand his campaign manager, Patty, a small envelope. Patty takes the envelope and places it inside a wall safe. Sherry waits until Patty has gone and opens up the safe to find an envelope addressed to the district attorney. Inside is a small microcassette, which Sherry pockets. A few minutes later, David comes into the safe room to find Sherry sitting there. She tells him she knows that he had a talk with Keith but when David suggests that she should talk to him too, to show that he has their support, Sherry seems keen in only blaming David for their son's predicament. David opens the safe to see the envelope missing and Sherry tells him she destroyed the tape because he is not seeing the situation clearly. It is then that David reveals that the tape she destroyed was not Keith's. He placed a duplicate in that envelope and he admits it breaks his heart to learn that he was right not to trust her. She defiantly tells him that she will do anything to protect her family and asks him if that makes her a bad person. David refuses to answer her. Instead he leaves the room and directs Mike to set up a press conference for one hour's time.

At **5:45 P.M.**, Jack installs his earpiece so he can communicate with Nina and Teddy. Almost immediately, Teddy begins to needle Jack, despite warnings from Nina. But when Teddy casually informs Jack that the wife of one of the agents he reported hung herself a few weeks ago, Nina calls George Mason to inform him that Teddy is compromising the assignment. George has Tony patch him in to Nina's communication channel and warns Teddy to bury whatever grievance he has against Jack until the operation is over.

By **5:53 P.M.**, Myovic has reached the Bauers' home. He checks out the house shortly before Agent Williams arrives. Myovic hides behind a tree, gun in hand.

Kim has realised that Frank is waiting for Dan to return with his payment from Gaines so he can use it for a drug deal. Knowing that neither Dan nor the money are going to turn up in time, Kim begs Rick to escape with her before Frank's contacts arrive and they end up in the middle of another mess. Frank tells Rick that he is indeed planning to use Dan's money – $20,000 – to buy ecstasy and sell it on for $50,000. Kim asks him what he'll do if Dan doesn't show up, but Frank dismissively tells her that Dan will be there.

The man with the red cap finally arrives at California Plaza. As he passes by, Jack calls to him, shows him his briefcase and directs him to sit down. The man asks him why he did not wait inside the nearby restaurant as arranged, but Jack tells him there is a cop there, which is why they are doing the transfer outside. Before he hands over the money, Jack tells the man to go over what he is supposed to do. Assuming he is talking to Alexis, the man tells him that he is being paid to shut down the power grid for a specified area for five minutes, starting at **7:20 P.M.** that evening. Jack asks him what else is planned and the man suddenly realises that Jack is not speaking in an accent like Alexis did. He bolts and Jack relays instructions to the team to cut off the nearby bridge. Teddy tells him that he can shoot the man to slow him down but Jack repeatedly tells him not to fire. Ignoring Jack's instructions, Teddy lines up the suspect in his sights and as he crosses a glass-walled bridge he fires. The man falls through the glass and down to the floor. Nina rushes to secure the area and keep people back from the contact's body while Jack calls for an ambulance. Furious, he repeats that his instruction to Teddy was *not* to shoot.

David Palmer gives the real microcassette to one of his aides for safekeeping. Meanwhile, Phil and Teri arrive at Teri's house. Myovic watches from the bushes, the dead body of Agent Williams at his feet.

NOTES

- **Who's Who?:** Kirk Baltz's (Teddy Hanlin) film credits include *Dances With Wolves* (Kevin Costner, 1990), *Reservoir Dogs* (Quentin Tarantino, 1992), *Natural Born Killers* (Oliver Stone, 1994), *Face/Off* (John Woo, 1997) and *Bulworth* (Warren Beatty, 1998).
- **Time Checks:** Nina estimates that the hotel is 20 minutes away from California Plaza, the location of the drop-off. At around 5:21 P.M., Andre tells Myovic that Alexis is expected at the meet-up in 20 minutes. David tells Mike to set up a press conference in one hour

(next episode) even though Mike tells him they already have one arranged for three hours' time. The contact tells Jack that he will be shutting down the power grid at 7:20 P.M. that evening.

- **Music:** As Kim and Rick look in Dan's room we hear 'Winter Notes' by Picastro. Frank walks into the room accompanied by John Frusciante's 'Remain', while Kim realises Rick is in trouble at the same time as we hear the Black Rebel Motorcycle Club's 'As Sure As The Sun'.
- **Death Count:** Agent Williams (shot by Myovic some time between 5:52 and 5:59 P.M.). Alan Morgan (shot by Agent Hanlin at 05:59 P.M.).
- **Trivia:** Up till now, ***24*** has been vague as to which party David Palmer represents, but this episode states for the first time that he is a Democrat. Agent Williams' car licence plate is G13 23846 – a government plate – while Phil Parslow's plate is 41BY911. The grid that Alexis's contact is due to shut down is 26 GG.

COMMENTS

Info-dump time: Los Angeles is located along the southern coast of California, in the Pacific Time Zone, which is GMT-8. California seceded from Mexico in June 1846 and declared its independence; it became the 31st state of America four years later. L.A. County consists of 88 cities, including Los Angeles, Beverly Hills, Santa Monica, Culver City and Long Beach. L.A. City covers 4,081 square miles (making it the second largest city in America). It has a population of 3.8 million people; L.A.County's population is 14.5 million. Infamous for its devastating earthquakes, L.A. also experiences dozens of minor tremors a week, though most register way below 5.0 on the Richter scale.

The people of Los Angeles are known as Angelinos. 45.6 per cent of L.A.County's population are Hispanic; whites account for 32.2 per cent; African-Americans 9.4 per cent. There is one car for every 1.8 people in

L.A. (including non-drivers like children!). The city has over 160 miles of freeway and 5,400 miles of other roads; 75 per cent of the water supply for L.A., some 525 million gallons a day, is brought there across the viaducts that William Mulholland (who lent his name to the famous Drive where Kevin Carroll takes Teri Bauer) and Fred Eaton constructed in 1908. L.A.'s first African-American mayor, Tom Bradley, served five consecutive terms from 1973-93.

Library Tower, with its 73 floors and height of 1,017 feet, is the tallest building in L.A. L.A. Downtown is 12 miles east of the ocean. California Plaza, where Jack poses as Alexis Drazen to meet Alan Morgan, can be found on Grand Avenue in the Financial District of Downtown L.A. Over 60 million passengers go through LAX airport (which services L.A.) every year. Griffith Observatory, which can be found within the 4,100 acres of Griffith Park, where Keith meets with Carl, is located on the side of Mount Lee, Hollywood. Both the park and the observatory take their name from the man who financed them both, Colonel Griffith J. Griffith, a gold-prospecting Welsh immigrant who also served two years in jail for the attempted murder of his wife.

The Hollywood sign was erected on Mount Lee in Griffith Park in 1923. Due to the amount of people who have tried to either commit suicide there or interfere with the letters, it is now illegal to hike up to the sign. Los Angeles and Long Beach Port, where the final episode is partly set, is the world's third busiest container port complex. No matter how fast you drive, even if you jump every red light on the way, you cannot get from the Bauers' house in Santa Monica to Van Nuys in 15 minutes.

QUESTIONS ARISING

- Will Alexis survive the stabbing?
- What will Frank do when he realises Dan is not going to turn up?

Will knowing he is dead make his mood any better?

- Can Teri escape Myovic a second time now that she can't even remember the first incident?
- What was Rick on probation for?

1:00 13:41 07:24 22:38 10:09 17:59 09:13 21:01 04:45 14:12 07:57 13:41 07:24 22:38 10:09 17:59 09:13

Production Code 1AFF18

First US Transmission: Tuesday, April 9, 9/8C

Written by Joel Surnow & Michael Loceff
Directed by Fred Keller

'The following takes place between 6:00 P.M. and 7:00 P.M. on the day of the California presidential primary... Events occur in real time.'

Cast: Penny Johnson Jerald (Sherry Palmer), Carlos Bernard (Tony Almeida), Zeljko Ivanek (Andre Drazen), Vicellous Shannon (Keith Palmer), Xander Berkeley (George Mason), Daniel Bess (Rick), Zach Grenier (Carl), Edoardo Ballerini (Frank), Megalyn Echikunwoke (Nicole Palmer), Henri Lubatti (Jovan Myovic), Vincent Angell (Dr Phil Parslow), Navi Rawat (Melanie), Kirk Baltz (Teddy Hanlin), Darin Heames (Detective Krugman), Randy J. Goodwin (Security Guard), Noel Guglielmi (Craig), Jason Matthew Smith (Chris), Lewis Dauber – credited as Lew Dauber (Jorgensen), Jenn McCullough (Elaine), Mariah Pasos (Sam's Partner).

EPISODE SUMMARY

Watched by Myovic, Phil and Teri make their way into the house via a key that Phil remembers Teri used to keep hidden in a garden ornament outside. They open the front door and immediately set off the burglar alarms. The noise makes Myovic scuttle back under the cover of the nearby trees. The telephone rings and Teri answers – it's the security company for her neighbourhood asking for the password, but unfortunately, Teri can't remember what it is.

Inspecting the dead contact's wallet, Nina learns that his name was **Alan Morgan** and that he worked for Pacific Electric. Nina tells Jack she'll ask Tony to check on the co-ordinates Morgan mentioned (26 GG) and then head back to the office.

Teri is startled by the arrival of armed security guards investigating her alarm. Phil tells the guards that Teri lives there but forgot her password (Teri claims that she doesn't usually set it). The guard sees the many family photos in the house and is satisfied that Teri lives there. He tells her they'll reset the alarm for her and goes to check around the house. As the guards set about their checks, Teri is transfixed by the pictures of a family that she can't remember.

Mason arrives at the plaza, joking that every time Jack is sent on an assignment someone ends up leaving in a body bag. Jack tells him that he gave Teddy Hanlin strict instructions not to shoot. As Mason goes to speak to Hanlin, Jack gets a call from David Palmer who has used his Pentagon contacts to retrieve the missing document from the Drazen file. It would appear to be a list of names and addresses pertaining to the last month of Victor Drazen's life. David gives Jack an address which Jack then checks with Tony at CTU to learn that it falls within the sector that Morgan was going to knock out, 26 GG. Jack is about to head over to the address when Mason stops him and asks for an update. Jack tells him that Ellis was murdered two hours ago to prevent him getting an address that he's just obtained from Palmer. Mason invites himself along and reluctantly Jack has to take Mason with him.

At Rick's house, Kim tries again to persuade Rick to escape with her, but Melanie stops him. Worried that Kim will tell the police about Frank's drug deal, Melanie repeats what Frank said – nobody is leaving until Dan shows up. Exasperated, Kim lets slip that Dan is not going to come. Frank overhears this and threatens Kim to explain what she means. Rick finally tells him that Dan was killed by Gaines and that Gaines didn't pay up. Frank realises that he has invited some very dangerous people to Dan's house to make a drug deal with money that he doesn't have. It's now too late to call it off.

At **6:15 P.M.**, the Palmers sit down to dinner. Sherry asks David what he intends to say at his press conference and when David doesn't reply, Keith tells his mother proudly that it will be 'the truth'. Sherry tells him off for his impudence and makes no secret of her belief that he is entirely responsible for the mess they are in. David points out that her decision to cover up Keith's mistake and his own absence as a father make them all to blame. But Sherry will not be silenced and accuses Keith of selfishly trying to ease his conscience at the risk of endangering his father's bid to become the first black President of the United States, something that is for the good of their country. Keith tells her that he has lived with his guilt for seven years, but he refuses to accept that covering up the murder of Dr Ferragamo is in the country's best interests. Sherry finally loses her temper:

> *'I never saw it until just this minute – you're your* father's *son! You cover up your weakness with a bunch of bleeding-heart sentimentality. [Turning to David] When are you going to be* man *enough to do what it takes to be President?!'*

As the row escalates, Keith notices that something is wrong with Nicole; his sister is sobbing uncontrollably. Sherry immediately calls for a doctor but David picks his daughter up in his arms and lets her lie down on a nearby couch. She apologises to her father – she blames herself for everything that happened.

As soon as she gets to the office, Nina begins working on the address Jack got from Palmer and calls him up to tell him it's the location of a wildlife sanctuary. This doesn't make sense as Jack knows Saugus is an industrial area. As Mason drives to the address, Jack apologises to him for shooting him in the leg with a tranquilliser. Mason laughs it off, though he is visibly unsettled by Jack's comment that he feels a lot less wound up just knowing his family are safe.

Teri goes to Kim's room to see if it jogs any memories. Phil is able to supply a little background information for her: he never got to meet Kim because Teri hadn't wanted her to know she was dating another man – Kim had been resolutely on Jack's side during the separation; Jack had grown distant from Teri and she had been the one who asked him to leave; after she met Phil she'd got scared of growing too close to him and of losing her family, so when Jack had asked to move back home, she let him. Although Teri cannot remember Phil, she thanks him for making her feel at ease.

Kim is growing increasingly uncomfortable about the situation and tells Rick she is going to try to escape. She quietly makes her way to the front door just as some of Frank's friends arrive. Knowing he can't make the deal without any money, Frank has decided to steal the drugs from his suppliers, and his friends have just arrived with guns to help him with his plan.

The doctor finishes checking on Nicole at **6:19 P.M.** Nicole insists she's fine and wishes her father well at the press conference. David urges them all to pull together and support each other, but Sherry appears distant and non-committal. Instead, she compliments his choice of tie. David leaves for the conference, escorted by Secret Service agents.

Teri looks through her diary but none of the events of her recent past help her recall anything. The doorbell rings – it's **Chris**, a friend of Phil's who he's asked to come over and keep an eye on Teri. Teri is alarmed by the sight of Chris's gun and she tells Phil to get him out of the house. Chris steps outside for a smoke while Phil tries to convince Teri to trust his judgement. Outside, Myovic continues to watch the house.

David Palmer and his entourage make their way through the hotel kitchens and into the conference room where a throng of reporters and cameramen are waiting. At **6:35 P.M.**, he informs the press about the telephone call he received last night involving his children that has since set off a tragic chain of events. He tells them that he will allow the voters to decide if what he has to say will affect his campaign; his only worry is his family. As with all campaigns, he says, his own has been financed by local businessmen. Regrettably, he has misjudged them – but they too have misjudged him. He goes on to describe Nicole's rape, Keith's failure to report the rapist's accidental death, and the subsequent murder of Dr Ferragamo as outlined in a recorded conversation that implicates his financial supporters in a conspiracy of corruption which he testifies he himself had no part in or prior knowledge of. The tape is now with the Justice Department. While he admits that the law might deem the taped evidence inadmissible, he affirms that he will stand by his son and is confident that his innocence will be proven, In the meantime, he begs the press to consider that his daughter is an innocent victim in all this and to respect her privacy.

'This is about the cover-up of an accidental death. This is not about rape. So I am asking you now, as a father, please find your humanity and spare Nicole the indignity of having to relive this nightmare...'

Upstairs in the suite, Keith and Nicole watch with a mixture of relief that the truth is out and pride in their father. Across town, Carl tells Palmer's supporters that he will fix their problem, but he is told that he is already too late.

Nina finally learns that Teri and Kim are missing and asks Tony why she was not informed. Tony tells her that was Mason's direct instruction because he didn't want her to tell Jack and distract him from his assignment. Fuming, Nina calls George Mason and warns him that if anything should happen to the women, when Jack finds out he will hold Mason responsible. Mason, who has just pulled over outside the wildlife reserve, replies vaguely in a manner that will not alert Jack, who is sitting right next to him. Pretending that his battery has died, Mason asks to borrow Jack's phone and then switches if off to prevent Nina calling Jack direct. Jack dramatically leaps over an iron-mesh fence, while Mason, smirking, moves the sections of the fence apart and casually steps through. As they walk through the reserve, Jack tells Mason about Drazen, how he was a 'shadow' for Milosevic, responsible for the massacres (or 'ethnic cleansing') of thousands of people in Kosovo, Sarajevo and Bosnia. Mason and Jack have come to the same conclusion – that Jamey could not have been acting alone and that someone had to have been helping her within CTU. The men reach a clearing with a power station in the middle. Jack observes that this makes an unlikely nature reserve with no stretches of water, no birds and no animals.

The drug dealers arrive at Rick's house, a man and a woman. When he sees Kim and Rick, the man asks them who they are and why they're present at the deal, but Frank tells him they're not important and to get on with business. Once the dealer has shown Frank his jar of pills, Frank opens a holdall and pulls out a rifle. The dealers instantly pull out their pistols only to be surrounded by Frank's armed friends. Once the dealers are disarmed, Frank turns on Rick. He blames Rick for not keeping his brother alive and causing this situation and with that he jabs his rifle into Rick's wounded arm.

It's **6:51 P.M.** and Nina is checking the hospitals for any sign of the Bauer women but to no avail. Tony tells her that they've traced the payphone that Kim called from and are searching the area, while Agent Williams is positioned at the Bauer house. He affirms that they are doing everything they can, but Nina is not convinced.

Frank packs all of the drugs into a bag while Rick and Kim cower in a corner of the room. The dealer asks Frank if he intends to kill them and he tells them he will if he ever sees them again. With that he breaks the dealer's nose with the end of his rifle. As the dealer gets up off the floor, his hand over his bloodied nose, he tells Frank he has the right to remain silent. The door to the house bursts open and a SWAT team flood the room, shooting one of Frank's friends – the dealer and his friend are cops. As the occupants of the room are cuffed and led away, Kim begs for help, telling the officer that she had no part in the deal.

Senator Palmer concludes his press conference at **6:55 P.M.** by taking responsibility for not ensuring he was fully aware of what has been happening in his own household, but notes that he would not be the first elected official to be guilty of making a mistake. Without waiting for questions, he concludes his conference and leaves. Outside the conference room, David finds his son waiting for him. Overcome with emotion, Keith hugs his father, sobbing.

Phil goes to make himself and Teri some coffee while Teri admires a home-made box with the word 'Mom' written across it, which, she recalls, Kim made for her. Phil's friend Chris steps in to use the bathroom but at that moment, Myovic enters the house and shoots both Chris and Phil. Teri collapses to her knees with fear and Myovic asks her at gunpoint to tell him where her daughter is. Teri sobs as she tells him in honesty that she doesn't know. Myovic is about to kill her when three shots send him to the floor – Tony Almeida is standing at the doorway, gun in hand. As he checks the assassin to make sure he is dead, Tony reassures Teri that she is safe. But the shock of being confronted by Myovic has brought back Teri's memory and she realises that Kim must have been killed when the car exploded.

Palmer returns to his suite and is lovingly hugged by his proud daughter. Sherry however walks casually but deliberately out of the room. Meanwhile, Jack and Mason use their handheld locating devices to find the address given by Morgan – it's in the middle of nowhere. Overhead they see a helicopter passing by. Mason wonders if it's reconnaissance, but Jack realises that it's something much more worrying:

'Someone knows we're here...'

NOTES

- **Who's Who?:** Randy J. Goodwin (Security Guard) played Davis Hamilton in the TV show *Girlfriends*. Noel Guglielmi (Craig) had a small role in the film *Training Day* (dir. Antoine Fuqua). Lew Dauber (Jorgensen) played the manager of the toy store in the Arnold Schwarzenegger comedy *Jingle All the Way* (dir. Brian Levant, 1996).

- **Time Checks:** Jack notes that Ellis died two hours ago. The conversation between Jack and Mason acts as a neat summary of the events since midnight.
- **Death Count:** An unnamed friend of Frank (shot by a member of the SWAT team at 6:54 P.M.), Chris (shot by Myovic at 6:57 P.M.) and Jovan Myovic (shot by Tony Almeida at 6:59 P.M.).
- **Trivia:** The address David Palmer gives Jack is 21911 Kipling Avenue in the city of Saugus. In amongst all the other posters on Kim's bedroom wall, a banner for 'nu-metal' band Linkin Park is just visible. According to Phil, Teri is a freelance interior design consultant with a friend and work colleague called Kitty. Phil's friend Chris asks to use the bathroom – he's been in the show for less than one episode and he's the first person to show any signs of normal bowel functions. Shame he dies before he gets to see if Teri has quilted kitten-soft loo roll...

COMMENTS

Back to the real-time thing. See, in the USA, they have this wonderful thing called 'adverts', little vignettes that are both informative and entertaining. They're used to break up the programmes and give viewers a chance for a toilet break or make a cup of tea. And naturally, TV shows don't just stop when the commercials run. No, life goes on. Time keeps ticking. Which is why, on ***24***, when we go to an ad break at 12:20:07 A.M. (plinkDONK, plinkDONK, plinkDONK), when we return to the drama it's 12:22:51 – a whole two minutes and 44 seconds later!

In the UK, of course, ***24*** is shown on the terrestrial channel BBC2 and cable/satellite channel BBC Choice, both non-commercial stations. As a result of losing the all-important ad break, though, the series loses about 18 minutes for every hour of on-screen drama, which tots up to over seven hours of lost time. So what have we missed during these vital hours? Is this when the characters themselves visit the bathroom? Maybe Palmer stops off between appointments for a burger and fries to go. Or possibly Sherry pops to her boudoir to have her hair refitted and her talons sharpened. Whatever they get up to, it does rather reduce the awesome promise of 24 hours of real-time drama. Perhaps the producers might consider a more honest title for the next series – ***17***, perhaps?

QUESTIONS ARISING

- Will David's announcement threaten his chances at the polls? Will this silence Carl Webb and his associates? And will Sherry forgive him for going against her wishes?
- Now that Teri has shaken off her amnesia, will she totally regain her memory? Will she recall the outcome of her conference call to Kitty?
- Now she's under police custody, can Kim consider herself 'safe'?
- Who is in the helicopter circling Jack and Mason? Will they be at all concerned that neither of them is poor Alan Morgan (deceased)?

00:00 13:41 07:24 22:38 10:09 17:59 09:13 21:01 04:45 14:12 07:57 13:41 07:24 22:38 10:09 17:59 09:

Production Code 1AFF19

First US Transmission: Tuesday, April 16, 9/8C

Written by Robert Cochran & Howard Gordon
Directed by Stephen Hopkins

'The following takes place between 7:00 P.M. and 8:00 P.M. on the day of the California presidential primary... Events occur in real time.'

Cast: Penny Johnson Jerald (Sherry Palmer), Carlos Bernard (Tony Almeida), Lou Diamond Phillips (Warden Mark DeSalvo), Zeljko Ivanek (Andre Drazen), Xander Berkeley (George Mason), Daniel Bess (Rick), Jude Ciccolella (Mike Novick), Megalyn Echikunwoke (Nicole Palmer), Tanya Wright (Patty Brooks), Vincent Angell (Dr Phil Parslow), Navi Rawat (Melanie), Darin Heames (Detective Krugman), Christian Hastings (Harris), Rick Garcia (Reporter), Jenn McCullough (Elaine), Dennis Hopper (Victor Drazen – not credited).

EPISODE SUMMARY

As the sun sets, Jack and Mason explore the area but find nothing useful. Jack is convinced that there are reasons why the helicopter flew past and why the Drazens tried to pay off an electrical company employee to cut off the supply to the very point they are standing on. Mason gets a call informing him that Alexis Drazen has been revived at the hospital and he decides to head there to be present when he comes round. Mason is convinced they've been fed bogus information. Jack however wants to wait around until at least **7:20**. Telling Jack he doesn't have time to argue with him, Mason returns to his car, leaving Jack alone.

Tony quickly evacuates Teri and a wounded Phil from the house and takes them to his vehicle, parked round the back. Teri is still traumatised by the memory of the car exploding but Tony is able to pacify her slightly by telling her about Kim's call to him shortly after the accident. He explains that Kim is fine, though she is still missing. Tony calls Nina to tell her what's happened. Nina is worried by Phil's presence and suggests Tony takes him to the clinic but brings Teri to CTU. In the meantime, she'll despatch back-up to the Bauers' house.

Kim is taken to a nearby police station along with the other suspects in the drug bust. She tells Detective Krugman (the man who posed as a dealer) that she needs to make an urgent call, but Melanie spitefully tells him not to believe her as 'she lies'. As Melanie is led away, Rick tells Kim not to tell the police anything about Frank. Kim has already decided to tell them she's an innocent bystander, but she warns Rick she'll have to tell them about everything else that has happened to them today, though after the safe house, she's unsure whether she can trust anybody. Rick asks her if she trusts him, and she jokes that trusting him has got her involved in the mess they're in. Rick advises her to tell the police everything, including his part in the kidnapping, and he'll back her up – it's about time he faced the consequences of his actions, he decides. At that point, Detective Krugman leads Kim away to be booked in as a prisoner.

David checks in on Nicole. She tells him she hadn't realised just how hard keeping her secret had been. David admits that there's every chance their hardship is not over – they are bound to be asked questions – but he is confident that, united, they will all get through the worst of it. Sherry enters the room and David asks Nicole to leave them alone for a while. Sherry apologises for interrupting David and Nicole's 'celebration', and when David suggests she could have joined in, Sherry replies bitterly that she's not in the mood to celebrate the end of his campaign. Sherry fears that, by airing his guilt like some 'guest on a bad afternoon talkshow', he might as well have conceded the election there and then, but David is not so defeatist. He thinks that some people might admire him for being that rare animal, an honest politician, and Mike agrees with him. Sherry scoffs that Mike is paid to tell him what he wants to hear, whereas it's her job to point out the truth. Now it's David's turn to mock as he reminds her she's hardly qualified to preach about 'truth'. Sherry says his speech has ruined everything they have spent the last 25 years working on and tells him she hopes his conscience comforts him after he realises that 'this is all over'. David asks her if she's referring to their marriage or his campaign, but she walks out without replying.

Walking around the area in the dark, Jack finds some stone steps leading underground. As he heads down them, some guards, submerged in camouflage, radio in to Drazen to warn him of Jack's arrival. Jack comes to a dead end, but as he turns to leave, a loud, ear-splitting alarm goes off. The noise temporarily confuses Jack, leaving enough time for a concealed door to open to reveal guards who shoot Jack with a laser dart and knock him out. They drag him into the bunker and allow the door to close behind them.

A few minutes later, at **7:13 P.M.**, Jack wakes up to find himself in a cell deep within the bunker. Within a few seconds, nausea takes hold of him and he is violently ill into a toilet. As he gulps water from a tap, the door to his cell opens and a man steps in. The man already knows who Jack is and introduces himself as **DeSalvo** of the Department of Defence. He informs Jack that he has found his way into a Class 3 government detention centre – effectively a prison that doesn't officially exist – and he should therefore justify what he is doing there. Jack explains that he is the lead investigator into an assassination attempt on a senator and that a trail he has been following has led him to where he is now. DeSalvo pushes him further so Jack reveals that the people he is tracking paid an employee of the electrical company to shut down the grid that powers DeSalvo's facility at **7:20 P.M**. DeSalvo watches him, stony-faced. Jack begs the warden to take him seriously – the people behind the assassination attempt are trained Serbian soldiers and have already killed a lot of people to get this far in their operation. Jack realises that the power cut was due to coincide with something that was going to happen in the detention centre. DeSalvo tells him that he is awaiting the arrival by helicopter of a new prisoner, a man who is moved from prison to prison every couple of weeks, but whose identity is classified – he doesn't even know who the man is himself. Jack narrows down the possibilities. Whoever this man is, the Drazens either want to free him or kill him. He suggests that the warden should call for back-up; even if they can't get here in under five minutes, they might help him save every life in the facility. Further, he should arm everyone, including his maintenance man and technicians, to make the bunker appear more secure than it actually is.

On the surface, Andre Drazen familiarises himself with plans to the underground complex. One of his team, **Harris**, expresses concern that none of them have heard back from Alexis in some time and worries about any deviations from the plan. Drazen tells him the plan will go ahead as arranged and despatches his soldiers to get into position.

Back in the bunker, Jack assists DeSalvo's untrained men with their guns while DeSalvo himself briefs his guards – all three of them. The men all head outside just as the helicopter comes in to land and position themselves in front of the lights so a strong security presence can be seen. With his army waiting on standby, Andre waits for the power to be cut to the complex, but already the small army is becoming wary of proceeding – Harris notes that they were expecting the warden and just three guards but they can clearly see as many as eight men including Bauer. Harris realises that the guards are expecting Drazen's troops. Drazen is not concerned, however, aware that when the power to the lights is cut, the sudden darkness will leave the warden's men disorientated and vulnerable. But the lights remain on well after the time they should have been cut. The helicopter lands and Jack leads the men into providing a guard as the prisoner is brought out into the open. Drazen insists the mission goes ahead as planned but Harris refuses to let his soldiers be put at risk when there are twice the number of guards they had anticipated and the power to the lights has clearly not been cut. By the time Drazen accepts defeat, the prisoner is safely underground. Harris radios for his men to stand down.

Kim is led to an interview room where Detective Krugman is waiting. She tells him that her father is the director of Los Angeles CTU but Krugman has never heard of that department and after being warned by Melanie about Kim's 'active imagination' believes Kim is just wasting his time. Kim tries to tell him about all that has happened to her over the last day but the more she speaks the less likely it all sounds. She writes the number for CTU on a piece of paper and asks Krugman to verify her identity. With that, she is led back to the cells.

With the transfer of the prisoner going off without a hitch, DeSalvo questions whether Jack's melodramatic concerns were at all genuine. Jack warns him that Drazen's crew have not attacked yet because the power didn't go down, but going on past experience they are bound to have a contingency plan. Reminding him that the impending attack on the complex is connected to the attempt on Senator Palmer's life, Jack tries to emotionally blackmail the warden into letting him speak to the prisoner, but DeSalvo tells him that even he doesn't have clearance to do that. Back-up is on its way but in the meantime he tells Jack he is free to go over his head if necessary. Jack recalls that DeSalvo works for the Department of Defence and asks if he can use the warden's phone...

At **7:34 P.M.**, Mike comes to see David. The Senator is worried that public reaction might be just as bad as Sherry had feared. But Mike turns on the TV without saying a word to let him see for himself – over 60 per cent of people polled say that Palmer's disclosures has had no effect on their decision to vote for him in the presidential election, 20 per cent have said it made them more likely to give him their support while only 18 per cent said they had changed their mind about him. The results completely vindicate David's decision to go public and, it has to be said, Mike's advice all along. A call comes through for David from Jack Bauer. Jack explains where he is and tells him he needs David to pull some strings to get Warden DeSalvo the authority to grant Jack access to the mysterious prisoner. Hanging up, Jack notices a security camera watching him. Mindful of the infiltration of CTU, Jack decides to follow the camera's feed to see where it leads. He eventually finds a small doorway and, behind it, a surveillance room that covers the entire complex above and below ground. Jack activates the camera inside the prisoner's cell, but before he can see the man's face, DeSalvo walks in, irate that Jack has breached their security. Jack apologises but again explains that he needs to know who the man is. On the monitor, Jack sees the man turn to look straight at the camera. He can't believe his eyes: the prisoner is **Victor Drazen**, the man he killed two years ago.

Outside the security room a few minutes later, Jack tells the whole story to DeSalvo, explaining that he led the government-backed mission against Victor Drazen two years ago, but that Drazen's wife and daughter died in the attack and – evidently – Drazen didn't. He needs to ensure that the Drazens don't get their father back or he will lose any leverage he has against them to protect his family. Though DeSalvo is not prepared to risk his career and a possible prison sentence just to appease Jack, he agrees to make a few calls on his behalf.

With Alexis having failed to call in for some time, Andre surmises that he must be dead. He decides their next course of action will be to blow up the nearby power station and then enter the complex through the front doors. Harris is concerned that this might draw attention to them, but Andre tells him it will help them free his father from prison, which is his only concern.

Having been unsuccessful in his interrogation of Alexis Drazen, Mason returns to CTU and almost instantly comes under a barrage of questions from Nina Myers about why he chose not to inform Jack about the disappearance of his family. Mason reminds her that as her superior he doesn't have to explain his decisions to her.

Sherry is revelling in her duties as hostess of a premature victory party and asks David to join his guests. His stern facial expression warns her that something is the matter. He asks her what she meant by her earlier comment that 'it's over'. Sherry tells him whatever she meant was said out of wanting to protect her family and asks him coyly if he holds her loyalty against her. David smiles and says:

'You're an amazing woman: smart, determined, sure of yourself... You always know what you want. But you don't want me – not really. I don't think you've wanted me for a very long time.'

Sherry dismisses his comments as nonsense, but David is not so sure. Her decision to keep the truth about Keith and Nicole from him for all those years leads him to think that he can't trust her any more. If he can't trust her, he asks, how can he love her? Sherry replies that he might not love her, but he will never leave her. With that, she tells him to take as long as he needs to pull himself together and then join her outside with their guests who have given up every day and night for the last year to put them both in office. She warns David that come next January, when he is being sworn in as President, she *will* be standing right next to him as First Lady of the United States. She leaves David alone to contemplate for the first time the full extent of his wife's ruthlessness.

At **7:54 P.M.**, Kim is placed in a holding cell with other female prisoners. Scared by the aggressive looks the other prisoners give her, Kim sits down meekly at one end of the cell.

DeSalvo is trying to understand why the government would keep Victor Drazen a prisoner if they'd already decided they wanted him dead. Jack realises that his mission must have been designed to fail from the start; somebody has already decided that Drazen is more valuable to the US government alive. DeSalvo receives a call from the DoD. Though they have to wait for a reply on Bauer's request to have Drazen moved, DeSalvo's superiors have given him permission to allow Jack to interview Drazen.

Jack enters Drazen's cell and introduces himself. He explains that, two years ago, he saw Drazen enter a bunker that he was not supposed to walk out of alive. He regrets that Drazen's wife and daughter were unnecessarily killed during the operation but points out that Drazen's fight is with himself, not his own wife and daughter. Drazen's wife and daughter have died already, but that doesn't mean his sons need to die too. Drazen tells him proudly that his sons are soldiers, but Jack says that if that is so his sons will die for nothing. He tells Drazen that he is aware of the attempt to free him and that his team have stopped it. Back-up is already on its way. He urges Drazen to tell his sons to call off their rescue attempt. Victor asks him how he is supposed to contact them and Jack, losing patience, tells him to use whatever method he has used to contact them all along. Having heard the conversation via the security camera, DeSalvo is now convinced that Drazen must be moved. He tells Jack his decision and Jack tells him to plan a route that will not be shown on any maps such as a flood or fire escape exit. The warden begins briefing his staff for an immediate evacuation of the prisoner.

As Teri says goodbye to Phil and leaves the clinic with Tony, and as Palmer's victory party continues, DeSalvo and Jack lead Victor Drazen towards a secret exit to the complex. Suddenly, the lights cut out. DeSalvo gets word that the power has been cut to the complex. Drazen looks Jack in the eyes. 'They're here,' he tells him defiantly.

NOTES

- **Who's Who?:** Born on February 17 1962, Lou Diamond Phillips (Warden Mark DeSalvo) came to fame as the rock star Ritchie Valens in *La Bamba* (dir. Luiz Valdez, 1987) before appearing in *Stand and Deliver* (dir. Ramón Menéndez, 1988), *Young Guns* (dir. Christopher Cain, 1988) and *Young Guns II* (dir. Geoff Murphy, 1990). The latter two also starred Kiefer Sutherland. Recently he's starred in the supernatural TV series *Wolf Lake*.

- **Time Checks:** After Mason gets the call about Alexis Drazen he tells the caller he'll be at the hospital within half an hour. Sherry accuses David of finishing their relationship in just 13 minutes with his speech (she's being a bit unfair – his speech lasted 20 minutes, including the ad break).
- **Trivia:** Tony's car licence plate is 4IZK505. Sherry and David have been married for 25 years.

COMMENTS

Getting an actor of Dennis Hopper's reputation for such a pivotal role was a major coup for the ***24*** team. He's one of Hollywood's true survivors, having crashed and burned more than once in his long career, only to return like the proverbial phoenix. Hopper was born on May 17 1936 in Kansas. When he first appeared on the silver screen (in two of the three feature films James Dean completed before his death in a car crash), he looked like the perfect, clean-cut boy-next-door type; handsome, enthusiastic, every inch the 'all-American boy'. But towards the end of the 1960s, having failed to make a major impression in something like 20 movies and earned himself a reputation of being 'difficult', Hopper began drifting away from acting towards the pop-art world, as a collector and photographer. But in 1969, actor Peter Fonda (son of the legendary Henry Fonda and elder brother of *Barbarella*'s Jane) convinced Hopper to appear in and direct his latest film, an experimental road journey into the anti-Vietnam counterculture of booze, sex and drugs. *Easy Rider* would not only come to epitomise the best and worst of late 1960s America, it would revolutionise Hollywood and the American film industry, removing the studio giants' stranglehold on the box office and giving power to independent mavericks like Fonda to make the kind of movies they wanted. As a result, film-makers like John

Cassavetes, Martin Scorsese and Francis Coppola became the kings of American cinema... for a time at least.

Just a decade later, the dream was slowly crumbling. The freedom of the 1960s gave way to the excesses of the late '70s. Hopper himself was struggling to come to terms with his lack of success after *Easy Rider* (his sprawling, drug-fuelled *The Last Film* received a justified critical mauling), and was more likely to find his life, rather than his work, reported in the newspapers. His marriage to Michelle Phillips lasted just a few days; in 1975, he was arrested and charged with reckless driving, failure to report an accident, leaving the scene of an accident and evading police officers; and on the set of Coppola's already out-of-control Vietnam epic *Apocalypse Now*, Hopper was seen to be drunk, drugged up and unreliable. His career in ruins, it was all Hopper could do to remember where to stand – remembering the script was out of the question.

Jump forward to 1986, where emerging film-maker David Lynch was auditioning for his new film, a sneak peek into the dark, disturbing underside of Americana called *Blue Velvet*. Having read the script, a cleaned-up, wiser Dennis Hopper called the young director and declared 'I *am* Frank Booth!', Lynch's lead villain. Lynch was convinced and Hopper was hired. Hopper's emotionally draining performance as the sexually deviant, immensely psychotic Frank suddenly catapulted him back into the big league. Few could wonder what dark well of emotion Hopper mined as research for the role. Suddenly, he was hot property again – which for a 50-something actor in the 1980s was quite an achievement. He went on to appear in films as eclectic as *Super Mario Bros* (playing a lizard king), *Waterworld* (playing an aquatic dictator) and *True Romance* (playing against type as a role-model father who finds himself at the wrong end of Christopher Walken's temper). For the makers of ***24***, casting Hopper as the mastermind behind the entire conspiracy must have been a double-edged bonus. Hired for just the final six episodes of the series, it was Hopper's name that the last run of trailers were trading on (although his name was kept off the cast list for this episode to maintain the pretence of a surprise). And of course, the fact that even on a low-grade video monitor he is recognisable means that the viewers can identify him and empathise with Jack's recognition of him a little more.

As luck would have it, the clothing company Gap just happened to launch their new brand commercials at the same time. In one of them, a serene, Gap-clad Dennis Hopper relaxes by a swimming pool sipping a long drink. A far cry from sitting in a stark prison cell in a secret government-owned underground bunker with a bag over his head...

QUESTIONS ARISING

- How can Victor Drazen be alive after all this time? Is he communicating with his sons in some way?

9:00 P.M.

Production Code 1AFF20

First US Transmission: Tuesday, April 23, 8/9C

Written by Robert Cochran & Howard Gordon
Directed by Stephen Hopkins

'The following takes place between 8:00 P.M. and 9:00 P.M. on the day of the California presidential primary... Events occur in real time.'

Cast: Penny Johnson Jerald (Sherry Palmer), Carlos Bernard (Tony Almeida), Lou Diamond Phillips (Warden Mark DeSalvo), Dennis Hopper (Victor Drazen), Zeljko Ivanek (Andre Drazen), Xander Berkeley (George Mason), Jude Ciccolella (Mike Novick), Tanya Wright (Patty Brooks), Paul Schulze (Ryan Chappelle), Navi Rawat (Melanie), Darin Heames (Detective Krugman), Christian Hastings (Harris), Jenn McCullough (Elaine), Angelo Pagan (Drake), Pete Antico (Barnes), Jon E. Epstein (Al), Gwen Stewart (Female Officer), Lisa Joyner (Reporter).

EPISODE SUMMARY

David Palmer watches a newscast announcing that he has won the primary election with an overwhelming clean sweep of California and the ten other states that held a 'Super Tuesday' at the same time. It would appear his announcement earlier today had little effect upon his victory.

Rick's girlfriend Melanie is placed in the same holding cell as Kimberly. The girl immediately begins harassing Kim by telling her she's sitting in her seat. Kim decides to avoid her by moving, but then Melanie follows her and repeats, 'You're in my seat.' Unwilling to be drawn into a fight, Kim vacates the seat and moves over to stand by the cell bars.

A few friends and colleagues have gathered in the Palmers' suite ahead of their victory party. Outside on the balcony, Mike Novick comes to tell David some good news. Not only did he take all 11 states in the election, *Fox News* have collated the results of an instant poll showing 83 per cent of the electorate in support of his handling of the Ferragamo situation. Mike warns against getting too confident, but despite the fact that there are many more primaries ahead, David feels confident enough to risk celebrating early.

Jack phones Nina at CTU but the call is intercepted by Mason. He's more than a little surprised when Jack informs him that the 'empty field' they were in was on top of a secret prison facility, that Victor Drazen is apparently alive, well and staring at Jack that very moment, and that the facility is under attack from Drazen's men. Mason agrees to send him some back-up and clear it with Chappelle after the event. As Mason gets off the phone, Nina begins to pester him to find out what's happening. Mason cuttingly points out what a shame it is that she's wasting the best years of her life 'on a married man, and picking up Almeida on the rebound'. He refuses to discuss the matter with her. Just then, Tony brings Teri into CTU, who understandably is desperate to know the whereabouts of Kim. Nina tells her they haven't found her yet but are still working on it, and that Jack has been sent out on an assignment. Teri is surprised and asks if he's aware of what happened to her and Kim at the safe house. When Nina admits that he isn't, Teri is not happy and demands to speak to him immediately. Nina pacifies her by explaining that Jack is in a dangerous situation and that she would help him best by explaining to her what happened at the safe house in detail.

In the bowels of the prison compound, while Jack holds Victor Drazen at gunpoint, DeSalvo tries unsuccessfully to speak to his guards by radio. As they make their way through the darkness towards the exit, the warden orders Drazen to tell him what his son is planning. Just then an explosion tears apart a section of the tunnel up ahead and DeSalvo is forced to order a retreat.

At **08:15 P.M.**, Teri goes to speak to Mason to ask about Kim. He tells her he's sure she's safe, if only because the man who attacked her at her house asked her where Kim was, suggesting they're still looking for her. He also assures her of Jack's importance to the team and that everyone is working their hardest to help him. With that, he deftly hands Teri over to his assistant... with instructions that she should keep Teri out of his way.

David checks in on his campaign manager, Patty, and is impressed that she has managed to incorporate changes that he's requested to his victory speech. Patty takes the opportunity to convey how much she admires him for standing by his beliefs. David is a little taken aback, but thanks her for such an unexpected compliment.

By the time Mason's back-up arrives, they see that the front entrance to the complex has been blown open and assume (correctly) that the hostiles have already made their way inside. As Jack and the prison team try to find another exit, Drazen's team use the cover of darkness to shoot all of DeSalvo's guards. Jack immediately grabs Victor and, holding him with a gun to his head, warns Drazen's men to drop their weapons or he will shoot. But then Andre comes forward with DeSalvo at gunpoint. Reluctantly, Jack releases Victor and is horrified when Andre callously kills DeSalvo anyway. Victor is overjoyed to see his eldest son again, though the reunion is soured by the news that Alexis is missing, presumed dead. Enraged, Victor grabs a gun and is about to shoot Jack when he is told about the CTU team making their way into the complex. He gives orders to collapse one of the tunnels to block their way and then tells his men to keep Jack alive as a bargaining tool.

Melanie continues to harass Kim. At first, she manages to keep her cool, but when Melanie describes Rick as a loser and then accuses Kim of being 'Daddy's little girl', Kim finally flips:

> *'You don't know anything about me! Last night I was kidnapped, tied up in the back of a trunk and then I got to see your friend Dan get shot in the head! You take all the bad luck you've had in your entire life it wouldn't fit into half of what's happened to me in the past 24 hours, so messing me up may not be as easy as you think, but if you wanna try,* bring in on!! *Here, outside, any place you like!'*

Their fight is disrupted by a guard, so Kim sits down, still fuming.

Victor accuses Jack of considering him a monster only because he believes the reports he has read, which in his opinion were written by men simply handing their superiors what they want to hear. Jack tells him he is insane, living out a 'psychotic fantasy' by trying to kill a list of enemies that stretches into the thousands. For such insolence, Drazen has Jack beaten. Andre comes over and hands his father a telephone – George Mason has called. Victor asks if George is the person he will be negotiating with but Mason corrects him – they do not negotiate with terrorists. He asks Victor to confirm that Jack is still alive, so Victor holds the phone to Jack's mouth. Jack takes his chance to warn Mason that Drazen has six armed men and is again silenced by a strike from one of Drazen's soldiers. Meanwhile, George asks Nina if she wants him to replace her with someone less 'emotionally involved' but she's insistent that she can still do her job.

One of the women in the cell with Kim is smoking a joint, but when the guards come she tells Melanie to take it from her. When Melanie refuses, she throws it at her and then tells the guard that it was Melanie who was smoking it. But then Kim backs up Melanie and the woman flares up and goes for Kim. She is dragged off by the guards, screaming threats at Kim. Surprised that Kim would stick up for her, Melanie decides to tell the guards that she is ready to tell the truth about the drugs bust.

Jack has realised that during 'Operation Nightfall' the man they thought was Victor Drazen must have been a decoy, but that as Drazen must have ordered him into the same bunker as his wife and daughter, he himself is to blame for their subsequent deaths. Victor tells him that his daughter had fallen ill and that she and her mother had returned to the bunker a day early. But he concedes that he should have been more careful. Jack tries to take advantage of Victor's reflective mood and attacks him, only to be overpowered by Andre. Victor looks down on Jack, sprawled on the floor, and tells him that while in prison over the last two years, he has accepted his share of responsibility for his family's deaths. But now it is Jack's turn to take his part of the blame. He steps back to allow Andre to deliver a vicious beating to Jack, warning his son to make sure their enemy doesn't die in the proceedings.

Patty comes to see David at **8:40 P.M.** on the pretext of checking her work with him, but as he reads some paperwork, sprawled on a couch, she tells him she feels bad about the way he worries about everybody else but no-one looks after him. He dismisses her concerns, saying he feels his entire team look after him. She moves towards him and begins to massage his shoulders. Although he appreciates the gesture, he tells Patty that he might be in danger of getting too relaxed to leave the couch. She makes her excuses and leaves, and David smiles to himself as he realises the girl might have a crush on him.

At just after **8:43 P.M.**, Ryan Chappelle calls to roast Mason for not keeping Jack on a 'tighter leash'. Chappelle spells it out for him: as Drazen didn't officially exist, he couldn't 'officially' escape; but now they have an assault team trying to stop him from leaving it's all suddenly become a major embarrassment for the Department of Defence, who are blaming Chappelle for the entire mess. As a result, Mason is compelled to order a final assault on the compound. When he informs Nina of this, he does so in a way that suggests Jack is not expected to survive. Nina goes to speak to Teri, who has just learned that Kim has been found safe and well at a nearby police station. Nina regretfully informs her that they believe Jack has been captured by the same people who had held her captive earlier. She tries to reassure her that the rescue team will reach Jack in time and that she knew Teri would want to be told, but for Teri it's just one more bit of bad news too much and she begins to cry.

At **8:48 P.M.**, the assault team prepare to enter the complex.

A few minutes later, Detective Krugman comes to find Kim. He tells her that thanks to the testimony of Melanie he was persuaded to call the number Kim gave him and verified that her story is true. He tells her that her mother is safe at CTU and, realising that she has had a pretty rough day and that he hasn't helped matters, he offers to drive her to CTU himself.

As the results of the election begin to come in, Mike urges David to smile a little more and enjoy his success, but David tells him he cannot put aside his concerns about Keith and Sherry. Mike tells him that when he is President, everything will defer to the position he holds; if his marriage helps him, then great, but if not, then he shouldn't worry about it.

Mason's assault team find the bodies of DeSalvo and his men. They report to Mason that the entire staff of the facility are dead and that there's no sign of either Drazen or Bauer. They find the Drazens' escape route – but it's heavily protected by mines.

Jack is led through the sewers to an outlet where the Drazens' transport is waiting for them. Andre is worried that they will not make the rendezvous for their escape. Now that they are free, Victor decides to kill Jack, taunting him that once he is dead his family will not be too far behind him, but when Jack tells him that his son Alexis is alive after all, he decides to take Jack with them and bundles him into their van.

On the way to CTU, Kim borrows Krugman's phone to call her mother and tell her she's on her way. Krugman apologises to her for not believing her story just as, from nowhere, a van crashes into them. Suddenly, masked men swarm out of the van, shoot Krugman dead and pull Kim screaming from the car...

NOTES

- **Who's Who?:** Lisa Joyner is a reporter for *Fox News*, though she usually specialises in entertainment news.
- **Time Checks:** David asks Patty to tell Mike he'll be ready for his speech in 20 minutes. Drake, head of Mason's assault team, estimates it would take half an hour or more to clear the mines from the tunnel that Drazen escaped through. Andre Drazen reminds his father that they have less than three hours left (presumably before they are collected to escape from the United States).
- **Death Count:** A guard called Lawrence (presumed to have been killed by Drazen's squad some time before 8:03) plus two other

unnamed guards (shot by Drazen's team) and DeSalvo (shot by Andre Drazen) during the attack on the compound at 8:20 P.M. Also, Krugman (shot by the masked kidnappers) and his driver (killed in the crash, both at 8:59 P.M.).

- **Trivia:** David Palmer's opponent during the primary is a man called Hodges.

COMMENTS

One of the most confusing elements of ***24*** is that David Palmer is not in fact campaigning for the post of President, but his party's candidacy in the presidential *primary* election. Presidential primaries are unique to the USA, a way for political parties to select their candidate for the election and create a little publicity for him ahead of the full elections the following November. To complicate matters further, though, the primaries are not necessarily held at the same time. Indeed, in the past, the first (New Hampshire) and last (California and New York) primaries were often held as much as six months apart. The first attempt at holding a substantial number of primaries at once – known as 'Super Tuesday' – occurred in the 1998 presidential campaign. The original aim of Super Tuesday was to encourage the support of the southern states and downplay the importance of the New Hampshire primary, which, coming early on in the game, had often been seen as the most influential and representative of the primaries. In the 2000 campaign, 12 states took part in Super Tuesday, including California for the first time.

Of course, some might accuse the American elections of being little more than personality-driven popularity contests, pointing to the elections of former actor Ronald Reagan and Bill 'Slick Willie' Clinton as evidence (though the successes of both generations of Bush in presidential campaigns might undermine that line of thinking). Another concern is that the corruption and financial influence that primary campaigns were created to eradicate still go on; primaries are expensive (though there are rules governing the amount of money that can be spent on promoting a candidate), and candidates often find themselves seeking assistance from the same kind of interested parties that controlled the original party conventions. Though rules restrict the amount of money a donor might give, this doesn't necessarily affect syndicates clubbing together to push a particular nominee. Certainly, this is something David Palmer can identify with.

Though Palmer's victory in the primaries might appear to make him the Democrats' first choice for presidential candidate, this isn't necessarily the case. As Palmer himself notes, although he has won the nomination of 11 key states, America has 39 other states (19 of which hold primaries) that might vote against him in the light of his revelations on election day. Historically, the south have never shown any likelihood to favour a black candidate (in fact, it was the southern Democrats that put up the most resistance to even allowing blacks the vote until the 14th Amendment to the Constitution started being more forcibly applied to some of their more restrictive statutes). There is also a precedent for the winner of the primaries to not gain the nomination from his party: in 1952, Senator Estes Kefauver won most of the primary elections but still failed to gain his party's support. In 1968, Vice President Hubert H. Humphrey avoided the primaries completely but still gained his party's nomination. Generally, though, a party would have to be foolish to reject a candidate with the wealth of support that Palmer has.

QUESTIONS ARISING

- Who are the masked men who have kidnapped Kim?

9:00 P.M.

Production Code 1AFF21

First US Transmission: Tuesday, May 7, 9/8C

Written by Joel Surnow & Michael Loceff
Directed by Paul Shapiro

'The following takes place between 9:00 P.M. and 10:00 P.M. on the day of the California presidential primary... Events occur in real time.'

Cast: Penny Johnson Jerald (Sherry Palmer), Carlos Bernard (Tony Almeida), Dennis Hopper (Victor Drazen), Zeljko Ivanek (Andre Drazen), Xander Berkeley (George Mason), Misha Collins (Alexis Drazen), Tanya Wright (Patty Brooks), Juliette Dudnik (Mila), Christina Moore (Dana), Eugene Lazarev (Nikola), Christian Hastings (Harris), Endre Hules (Serge).

EPISODE SUMMARY

Kimberly's abductors throw her into the back of their van, tape her mouth up and bind her arms, all the while speaking to each other in Serbian. Meanwhile, David Palmer makes his victory address to his campaigners. He tells them that they can all proudly consider themselves part of history.

Jack calls Nina from the back of the Drazens' SUV and asks her to confirm to Victor that his son Alexis is still alive. Nina gets Tony to patch through a telephone at the hospital so that Alexis can speak to his father. The man is still weak from the attack and begs his father for forgiveness for failing him. Victor tells him he has not failed – he is free and soon they will be together again. Turning his attentions to the CTU staff that he knows are listening in, Victor tells them that he is willing to make a trade – Jack for Alexis. George Mason speaks to Victor and informs him that he is not authorised to agree to such an arrangement, but Victor refuses to discuss the matter further. He tells George to speak to his superiors and that he will contact him again in 15 minutes for his answer.

While David continues his speech, Sherry tells Patty that she will not be joining David tomorrow as she has an appointment with the National Youth Service. Patty tells her she can rearrange David's schedule so that he can join her, but Sherry claims she's happy to go alone, but suggestively asks Patty to make sure David doesn't 'feel alone'.

At **9:09 P.M.**, Mason tells Nina that Ryan Chappelle has refused permission to agree to Drazen's trade offer. Apparently, it is felt that Drazen's mere existence is an embarrassment to the Department of Defence; especially because he has escaped after they have spent so much time and effort secretly keeping him their prisoner when the world thought he was dead. Nina asks what they intend to do about Jack and Mason tells her that, like the rest of them, he is considered 'expendable'. Desperate to save Jack, Nina asks how they intend to capture Drazen if they don't make the trade, but Mason reveals that they probably won't even bother as it will draw attention to the situation. Nina goes to speak to Teri and reveals bit by bit that they've had confirmation that Jack is now the Drazens' hostage and that although they are offering to return him in exchange for Drazen's son, the US government are not willing to trade with terrorists, which means that Jack is out on his own.

The Drazens take Jack to their secret base, a basement owned by an old friend of Victor's called **Nikola**. Victor is offered a warm welcome by Nikola and his daughter **Mila**.

As Mason argues with his superiors, trying to persuade them not to abandon Jack, Teri forces her way into his office to demand to know what he intends to do to rescue her husband. Mason glibly tells her that Jack is in a better position than any other agent in his position because he has exceptional training, but when Teri accuses him of patronising her he gives it to her straight – when he calls up Division to ask them one more time to change their mind, they will say no. Teri interprets his realism as an unwillingness to help her husband. She leaves Mason's office and begs Nina to help Jack. Nina tells her that she's already working on a plan, but that as it's unconventional she can't tell her what it is. She'll just have to trust her.

At the victory party, David proudly introduces some guests to his campaign manager, Patty, telling them that she is the brains behind his speeches. Just then, a call comes through from Nina Myers. She tries to summarise the events of the last hour and her first bombshell is the fact that Victor Drazen is alive and up until an hour ago was the prisoner of the US government. David hardly has time to comprehend this before Nina tells him about the Department of Defence's unwillingness to agree to a trade for the recently captured Jack in return for Drazen's son.

Nobody else knows that she has called him and currently the only person negotiating with Drazen is George Mason, who Nina describes as 'by the book, he's very ambitious and political'. The Senator agrees to make a few phone calls to help Nina, much to her immense gratitude.

Tony learns that the car carrying Kim to CTU has been attacked. Two officers have been killed and Kim is missing. He is about to inform Nina when Teri comes over asking about Kim. Tony tells her everything's fine, but Nina can sense that he's lying and asks Teri to wait in the conference room. Once Teri's out of earshot, Tony tells Nina the news and debates whether or not to tell Teri.

At **9:26 P.M.**, George Mason gets a call from Senator Palmer and is momentarily thrown when Palmer demands that he reverse his decision over the trade with Drazen. Mason is not sure how much Palmer knows about the situation but cautions him that the CTU does not fall under his jurisdiction. Palmer reminds him that as part of the Department of Defence, however, it does fall under the jurisdiction of the President. He orders George to go against his superior's orders and break a few rules to save Jack Bauer. Though he might be reprimanded, maybe even demoted, he guarantees him a promotion to a higher position in Washington within one month of him being inaugurated as President. Mason asks him what will happen if Palmer fails in his bid for the White House and David confidently tells him, 'That's not going to happen.'

Enjoying being spoiled by Nikola's daughter Mila, Victor taunts Jack. Jack seizes an opportunity and knocks down a guard, grabs Mila and, holding a steak knife to her throat, orders everyone to drop their weapons. Victor instructs everyone to do as Jack asks, but then with expert marksmanship he shoots Mila through the head. As the guards grab Jack and beat him into submission, Victor tells him that Mila's death is another on his conscience and then directs Andre to call Mason.

When Andre calls, Mason agrees to the trade but on his terms. Andre instantly dismisses any conditions Mason might offer and tells him the trade will take place in half an hour on 2127 Grand Avenue where a green SUV will be waiting. Once Alexis has been placed inside the vehicle, they will receive directions to Jack's location. Tony swiftly locates the address, a repair garage, while Mason tells him he's off to the hospital to collect Alexis.

At **9:31 P.M.**, Sherry infuriates David by criticising him for making calls when he should be greeting guests. He doesn't appreciate being lectured by her on his duties, but Sherry tries to dismiss his attitude as being the result of missing a night's sleep. Patty comes to David to tell him she's compiled some standard quotes for use in the *Wall Street Journal*. David smiles at her and tells her she looks gorgeous, then changes tack and warns her that his press conference about Keith is bound to shift the focus of future interviews. Patty says that she has already prepared a list of possible questions for him to go through whenever he likes but is surprised when he says he would like to look at her work straight away. Though he's willing to go through the papers alone, Patty says that she'd prefer to talk him through them so he arranges to meet her upstairs in his suite in five minutes.

Victor tries to convince a sobbing Nikola that his daughter's death was the fault of their enemy, Jack, but when Nikola turns against him, Victor shoots him too. Just then, Kim is brought into the cellar. Jack calls out to her but a bag is thrown over his head and he is dragged up the stairs in preparation for the hand-over.

Nina is pleased to inform Teri that Mason has sanctioned the trade for Jack. Teri again asks after her daughter and suggests Nina might be able to patch her through to the police car to at least let her speak to Kim. Unable to tell her the truth, Nina says she'll see what she can do. To make matters worse, Teri thanks Nina for being so honest with her. Nina goes straight to Tony to confess she'd been unable to tell Teri about Kim and that she thinks maybe she's just not tough enough to do her job, but Tony tells her he disagrees; their job is about helping people, something he believes she's very good at. This goes some way to making Nina feel a little better about herself.

Once more in the back of the Drazens' SUV, Jack begs them to let his daughter go. Tiring of the sound of his voice, Andre threatens Jack and warns him to shut up and let his father rest. Too tired to argue any more, Jack falls silent.

David discusses the way he wants to handle the Ferragamo issue with Patty. She tells him she has already briefed Mike to speak to their lawyers and set up interviews with all the major papers. He is amazed that she has been able to organise all this *and* write two speeches for him. She jokes that if she doesn't help him get into the White House then she's out of a job. David offers her a glass of champagne and they begin to discuss their respective private lives. David becomes aware that Patty is flirting with him and although he doesn't appear too uncomfortable about it, he returns to matters of work before inviting Patty to accompany him back to the party.

It's **9:45 P.M.** and the Drazens arrive at their first stop, a remote oil field. Jack is dragged out of the vehicle and handcuffed to a small pump where Andre says he will remain until they have collected their brother. If everything goes to plan, he will live; if not, he says, a sniper will be instructed to shoot him. He puts a scrambled cellphone into Jack's pocket and tells him he will be in touch. With that, he leaves Jack wondering what on earth they can want him to do next.

At **9:51 P.M.**, while David asks representatives of AIDS research what he can do for them in his first term, Sherry pulls Patty aside. Patty tells her that she flirted with David as Sherry had told her to, but that she felt uncomfortable with where it might lead. Sherry tells her not to concern herself with that; all she needs to know is that what she is doing is for the good of the campaign. Patty is not happy with deceiving David and repeats that this course of action might lead to other things. Sherry smiles and tells her they'll deal with that problem if and when it happens.

Mason supervises the hand-over of Alexis Drazen. He is met by Andre's man Harris who proceeds to move the gurney carrying Alexis into his vehicle. Harris makes to leave but Mason stops him, reminding him that the deal was they get Jack in return. Harris says that once he is sure they have not been followed they will inform him of Jack's location. Mason refuses to let him leave until Harris reveals that they also have Jack's daughter. Mason asks if they'll be getting both Bauers but Harris tells him clearly that he gets Jack; the daughter is no concern of his. Mason instructs his team to pull back and let Harris leave with Alexis.

Nina begins tracking Harris's SUV from CTU and tells Mason that as soon as they have Jack the SUV will be taken down, but when they lose the trace Nina realises that Harris has found the trace that they hid on Alexis.

As Jack looks around him anxiously, a shot rings out and his handcuffs are severed. The phone that Andre gave him begins to ring and Jack answers it. Andre tells him that if he wants to see his daughter alive he should make his way to a car that has been left for him nearby and, without speaking to anyone, head towards Century City. Jack finds the car, one of the Drazens' SUVs, and uses the keys inside to remove his handcuffs before driving off towards his next destination...

NOTES

- **Who's Who?:** Eugene Lazarev (Nikola) is one of Russian cinema's biggest actors, though Western viewers might recognise him from the film *The Saint* (dir. Phillip Noyce, 1997) and his guest role in two episodes of the first series of *Alias*. Endre Hules (Serge) had small roles in Imagine's *Apollo 13* (dir. Ron Howard, 1995), *Se7en* (dir. David Fincher, 1995), *The Peacemaker* (dir. Mimi Leder, 1997) and *Zoolander* (dir. Ben Stiller, 2001).

- **Time Checks:** At 9:04 P.M., Victor Drazen tells Mason he will call him again in 15 minutes, while Andre tells him they will make the trade at the end of the episode.
- **Music:** At David's victory party, we hear astoundingly soulless versions of Sister Sledge's disco classic 'We Are Family', Kool and the Gang's 'Celebration', and 'I'm So Excited' by the Pointer Sisters.
- **Death Count:** Mila (9:28 P.M.) and Nikola (9:34 P.M.), both shot by Victor Drazen.

COMMENTS

Behind every great man, as Annie Lennox almost sang, there's usually a great woman. In ***24***, we have the determined Teri Bauer and the ruthless Sherry Palmer who, in their own ways, support their husbands' work while struggling to keep their children safe and their family together. But while there are many similarities between the women, it's the differences that make them interesting. The role of women in drama tends to fall into two basic functions; either the victim, or the aggressor (more commonly referred to as 'the bitch'). Now although Teri is a strong independent woman, it has to be said her function in the dynamics of ***24*** is that of the victim, the woman in peril in need of being rescued. Sherry Palmer, on the other hand, actively pursues her goals, whether they be the suppression of a negative news story about her son or the positive promotion of her husband as the most suitable candidate for the position of president. As she urges David to wear a smile to mask his fears, one is reminded of another arch manipulator who pushed her husband into 'public office' – Lady Macbeth.

As all literature scholars will recall, Lady Macbeth's husband, Macbeth, had an encounter with three witches who rather cruelly put into his head the idea that he would one day be King. Egged on by his wife, Macbeth indulged in a spot ('out, damn spot!') of regicide and soon found himself sitting on the throne – which is when his troubles really began.

While up to this point Sherry hasn't suggested David murder his rival candidates, her single-minded determination to make sure he gets to the White House, whatever the cost, is reminiscent of Lady M's urging of her husband to 'screw [his] courage to the sticking-place' (while also encouraging his campaign manager to... actually, I'd best not continue that analogy...). For Sherry, nothing – her daughter's rape, her son's involvement in the death of a teenager, her part in the cover-up or her husband's doubts – can stand between her and success. For when David is inaugurated almost a year later, Sherry is determined to be by his side, no matter what. But this is where Sherry reveals herself to be even more devious than Lady M. Remember in Episode 1, Sherry questions her husband about the mysterious phone call he received, asking him, 'Since when don't we talk about things?' Sherry Palmer points to the one thing that keeps all dramas ticking over – characters hiding information from each other until it's too late to do anything about it. Of course, as we've seen since, Sherry's not exactly innocent of keeping things to herself. But now that David is close to discovering the full extent of his wife's continual manipulation of events to suit her own purposes, Sherry's downfall can't be too far ahead. At least she can take consolation in the fact that, unlike Lady Macbeth, she won't have to swallow hot coals to escape her guilt.

QUESTIONS ARISING

- What will the Drazens do next? Will Alexis survive the journey to be reunited with his father and brother?
- Will Kim ever last more than an hour without ending up kidnapped?
- Will Mason face demotion after disobeying orders?
- What does Sherry think she's playing at, asking Patty to seduce her husband, the future President of the United Sta- *Oh*, she's going to *blackmail* him. Ooh, the scheming *cow*!!

7:24 22:38 10:09 17:59 09:13 21:01 04:45 14:12 07:57 13:41 07:24 22:38 10:09 17:59 09:13 19:47 05:20

Production Code 1AFF22

First US Transmission: Tuesday, May 14, 9/8C

Written by Robert Cochran & Howard Gordon
Directed by Paul Shapiro

'The following takes place between 10:00 P.M. and 11:00 P.M. on the day of the California presidential primary... Events occur in real time.'

Cast: Penny Johnson Jerald (Sherry Palmer), Carlos Bernard (Tony Almeida), Dennis Hopper (Victor Drazen), Zeljko Ivanek (Andre Drazen), Xander Berkeley (George Mason), Misha Collins (Alexis Drazen), Tanya Wright (Patty Brooks), Paul Webster (Agent Ron), Josip Kuchan (Serbian Doctor), Yvette Fernandez (Reporter), Emile Williams (Secret Service Agent).

EPISODE SUMMARY

Now that Jack is on the road, Andre contacts Jack to give him his instructions. He tells him to proceed to Palmer's suite at the hotel. Having proven he can persuade Palmer to do practically anything, the Drazens want Palmer to release $200 million of the Drazens' assets that have been frozen ever since Victor was captured. He tells Jack to call him back at 10:45 P.M. for further instructions. Jack realises that eventually they will ask him to kill David Palmer, and that they have taken his daughter to make sure he obeys their commands.

Patty notices that David has left the party early and goes looking for him. She finds him upstairs in his suite reading through some paperwork. Having checked that he's happy with the schedule she's drawn up for him for his visit to Dallas tomorrow, she asks if there's anything else she can do for him. David instructs his Secret Service bodyguards to leave them alone and then invites Patty to sit with him. He asks her about her flirting with him earlier and she admits that she is attracted to him. David then removes a keycard for a room elsewhere in the hotel and asks Patty to meet him there in 20 minutes. Sherry walks in on them and acts as if she's caught them in a compromising position. Patty makes her excuses and leaves. Sherry cautiously tells David that she's informed their children that she will be campaigning separately to him and that they have agreed to go with her. David tells her he thinks it's a good idea for him to spend time alone and then returns to his paperwork. Taking this to signify that their conversation is over, Sherry leaves the room.

Mason and Nina discuss the current situation. They can't find Jack without finding the Drazens, and they can't find the Drazens now that their tracker on Alexis has been destroyed. Mason suggests Nina uses satellite simulations to find Alexis. Just then, Jack calls Mason to tell him that he's free but unable to come back to CTU. He asks him to tell Teri he's fine, but not to mention their conversation should Drazen call back in case it endangers Kim. Once Jack has hung up, Mason begins to follow a train of thought: Jack won't let them help him and won't tell them what he's doing and he's trying to protect Kim. He asks Nina rhetorically what is the one thing they know the Drazens want. Nina realises that the Drazens are forcing Jack to kill David Palmer. Mason calls the Palmers' suite and asks to speak to Secret Service.

The Drazens arrive at a warehouse near the docks where Kimberly Bauer, still bound and gagged, and Alexis have both been taken. A doctor who has been caring for Alexis regretfully informs Victor and Andre that Alexis has suffered massive internal bleeding and that there is nothing he can do. Alexis calls out for his father but then dies. Having already lost his mother and sister, Andre snaps and is about to shoot Kim when his father orders him to stand down. They still need her alive.

At **10:14 P.M.**, Sherry meets with Patty, who is still very unhappy with what she is being made to do and can't understand why Sherry is going to such lengths. Sherry explains that it is important for her husband to have her by his side. At the moment, though, he doesn't feel like confiding in her, so she needs Patty to win his confidence and then report back to her. She admits that she's not 'OK' with the idea of Patty sleeping with her husband, but she accepts that it's necessary. With that, she sends Patty off on her way.

Tony notices that the schematics of the compounds where Drazen had been held have been tampered with and asks Nina if she thinks it suggests there's another dirty agent involved. Nina thinks so and tells him to check who has had access to the schematics files in the last month. Mason comes over to ask Nina to look after Teri, who he describes as a 'basket-case'. Unwillingly, she agrees to have a word with her. Nina tells Teri that Jack is free but isn't coming back to CTU because the Drazens have got him doing something for them. Teri cannot understand what would possess Jack to work with those people and reluctantly Nina is forced to tell her that Kim has once again been kidnapped. Teri refuses to listen, unable to cope with any more stress.

Victor tells Kim that Jack is doing a task for him. Kim asks whether she will be freed once he is finished. Victor mutters, 'We will see...'

Jack calls David to tell him he needs to see him urgently. David replies that Jack's office have already told him that the Drazens have Jack's daughter and that he might be a danger to him. Jack says that although the Drazens do have his daughter, he doesn't wish to hurt him. At **10:45 P.M.**, they will call him on the phone he is currently using (which has been scrambled so they can't trace the call) and will expect to speak to Palmer about some money. He assures him he will tell him all the details when he gets there. Knowing what the Drazens are capable of, David is wary of letting him anywhere near him.

A few moments later, David waits in the hotel room for Patty. When she arrives, he tells her she is fired. He knows that she has been conspiring with his wife and tells her she is to remove her belongings and leave the hotel immediately.

Inspecting the logs on the schematics, Tony and Nina discover that George Mason accessed the file four days ago. Concerned that Mason is a traitor, Tony suggests they should call his superiors, but Nina tells him to just shut down his network access instead.

David tells Sherry that he has just fired Patty having realised that she was conspiring with her. His wife accuses him of cutting her out from his inner circle, an act that she boasts will be his undoing because without her looking out for him he is destined to fail. They are interrupted by one of David's bodyguards, who informs him Jack Bauer has arrived. As David leaves the room, he warns Sherry that their discussion is not over.

Although the Secret Service have allowed Jack through their cordon, they are unwilling to leave him alone with the Senator, which Jack understands. He tells David that the Drazens will be calling in just a few minutes. They claim that David has the necessary clearance to release the money that was seized when Victor was captured. As soon as they have confirmation that the wire transfer has taken place, they will instruct Jack to kill him. Jack reassures him that he has no intention of harming him and that he's just trying to buy time in order to save his daughter. David tells him that there's no way he could ever get their money for them – it's been reallocated by the government and, more to the point, he's certain Drazen knows that. He doubts that the money could be the real reason Drazen is calling. However, he agrees to listen to Drazen's demands.

At the warehouse, Kim listens in as Victor makes the call. Drazen taunts Palmer, but when Palmer asks him what he wants, Drazen doesn't reply. Jack realises it's a trap, grabs the phone and throws it out of the window just as a massive explosion tears the suite apart. On the other end of the line, Kim hears the sound of the bomb and cries out.

Sherry runs into the apartment fearing the worst and is relieved to discover that David is unharmed. He introduces her to Jack as 'the man [who] has saved my life twice today' but Sherry scowls at him and accuses him of being responsible for David's life being at risk. Jack asks David to help him buy time to rescue his daughter by leaking a story to the press claiming he has died. Sherry can't believe he could suggest such a thing, thinking only of the damage that might do to David's presidential campaign if the public think he is playing games with them. But David reminds Sherry that the life of an innocent girl is more important and tells her to fetch their children, warning her not to speak to anyone. Jack meanwhile briefs the Secret Service agents present and asks to speak to Mike Novick. Once Mike and the children are in the room, Jack gives instructions that nobody is to enter or leave.

By **10:39 P.M.**, George Mason has discovered that his network access has been shut down and asks Tony what's going on. Trying to stall him, Tony tells him he'll call their IT services, but Mason isn't prepared to wait and orders Tony to get his network access back. Tony and Nina discuss their suspicions but realise that without evidence they can't proceed any further. Nina tells Tony to restore Mason's access but to log everything he does and report back to her. Just then, Mason comes running down into the office telling everyone to turn on their TV monitors. The news has reached the TV stations that David Palmer has been killed in an explosion at his campaign headquarters. CTU is filled with stunned faces.

The Drazens congratulate themselves on a job well done in front of a distraught Kim. Andre offers to dispose of Kimberly but Victor tells him that the girl must live until they are sure that Jack Bauer is also dead. Andre calls the Palmer suite to speak to Jack. Jack tells him that, having killed Palmer with his bomb, he is the last name on their list and offers to hand himself over in return for the release of his daughter. Andre agrees to the swap and assures him that Kim will remain unharmed:

> *'We have decided the sins of the father need not be visited on her.'*

Andre warns him not to bring any of his colleagues. As he leaves, Palmer wishes him luck. Jack calls Nina to tell her that he is OK but refuses to tell her where he is. He asks to speak to Teri. Relieved to hear his voice, Teri tells him she can't take much more. Jack tells her that he loves her and Teri tells him that she's been waiting for the right time to tell him that she is pregnant. Jack is overcome with emotion and begins to weep, aware that he might never see her again.

10:51 P.M. Andre tells Kim about his sister and how she and their mother were killed by Jack. Kim refuses to believe him, confident that her father would not kill innocent people. Andre asks her if her father has ever spoken to her about his work and tells her he is not a 'good man'.

Mason tells Nina and Tony that Palmer is in fact alive but that his death has been reported to fool the Drazens. He asks them if either of them have spoken to Jack since he last called in and Nina lies, saying that she hasn't. Mason doesn't seem too worried either way as he is confident that the situation will soon be over. Outside Mason's office, Nina admits to Tony that she has spoken to Jack but that he won't let them help him.

Kim is left alone with a guard and asks permission to make some coffee to warm herself up. The guard approaches her and she throws scalding coffee into his face and escapes from the warehouse. The Drazens and their men are soon swarming over the docks and eventually find Kim standing on the end of a pier, her hands still bound. Pointing a gun at her, Andre warns her not to be foolish as she might drown, but Kim is desperate and throws herself off the pier. Underwater, she undoes her bonds and swims under the dock, out of sight.

Andre asks his father how he hopes to succeed without their hostage. Victor is confident that Jack will be forced to trust them. Andre receives a call from a woman calling herself Yelena. Speaking in his native language, the woman informs him that Palmer survived the explosion and that the press were wrongly informed of his death to give Jack time to save his daughter. From her hiding place within CTU, Yelena can see and hear everything that is going on. For Yelena is Nina Myers...

NOTES

- **Time Checks:** Andre Drazen tells Jack to call him at 10:45 P.M. David asks Patty to meet him in the hotel room and gives her 20 minutes to prepare. When Andre tells Jack to meet them at the docks, Jack tells him he will be there in 30 minutes.
- **Death Count:** Alexis Drazen (10:08 P.M.) of internal bleeding.
- **Trivia:** The Drazens' warehouse is at Dock 11A, Port of Los Angeles.

COMMENTS

The revelation that Nina is a traitor does appear to come from nowhere. Even after the possibility was raised and then dismissed early on in the series, this revelation struck many as just illogical. Why hadn't we seen any evidence that Nina was involved before? Why hadn't any of the Drazens mentioned that they had been receiving information from her all day if, as it would appear, they had been?

Some might point towards the opening narration on all the later episodes in which Jack's voiceover states that the people that he works with might be involved in the conspiracy just as Nina comes into shot. The tease is similar, in fact, to that of another great conspiracy drama, *The Prisoner*, the opening narration of which can be interpreted as revealing: 'Who is Number One?' Whether the reply is the dismissive 'You are Number Six' or the more leading '*You* are, Number Six' has been debated among *Prisoner* fans for over 30 years. With this in mind, the main complaint has been that implicating Nina was just *too* obvious, a sign that the writers hadn't even bothered to come up with anything clever and just took an easy way out without thinking it through. There were so many more likely candidates for the traitor. Tony, for example. Or George Mason. Or Walsh (apparently a small but vocal minority were convinced that, as Jack hadn't been able to check his pulse, Walsh could easily have been *pretending* to bleed to death from a shower of gunshot wounds... oh yeah!). Even *Teri* would have been a better choice – serve him right for leaving her in the first place!

In an interview with American magazine *Entertainment Weekly* (June 7 2002), Robert Cochran admitted that they didn't decide to make Nina a villain until halfway through writing the show. From then on, there are a number of moments where Nina is seen quickly ending conversations on the phone that we haven't been privy to, telling Tony that she's been unable to speak to Jack. Might she in fact have been speaking to someone else and using Jack as a cover? Watching the previous nine episodes again makes for interesting viewing if you're now looking out for alternative possible interpretations of Nina's actions. Was she posted to CTU merely to pass on information or has she been actively hindering the operation from the very beginning? It does seem suspect, for example, that she vacated the safe house minutes before Myovic and his friend moved in and started shooting. Coincidence? Just good timing?

QUESTIONS ARISING

- Forget any other questions you have – what the bloody hell is Nina doing?!

> ***'After 23 hours on the edge of your seat, the most thrilling... the most powerful... the most shocking hour... will be the last! The season finale of 24, next Tuesday at 9 (8 Central) on Fox.'***

Fox's trailer for the final episode of *24*

0:00 13:41 07:24 22:38 10:09 17:59 09:13 21:01 04:45 14:12 07:57 13:41 07:24 22:38 10:09 17:59 09:13

Production Code 1AFF23

First US Transmission: Tuesday, May 21 9/8C

Teleplay by Joel Surnow & Michael Loceff
Story by Robert Cochran & Howard Gordon
Directed by Stephen Hopkins

'The following takes place between 11:00 P.M. and 12:00 A.M. on the day of the California presidential primary... Events occur in real time.'

Cast: Penny Johnson Jerald (Sherry Palmer), Carlos Bernard (Tony Almeida), Dennis Hopper (Victor Drazen), Zeljko Ivanek (Andre Drazen), Xander Berkeley (George Mason), Jude Ciccolella (Mike Novick), Karina Arroyave (Jamey Farrell), Kevin Chapman, Terrell Tilford, Rey Gallegos (Sergeant Devlin), Tico Wells (Karris), Endre Hules (Serge), Jane Yamamoto (Field Reporter).

EPISODE SUMMARY

Kim manages to avoid Drazen's men and makes her way out of the docks to the main road where she narrowly misses being knocked over by a truck. Andre is not too concerned – as long as Jack Bauer *believes* they have his daughter they can control him.

Sherry continues to berate David for 'playing dead' and forcing her to play the grieving widow. As no body has been removed from the scene, the press and news crews that are swarming outside are beginning to speculate all kinds of wild theories. She tries to get Mike Novick on her side but he refuses to be drawn into it. David finally snaps and reminds Sherry that Jack has saved his life twice today. He will not allow Sherry to sacrifice the man's daughter.

At CTU, Mason speaks to **Sergeant Devlin**, a highway patrolman, who tells him they have found Kim. Mason speaks to her and she tells him that she has escaped from the Drazens but her father is walking into a trap. Mason asks to speak to the officer again and learns that Kim was found near dock 11A. He tells Nina to despatch two tactical teams to the port immediately.

Andre calls Jack to ask him where he is. Jack tells him he has only just arrived at the port, but really he is wary of walking straight into a trap. He tells Andre that he doesn't trust him but Andre questions his idea of trust, telling him that they know Palmer is alive. Jack demands to speak to his daughter and when Drazen refuses he hangs up. Andre tells his father that he doesn't think Bauer is coming, but Victor coolly reassures him: 'He will come.'

Jack phones Nina to warn her that someone in CTU has leaked Palmer's survival to the Drazens. She tells him that apart from herself, only Tony, Mason and Chappelle knew that the news of Palmer's death was a lie. Jack is convinced that one of them is their mole and tells her not to trust anyone. He confides in her that the Drazens want to trade him for Kim and that he might not get out alive. Nina allows Jack to hang up without telling him that Kim has already escaped, but as she looks up she notices that Mason is watching her suspiciously.

David tells Mike that he fears by doggedly focusing on 'truth' he might just have torn his family apart. Mike, however, suspects the events of the last day might help him discover who he really is. Just then, Mike gets a tip-off to check the TV. The men watch flabbergasted as a TV news bulletin reports that he was unharmed by the explosion. In a fury, David hunts down Sherry. He finds her cowering in a bathroom and still insisting that everything she has done has been to protect him. David cannot believe that she is continuing to undermine him at every step and makes to hit her. Mike pulls him back and tells him that it is now essential that he makes a statement to the press – the longer he leaves it the more power he is granting them to destroy him. Burning with anger, David smashes a vase against a wall.

Nina phones Andre at **11:17 P.M.** and warns him that Kim has been found and is on her way to CTU. Bauer doesn't know, she says, but there are two CTU teams heading straight for the harbour. Keeping Nina on hold, Andre passes on her news to his father, warning him that he doesn't want to risk him being captured again. Victor asks to speak to her. He asks her to tell Jack that his daughter's dead body has been found in the docks in the hope that it will unhinge him and make him come after the Drazens. Nina is worried that her cover will be blown if she openly lies to Jack but Victor tells her that Jack will soon be dead.

Jack answers his phone thinking it will be Andre and is surprised to hear Nina's voice. She tells him that a coastguard has just called them to let them know they have just pulled Kim's body from the river. Jack collapses in shock and breaks down crying. Eventually he manages to pull himself together. Returning to his SUV, Jack collects a full clip of bullets for his gun and heads towards Drazen's warehouse. But then he changes his mind and breaks into a nearby van...

Andre is unsure whether his father's plan will work, but Victor is sure Jack won't be able to resist trying to hunt them down. They are both taken by surprise, however, when Jack drives his stolen van straight through the warehouse wall. He leaps from the van via the rear doors, leaving the vehicle to plough into Drazen's men. Andre quickly grabs his father by the arm and the pair make towards a jetty where an approaching boat will collect them. Jack pursues them and manages to shoot Andre dead, but Victor returns fire and shoots Jack in the stomach. As Jack crawls along the wooden jetty, Victor holds him in his sights and pulls the trigger, only to find he has run out of bullets. He puts his hands up to surrender as Jack struggles to his feet. The men stare at each other for what seems like an eternity but then Jack shoots Victor Drazen at point-blank range and keeps shooting until Drazen falls into the water. Once his clip is completely empty, Jack collapses to his knees. The pick-up boat turns and speeds off

At **11:28 P.M.**, David makes a statement to the press apologising for the misinformation that led to reports of his death. He confirms that his family are safe and well and thanks everyone for their support. Upstairs, Mike goes to see Sherry. She assumes he too is going to lecture her about disloyalty but Mike tells her that he actually supports her on the matter and agrees that David should not have misled the electorate. Sherry asks him to find out how the day's events have affected David's popularity and suggests that in her opinion he should cancel his planned trip to Dallas tomorrow. Mike tells her he thinks those kinds of decisions should be made by David. He then mentions that David wants to meet with her in the hotel ballroom once he's finished delivering his statement to the press and tactfully urges her to take the opportunity to make the first step to patching things up between them.

Mason strides into the CTU main office to tell the staff that the two teams he sent to the port weren't needed after all – Jack single-handedly took down the Drazens and five of their men. He congratulates Teri, telling her that she will soon be reunited with her family. When she hears that the Drazens are dead, Nina panics. She takes advantage of the excitement to slip out of the office and races towards one of the server rooms to collect a briefcase hidden inside one of the wall panels. A technician wanders in and Nina ruthlessly kills her before calling her real superiors. She speaks to them in German and is told to erase all evidence that might expose her as a traitor. Teri has come looking for Nina, confused over the reports about Jack. She overhears some of what Nina has said but Nina switches to English as soon as she realises Teri is there, alerting her superiors that she has been disturbed. Terminating the call, Nina explains that she was calling their counterparts in Frankfurt. Teri puts her surprise at Nina's hitherto unknown linguistic ability aside to ask Nina to tell her what has just happened with Jack. When she last spoke to him he was on his way to collect Kim, yet now she learns that he's been involved in a big shoot-out. Nina tells her to stay calm and that Jack and Kim are both on their way back to CTU. Nina's phone rings again and Teri steps away to let her answer it, but then she sees a pool of blood from the murdered technician and realises that something is wrong. She tells Nina that she can see she's busy and makes to leave, but Nina dashes to block her way. Holding her at gunpoint, she tells Teri she can't let her leave. She binds her arms and tapes her mouth up while she continues to delete a series of files from the network.

Jack is being tended to by a paramedic when he notices one of the coastguards walk by. He asks to claim the body of the girl who was fished from the river, explaining that he is the girl's father. The man tells him he doesn't know what he's talking about and calls the harbourmaster to confirm that no-one had reported a dead body. Jack calls Mason who jokes that he doesn't know whether to congratulate him or demand his resignation. Jack cuts him short and asks him if he knows where Kim is. When Mason confirms that she's on her way to CTU, safe in the care of the highway patrolman, Jack tells him to arrest Nina and stop her from leaving the building, explaining that Nina has been working for the Drazens and helped them set a trap for him. Mason asks him if there's any way he might have misunderstood, but Jack tells him bluntly – Nina told him that Kim was dead; it was a clear lie. Mason tells him he needs proof of the accusation. Jack promises he'll get it just so long as Mason keeps an eye on Nina.

At **11:42 P.M.**, Jack contacts Paul Wilson from CTU archives and asks him to retrieve security footage for the ITF room from around the time of Jamey's suicide. Wilson is surprised to discover that the security footage has been wiped from the network so Jack gives him security clearance to access the security cameras' back-up. Wilson tells him he'll need just a few minutes so Jack asks him to get back to him as soon as he can.

Sherry meets with David and says that she admits they need to talk but asks if whatever he has to say can wait until the morning when they've had some sleep. She says she knows he must be angry with her but hopes that when he has chance to put the day into perspective he'll see how she's been acting in his best interests all along.

> *'I feel sorry for you... You've lost touch with what it is to be a parent... a friend... a wife...'*

He tells her he never wants to see her again, regardless of how it affects his presidential campaign, not because he doesn't want to be President but because he feels she is not fit to be First Lady. Sherry warns him that he can't succeed without her and that he won't get rid of her so easily. David, however, has made his mind up. He tells Sherry that Secret Service will collect her and return her to Washington. Leaving Sherry's rants behind him, David walks away from the ballroom and his marriage.

Wilson uploads the security footage to a monitor in Jack's car and Jack watches horrified as he sees images of Jamey being grabbed from behind by Nina and shocked into unconsciousness before slashing her wrists in an attempt to make it look like she has committed suicide. Jack tells Wilson to send the file to Mason for his eyes only and patch him through to him. When Mason sees what Nina has done he can't believe his eyes. Jack urges him to find Nina quickly.

At **11:53 P.M.**, Nina discovers that a CTU emergency lockdown is in progress, freezing her out of the network. Pocketing a CD ROM of valuable data, she calls her superior and is instructed to escape to Munich and lie low for three days, ensuring before she leaves that no-one can trace her back to Germany. She turns to Teri and tells her that she is leaving but that someone will find her soon. Then she picks up her gun...

With the emergency alarms sounding, Nina carefully makes her way towards the exit of CTU, shooting two agents before reaching the car park. She gets into her car and drives towards the exit just as Jack enters. The two agents try to shoot each other and Nina crashes. Jack pulls over and drags Nina from her car with his gun held towards her head. Nina tells him that if he kills her he'll never discover who she was working for – because it wasn't the Drazens. She tries to excuse her actions as just doing her job, but Jack refuses to listen:

'My wife and daughter almost died today! How many people that trusted you lost their life today because you were "doing your job"? Walsh, Jamey, Ellis, how many others?!'

Mason and Tony arrive and succeed in talking Jack down, telling him Kim has just arrived at CTU. Persuaded to rejoin his family, Jack releases Nina and Tony watches her being led away.

Jack and Kim are finally reunited. Jack promises his daughter that their ordeal is over. Realising that Teri is nowhere to be seen, Jack goes looking for her and follows the trail of bodies while on TV, Jack is named as the man who saved Palmer's life. Finding two men trying in vain to resuscitate the first officer Nina shot, Jack follows the corridor along to the server room where Nina left Teri. He runs to untie her hands and gasps as he sees that she is bleeding from a gunshot to the stomach. He gathers her up in his arms and only then does he realise she is dead. He falls to the floor, hugging her lifeless body tight, overcome with feelings of guilt...

NOTES

- **Who's Who?:** Terrell Tilford played David Grant (or one of them at least) in the soap opera *Guiding Light*. Tico Wells's (Karris) filmography includes *The Five Heartbeats* (dir. Robert Townsend, 1991), *Universal Soldier* (dir. Roland Emerich, 1992), *The Relic* (dir. Peter Hyams, 1997) and *Bram Stoker's Legend of the Mummy* (dir. Jeffrey Obrow, 1997) in which he played the young Louis Gossett Jr. Kevin Chapman also appeared in the films *In Too Deep* (dir. Michael Rymer, 1999) and *Blow* (dir. Ted Demme, 2001), while Jane Yamamoto is a general assignment reporter for *KTTV Fox 11*.
- **Time Checks:** Kim tells Andre that Kim will be back at CTU before the

end of the episode, within the hour. When Mason views the security footage of Nina, Jack tells him he is just five minutes away.

- **Death Count:** Five unnamed members of Drazen's team (11:21 P.M.), Andre Drazen (11.22 P.M.), Victor Drazen (11:23 P.M.), all shot by Jack Bauer, a CTU technician (11:33 P.M.), two CTU agents (11:55 P.M.) and finally Teri Bauer (some time between 11:54 and 11:55 P.M.)
- **Trivia:** The access code Jack gives Wilson in archives is C22717.

COMMENTS

Speaking to *Entertainment Weekly*, co-creator of ***24*** Robert Cochran spelled out the approach to the show: 'It's not a show that says "don't worry, be happy". That would be false to the tone we set.' Hence the brutal murder of Teri in the final moments of the last episode. To say this decision polarised their fan base is putting it mildly. The day after the first broadcast of this final episode, the internet was flooded with complaints from ***24*** fans furious at what they saw as a cheap exploitative cop-out. To have sat through the entire series (which, thanks to the way American TV draws things out, accounted for more than six long, fraught, irretrievable months) willing Jack on in his attempt to keep his family safe, only for Teri (and her unborn child) to be callously murdered at the end was robbing them of the happy ending they so desperately needed. Surely this undermined everything Jack had risked his life for? And coming so soon after the discovery that Nina was a traitor (not only assisting the Drazens but also, we discover, in the employ of a 'phantom menace' operating out of Germany), the viewers' comfort zones were being deliberately, maliciously targeted, particularly after the manipulative way Nina claimed to be willing to let Teri live, only to kill her off screen to protect her German connections.

Such a nasty, downbeat, 'sick' ending was not what these viewers had wanted or expected and to have been denied a 'safe' ending after everything the characters had been through was just the dirtiest trick the producers could have pulled. Linking the horror of the finale to the incalculable loss at the World Trade Center the previous year, one fan wailed 'DON'T YOU THINK WE'VE SUFFERED ENOUGH?' Another accused Cochran and Surnow of being talentless for resorting to an unnecessary downbeat ending, suggesting that this sort of thing wouldn't happen with true greats like Shakespeare and Hitchcock (the author of this e-mail clearly hadn't seen *King Lear*, *Macbeth*, *Othello*, *Vertigo*, *Psycho* or *Topaz*, all of which have particularly bleak endings with strong parallels to ***24***).

As you might expect, I don't hold with any of that. All power to Surnow and Cochran for creating a show that inspires people to become so impassioned by such a ruthlessly shocking and uncompromising climax. Every complaint I read about it being a dumb cheap shot is countered, in my mind at least, by praise for the brave decision not to 'Hollywoodise' it all and allow everyone to live happily ever after. War isn't a fairytale, after all. Despite the need for many to feel happy again after the tragic deaths of thousands of American people so recently, most fans recognised that the controversial ending was at least dramatically true to itself. For Bauer to walk off into the sunset arm in arm with his family would have been too clichéd, too phoney. Besides, you don't really get sunsets at midnight in L.A....

24 has revolved around two basic goals: the physical and political survival of David Palmer and Jack's rescue of his daughter, Kim. To achieve the first, Palmer was forced to sacrifice both his wife and his campaign co-ordinator (a person who only a few hours earlier he has credited for his election victory) while overcoming his fear that the system might fail him for trying to be honourable and honest. But Jack's goal was complicated by the involvement of his wife. She'd been forced to take on his responsibilities when he left the family home, and now that he is kept away from his family by work, she is forced to take his place as the hero and search for Kim herself. She substitutes herself for Kim too, we recall, to protect her from Eli's lust, and denies herself the chance of a new beginning with Dr Phil because she knows that she needs to reunite Jack with his daughter. Ultimately she stands in for Jack once more by being killed by his enemies. Her death isn't a 'cheap shot', it's the logical climax to the thematic development of her character as the victim in the play. Far from Jack's entire day being wasted, he's saved his daughter twice while also learning, as David has, that he cannot risk letting his work come before his family. Both men have now lost their wife in an attempt to protect their offspring. Jack's prediction that this would be the longest day of his life is more accurate than he could ever have imagined and the aftershock of the closing moments will be felt by both the characters and the viewers for a long time to come.

QUESTIONS ARISING

- Who is Nina/Yelena really working for? As her masters appear to be working out of Germany, and as Mandy, the terrorist from the first few episodes, flew out from Germany, is there a link there?
- Come to think of it, whatever happened to Mandy and Jonathan?
- Will Keith now face a prison sentence or will his much-publicised side of the story convince a jury of his innocence?
- Will David Palmer become America's first black President, or will Sherry sabotage his campaign 'for his own good'?
- What now for Jack? Can he continue working at CTU as a single parent when he blames himself for the deaths of his wife and unborn child?
- And probably the most important question of all – how can Series Two possibly top that?

THE LAST WORD

5 00:00 13:41 07:24 22:38 10:09 17:59 09:13 21:01 04:45 14:12 07:57 13:41 07:24 22:38 10:09 17:59 0

Before the final episode reached American screens, a second series of ***24*** was commissioned. Rumours began circulating that the format would be changed to make each episode one day, retaining the '24 hours' gimmick but spreading it out over 24 days (one wag suggested they should rename the show 'Month' and have done with it). But, said Robert Cochran, 'If we tried to do something different, it wouldn't be ***24***.' So apparently the new series will be another day in the life of Jack Bauer, one year on from the events of the first series. David Palmer will, I gather, be successful in his election bid and so will already be a few months into his first term as America's first African-American President. Jack will still be at CTU, though we can assume some new faces will be around to fill the 'vacancies' left by Jamey, Nina and the rest. As for Nina, last seen under arrest for treason, murder and (possibly) dangerous driving in a government car park, whether she plays any part in the proceedings remains to be seen. As Cochran cryptically says, 'We'll deal with that next year.'

Roll on Series Two!

SUPPORTING CHARACTERS

18:19 18:05 00:00 13:41 07:24 22:38 10:09 17:59 09:13 21:01 04:45 14:12 07:57 13:41 07:24 22:38

Just to preserve some mystery for readers who've yet to see every episode, I've saved this until the end. Here's a quick run-down of some of the additional characters:

The Villains

The small terrorist operation behind the threat on Palmer is funded by **Alexis** and **Andre Drazen**, Serbian brothers and son of **Victor Drazen** who have financed **Ira Gaines**'s team via **Ted Cofell**, an investment banker in L.A. Gaines's team includes **Mandy**, a highly trained terrorist, Mandy's friend **Bridgit**, a motorcyclist and the pick-up for the I.D. that Mandy has been hired to acquire, **Jonathan**, a marksman who has undergone extensive plastic surgery to resemble Belkin, **Rick** and **Dan**, two young men hired to kidnap Kim Bauer, and **Kevin Carroll**, a former member of the Drug Enforcement Agency in Florida and skilled undercover operative. The Drazens also have assassins **Mishko Suba** and **Jovan Myovic** waiting in the wings, a small army, headed by **Harris**, and a contact known only as '**Yelena**'...

CTU

Richard Walsh was head of the Counter Terrorist Unit of L.A. until his untimely death. Reporting to him are regional director **Ryan Chappelle** and district director **George Mason**, and beneath them, **Alberta Green** and **Jack Bauer**. As well as his full-time team, Jack occasionally hires in technical experts such as **Milo Pressmann**, a whizzkid with computers.

Palmer's Campaign Office

Though the most important decision-maker in Palmer's campaign (aside from himself) is his chief of staff, **Mike Novick**, Palmer credits much of his success to his campaign manager, **Patty Brooks**, and his assistant, **Elizabeth Nash**, the daughter of an old friend of the Palmers. Currently stationed there is **Agent Aaron Pierce** of the Secret Service. Lurking in the background is **Carl Webb**, the go-between for the consortium funding a large part of Palmer's campaign.

Friends and Confidantes

David Palmer has been good friends with celebrated TV reporter **Maureen Kingsley** for many years. But their relationship is threatened by a news story that reaches Maureen via **Dr George Ferragamo**, the psychiatrist to David's son, Keith.

Kim Bauer's best friend is **Janet York**, a fellow student at Santa Monica High. Janet has recently started dating a boy called Dan. Kim's mother, Teri, has a close friend called **Phil Parslow**, who she met while she and Jack were separated. Though their relationship was purely platonic, it was always clear to her that Phil wanted it to be much more.

Rick, the kidnapper, lives with his girlfriend, **Melanie**. His partner in crime, Dan, has a bullying older brother called **Frank** who is trying to put together a major drugs deal.

REFERENCES

00 13:41 07:24 22:38 10:09 17:59 09:13 21:01 04:45 14:12 07:57 13:41 07:24 22:38 10:09 17:59 09:13

Books

Los Angeles, Andrea Schulte-Peevers, Lonely Planet, 2001

Made in America, Bill Bryson, Black Swan, 1994

Magazines

'The Man with the Golden Globe: Andrew Duncan meets Kiefer Sutherland', *Radio Times*, 6–12 April 2002

'Rush Hour', *Entertainment Weekly*, June 7 2002

'The Time of Their Lives', James Poniewozik, *Time Magazine*, November 12 2001

WWW Sites

The official ***24*** site from Fox (http://www.fox.com/24/) contains plenty of background information to the characters not revealed in the show itself, and boasts a thriving online community.

Over on Yahoo!Groups, the ***24*** group (http://groups.yahoo.com/group/24/) have helped me with a number of the topics discussed in this book... although to be honest, they didn't know they were helping me as I sneaked in, Nina-style, and lurked for most of the time. They're a great bunch though.

Odd facts and figures have come from h2g2 (http://www.bbc.co.uk/dna/h2g2/), the interactive Douglas Adams-inspired guide to life, the universe and everything.

And, as ever, I cannot recommend the Internet Movie Database (www.imdb.com) highly enough.

Additional Online Articles

'Working Around The Clock', Elina Shatkin, DirectorsWorld.com: http://www.directorsworld.com/article/mainv/0,7220,31363,00.html

'A Day In The Life', Ian Rothkerch, Salon.com: http://www.salon.com/ent/tv/int/2002/02/05/surnow/index.html?x

'What If '24' Calls It A Day After 13 Hours?' Cheryl Klein, TV Zap2it.com: http://tv.zap2it.com/shows/01-02/fall/feature.html?19351

'It's Been A Long Day', Bernard Weinraub, *The Observer* online, March 3 2002: http://www.observer.co.uk/Print/0,3858,4366403,00.html